BUYING AND SELLING
CIVIL WAR MEMORY IN
GILDED AGE AMERICA

Buying and Selling Civil War Memory in Gilded Age America

EDITED BY JAMES MARTEN
AND CAROLINE E. JANNEY

The University of Georgia Press *Athens*

Most University of Georgia Press titles are
available from popular e-book vendors.

Printed digitally

Library of Congress Cataloging-in-Publication Data

Names: Marten, James Alan, editor. | Janney, Caroline E., editor.
Title: Buying and selling Civil War memory in Gilded Age America /
    edited by James Marten and Caroline E. Janney.
Description: Athens : The University of Georgia Press, [2021] |
    Series: Uncivil wars | Includes bibliographical references and index.
Identifiers: LCCN 2020055801 | ISBN 9780820359663 (hardback) |
    ISBN 9780820359656 (paperback) | ISBN 9780820359670 (ebook)
Subjects: LCSH: United States—History—Civil War, 1861–1865—Collectibles. |
    United States—History—Civil War, 1861–1865—Social aspects. | Material culture—
    United States—History—19th century. | Selling—Collectibles—United States—
    History—19th century. | Collective memory—United States—History—19th century. |
    Popular culture—United States—History—19th century.
Classification: LCC E468.9 .B896 2021 | DDC 973.7/1—dc23
LC record available at https://lccn.loc.gov/2020055801

Contents

Acknowledgments

Thanks first to our authors, who displayed patience and professionalism through an unusually long process of articulation and revision; we appreciate their willingness to meet deadlines and expectations and to aim at a sometimes moving target. Thanks also to the anonymous, extraordinarily thorough, and exacting readers of the manuscript. They might not recognize their hard work in the finished book, but their engagement with the manuscript deeply influenced the final product nonetheless.

Amy Murrell Taylor and Stephen Berry welcomed this book into their UnCivil Wars series with open arms and offered typically fresh and practical ideas for improving it. And thanks to the staff at the University of Georgia who eased this project through the publication process: Mick Gusinde-Duffy, Jon Davies, and Beth Snead.

John Neff, who wrote the essay on Libby Prison, died suddenly not long after finishing his essay. He will be remembered by all who knew him as a wonderful colleague, excellent historian, and beloved teacher.

BUYING AND SELLING CIVIL WAR MEMORY IN GILDED AGE AMERICA

Introduction

JAMES MARTEN AND CAROLINE E. JANNEY

In the spring of 1871, the Southern Agricultural Works, H. M. Smith & Co. of Richmond, mailed its annual catalog of agricultural implements to agrarians throughout the state of Virginia. Flipping through the pages, farmers found a host of tools that might make their arduous labor at least somewhat less taxing. Some gravitated toward the garden and field rollers for breaking and pulverizing clods of dirt, others eyed the wooden barrows for loading vessels with cord wood, and still others wondered whether the twenty-three-quart Arctic Freezer ice-cream maker might be worth its steep price of twenty dollars. But at least a few no doubt found exactly what they needed on page 73: "the dirt scraper, or ox shovel." Drawn by a team of horses or oxen, it had been designed "for carrying away earth and scooping out ditches, drains, and any excavations" and was, the ad promised, "especially useful in leveling earthworks and filling rifle pits."[1]

The matter-of-fact description illustrates just how much the Civil War remained a part of U.S. life for years after the fighting ended, not only in the great political issues being decided in Washington, D.C., and in state capitals throughout the old Confederacy, but also in the everyday lives of southerners and northerners alike. In this case, the ox shovel would have particularly appealed to Virginia farmers trying to make a living on the old battlefields, in places such as Spotsylvania County, where the armies had clashed four times during the war, or along the defenses of Richmond and Petersburg that had witnessed months of trench warfare that left the land denuded of trees and crisscrossed with earthworks. The entrenchments and fortifications that had come to dominate the last year and half of the war cut deep scars on the landscape and prevented farm-

DIRT SCRAPER, OR OX SHOVEL.

This is drawn by a team of horses or oxen, for carrying away earth and scooping out ditches, drains and any excavations, and at this time is especially useful in leveling earthworks and filling rifle pits.

PRICES.

No. 1...........................$10 00
No. 2........................... 12 00
No. 2½......................... 14 00
No. 3........................... 16 00

In 1871, the *Illustrated Annual Catalogue of Agricultural Implements* published by the Southern Agricultural Works, H. M. Smith & Co. of Richmond, Virginia, advertised a dirt scraper that might be used to remove field fortifications and earthworks that remained six years after the fighting ended. (Courtesy of Eric Mink)

ers from plowing, much less planting, their fields. Yet as with so many products and services sold in the years after 1865, the Civil War had not spawned a brand-new tool, but it had both shaped the advertising and given new meaning to a common object. In purchasing and wielding the ox shovel, a farmer might remove the scars of war and restore fields to their agricultural bounty. The war might thereby be erased from the landscape even as it was deployed to sell more products.

To the north in the small town of Gettysburg a similar process of removing the visible traces of war unfolded. Here, too, the war had transformed the value and meaning of objects. Visitors to the town would be besieged—at least as portrayed by *Harper's Weekly*—by young boys peddling spent bullets, bayonets, canteens, and other detritus of war scavenged from the battlefield and converted into souvenirs. In the years that followed, Gettysburg would become the most famous and most popular battlefield of the war, drawing tourists and veterans to reunions, historic tours, exhibits, and even amusement parks. Commerce mixed with patriotism and a dedication to preserving a certain version of the battle's memory to create plenty of opportunities for profit making.[2]

These large and small examples of Civil War commerce and memory foreshadowed the central place such business efforts would assume during the Gilded Age. The Civil War had consumed Americans over four long, bloody years. For the thirty or forty years after the war, the generation that survived and their children consumed the Civil War in products and services ranging from ox shovels to tobacco. Some individ-

"Relic-Sellers, Gettysburg." (*Harper's Weekly*, July 17, 1869)

uals and companies offered products or services exclusively for veterans. Within days of the Confederate capital's occupation by Union troops, a Richmond newspaper ran a New York jeweler's ad for a medal commemorating the surrender hanging from a pin inscribed "Lt. Gen. U. S. Grant." For three dollars, veterans of the Army of the Potomac could have their name, regiment, and company engraved on the top bar. Not only was the jeweler offering these medals before many believed the war was over, but he was also seeking sales agents "to whom especial inducements are offered."[3] In the decades that followed, annual encampments of veterans of both the Union and Confederate armies became veritable bazaars of Grand Army of the Republic and United Confederate Veterans paraphernalia such as medals and uniforms. Other companies peddled war kitsch to nonveterans. Well into the 1870s, children could play with a walking General Butler doll, along with tin monitors and paper soldiers.[4] And some savvy businesses marketed their wares and services to veterans and civilians alike. State and federal homes for disabled soldiers in both the North and the South offered an astonishing array of souvenirs, from guidebooks and postcards to commemorative plates, cups, bookmarks, spoons, bars of soap, moustache cups, and toothpick holders all decorated with images of the home or patriotic emblems.[5] In 1889, the Pabst Brewing Company helped sponsor the national reunion of the Grand Army of the Republic in Milwaukee, printing a full-color program and handing out thousands of glass beer mugs embossed with a GAR medal.[6]

The extraordinary interest in the war—among civilians who wanted to experience history, and among veterans who wanted to ensure that their valor and sacrifice were represented accurately and honorably—created major industries in monuments, markers, guidebooks, and maps.[7]

In most instances, the war did not create new products. Ox plows, stereoviews, tobacco, medicines, panoramas, and children's literature all existed before the conflict. The war did, however, create new markets and advertising strategies for goods and services. With the war and Reconstruction behind them, these Gilded Age buyers and sellers rushed forward into a period of unprecedented economic boom and bust. The tremendous growth of the industrial sector marked an era of big business led by so-called robber barons such as Cornelius Vanderbilt, Andrew Carnegie, and John D. Rockefeller even as the poorer classes found themselves relegated to twelve-hour working days and grime-encrusted slums. In the burgeoning urban centers, people stood in awe of the first skyscrapers, rode on streetcars to their new homes in the suburbs, and shopped in magnificent department stores. Spectator sports such as boxing, baseball, and college football, as well as vaudeville halls and amusement parks like Coney Island, offered leisure and entertainment. Labor strife, Populist revolt, political corruption, unbridled materialism, social Darwinism, state-sanctioned segregation, and the scourge of lynching were hallmarks of this period. But so too were reform efforts such as Jane Addams's Hull House or the antidrinking campaign launched by the Women's Christian Temperance Union, not to mention the burgeoning conservation movement that preserved magnificent natural landscapes such as Yellowstone.

These stirring developments pointed toward the future, but during these same years, a nostalgia for the Civil War emerged. Declining throughout the 1870s, by the mid-1880s the ranks of the largest Union veterans' association, the Grand Army of the Republic (GAR), had grown to more than 350,000 members and Confederate veterans had begun to organize their own official organizations. Union and Confederate women, likewise, sought to honor their respective causes through groups such as the Woman's Relief Corps and the United Daughters of the Confederacy. African Americans, too, commemorated their roles in the war and emancipation, both in segregated associations and in those devoted exclusively to the United States Colored Troops. Through Memorial Days and Emancipation Day celebrations, monument dedications, and the writing of memoirs, individuals and groups—Unionists and Confederates, men and women, white and black, veterans and civilians—attempted to both shape and harness the war's meaning for political and social power. For more than thirty years, Gaines Foster, Nina Silber, David Blight, William A. Blair, and other scholars have mined these associations and events to remind us that interpretations of the war had—and in many cases continue to have—profound implications for partisan politics, government policy, citizenship, ideas about gender and race, and the future of the nation.[8]

While scholars have extensively examined the various strands of Civil War memory and their implications for society and politics, only recently have they begun to consider how the war fit into larger patterns of nineteenth-century consumer culture.[9] Wendy A. Woloson argues that Jacksonian-era technological and economic changes planted the seed of a "shopping ethic" that would be fully realized after the Civil War.[10] Indeed, as Joanna Cohen reminds us, the war "sparked a dramatic fusion of patriotism with a broader consumer culture," in the Civil War North. Capitalizing on the technological changes in printing, mass production, and transportation, manufacturers and entrepreneurs offered a flurry of new and often cheap goods that allowed Americans to "stimulate and articulate their emotional bonds to each other and their country." Unionists might purchase flags, books, board games, prints, songbooks, or stationary packages all in the name of patriotism.[11] In *Marketing the Blue and Gray*, Lawrence A. Kreiser Jr. shows how wartime advertisers framed consumption in the contexts of politics and patriotism—ensuring that the war would infuse almost every element of U.S. culture.[12] This would continue long after the war, as retailers, publishers, entertainers, and manufacturers—aided by the new professional advertising agencies—tapped into the anxieties, animosities, and physical needs unleashed by the war to sell their wares and services.[13] The outpouring of Civil War–related products paralleled the startling rise of consumer culture after the Civil War as part of the transition from what Jackson Lears calls the "irrationality" of the economy of the early republic to the "rational" economy that emerged later in the century, driven by national confidence, a faith in progress, and the knowledge of abundance.[14]

But it was not only in producing, marketing, or selling goods that these objects mattered. As Joan Cashin's recent collection of essays on material culture reminds us, "the war transformed the physical world and ideas about that world in ways that were national in scope yet very personal in effect."[15] The physical property of an object could shape both its potential and its reception, as demonstrated in John Neff's essay about the relocation of Libby Prison. For the investors, dismantling the Richmond warehouse, reassembling it in Chicago, and opening it to visitors was a business venture. For white southerners, it was a crass move calculated to rile up sectional wounds. For former Union prisoners, it could be either a visceral experience or a memorial to their suffering. Though the size of a city block, one object could contain all of these meanings—individual and national, celebration and mourning, healing and renewed suffering.

Buying and Selling Civil War Memory in Gilded Age America does not offer a history of capitalism in the aftermath of war, nor does it presume to provide a new interpretation of the emerging professionalization of marketing—even though both of those fields intersect with a number of the essays. In addition, we do not follow the path of previous studies on Civil War memory, which tend to focus on those organizations and political movements, monuments and ceremonies, and memoirs and novels that reflected bedrock northern and southern values, the continuing sectional conflict, and the grand narrative of the nation's history during the transformative second half of the nineteenth century.

Rather, the essays show how memory of the war became a practical thing for many—not necessarily, or at least not only, a framework for politics or race relations or sectional identity—and how it intersected in large and small ways in Americans' daily lives. Readers follow stereoview and subscription book salesmen into middle-class homes, where they hawk images of the conflict; look over the shoulders of veterans as they surreptitiously scan ads in newspapers for addiction cures; sit alongside audiences who laugh, cry, and applaud at famous lecturers' war stories; stroll with customers through museums and massive art projects; peer with hopeful English investors into musty London bank vaults; shop with Confederate veterans and their wives and daughters for spiffy new uniforms to wear proudly at their next reunion. Here and there, sellers take advantage of war nostalgia, entrepreneurs cash in on buyers' desperation and pride, and opportunistic merchants shrewdly connect their wares in somewhat dubious ways to the war.

Extending the study of Civil War memory, the essays in this collection demonstrate the ways in which the products and services born of the war reflected and affected American consumerism and financial interests throughout the late nineteenth century. What financial and social opportunities did the war continue to offer? What new services and products did it necessitate? How did the short- and long-term effects of the war create new markets? How did merchants, entrepreneurs, printers, and advertising agencies capitalize on the war's lingering effects? How did they reflect and deploy the various strands of memory? Or ignore it all together? Rather than examining the ideas and rhetoric that are so often the focus of memory studies, *Buying and Selling* looks at the objects, art, and services that retained the war as a tangible presence in the lives of many for years and even decades after Appomattox—even when some would have rather forgotten. The time frame—roughly 1865 to 1900—also offers a window into how the war continued to shape products and services consumed by those who survived it. For some, this necessitated new products like opiate cures. For others, this meant purchasing newspapers, subscriptions, or tickets to entertainments peddling a particular memory of the war. But these years are likewise relevant because they witnessed such profound transformations in printing, mass production, and transportation alongside new professional advertising agencies that tapped into the anxieties, animosities, and physical needs unleashed by the war to sell their wares and services. These essays showcase only some of the ways in which individuals, communities, and businesses leveraged the war in the decades after Appomattox.

Buying and Selling Civil War Memory is organized around the ways in which late nineteenth-century Americans would have consumed the Civil War. The first section, "Defining Veteranhood," focuses on publishers, pharmaceutical companies, Lost Cause organizations, and clothing manufacturers. "Marketing and Advertising" takes up the question of money more directly, focusing on the long, strange history of Confederate bond investors and on the ways that Gilded Age advertisers continued to draw on wartime images for their own purposes. Section 3, "Imagining the War," turns to popular images of the war in print culture and other media and introduces some of the ways in which the war was marketed as entertainment.

Historians have long debated the ways in which Americans applied the meanings of the Civil War to the nation's big issues and guiding ideologies. This collection takes a ground-level view. The war certainly disrupted U.S. society in ways that were sometimes hard to fathom, but it also provided endless possibilities for creating a culture shaped by commerce. These simple, everyday acts of buying and selling made it possible for images and words to transport consumers to other places and times; gave entrepreneurs the opportunity to deploy familiar technologies and media to the inspiring and tragic stories of the war; and provided paths for veterans of that war to make sense of their own experiences long after they had endured the trial of battle.

NOTES

1. *Illustrated Annual Catalog of Agricultural Implements*, published by the Southern Agricultural Works, H. M. Smith & Co. of Richmond, Va., 1871.

2. Jim Weeks, *Gettysburg: Memory, Market, and an American Shrine* (Princeton, N.J.: Princeton University Press, 2003.

3. *Richmond (Va.) Whig*, April 21, 1865.

4. Bernard Barenholtz and Inez McClintock, *American Antique Toys, 1830–1900* (New York: Abrams, 1980), 92; Blair Whitton, *Paper Toys of the World* (Cumberland, Md.: Hobby House Press, 1986), 85; *American Clockwork Toys* (Exton, Pa.: Schiffer, 1981), 92.

5. James Marten, *Sing Not War: The Lives of Union and Confederate Veterans in Gilded Age America* (Chapel Hill: University of North Carolina Press, 2011), 153–54.

6. Ibid., 128–30, 153.

7. Timothy B. Smith, *This Great Battlefield of Shiloh: History, Memory, and the Establishment of a Civil War National Military Park* (Knoxville: University of Tennessee Press, 2004), 101.

8. See, for example, Gaines M. Goster, *Ghosts of the Confederacy: Defeat, the Lost Cause, and the Emergence of the New South* (New York: Oxford University Press, 1987); Nina Silber, *Romance of Reunion: Northerners and the South, 1865–1900* (Chapel Hill: University of North Carolina Press, 1993); David W. Blight, *Race and Reunion: The Civil War in American Memory* (Cambridge, Mass.: Belknap Press of Harvard University Press, 2001); William Blair, *Cities of the Dead: Contesting Memory of the Civil War in the South, 1865–1914* (Chapel Hill: University of North Carolina Press, 2004); John R. Neff, *Honoring the Civil War Dead: Commemoration and the Problem of Reconciliation* (Lawrence: University Press of Kansas, 2005); Marten, *Sing Not War*; Barbara Gannon, *The Won Cause* (Chapel Hill: University of North Carolina Press, 2011); Caroline E. Janney, *Remembering the Civil War: Reunion and the Limits of Reconciliation* (Chapel Hill: University of North Carolina Press, 2013); and M. Keith Harris, *Across the Bloody Chasm: The Culture of Commemoration among Civil War Veterans* (Baton Rouge: Louisiana State University Press, 2014).

9. Historians have not addressed the commerce of Civil War memory as such. Among the books dealing with "selling the South" are Grace Elizabeth Hale, *Making Whiteness: The Culture of Segregation in the South, 1890–1940* (New York: Pantheon Books, 1998); Karen L. Cox, *Dixie's Daughters: The United Daughters of the Confederacy and the Preservation of Confederate Culture* (Gainesville: University Press of Florida, 2003); and Reiko Hillyer, *Designing Dixie: Tourism, Memory, and Urban Space in the New South* (Charlottesville: University of Virginia Press, 2014). Ross A. Brooks, *The Visible Confederacy: Images and Objects in the Civil War South* (Baton Rouge: Louisiana State University Press, 2019), examines the purposes and meanings of Confederate art, currency, uniforms, and other objects and images,

but stops at the end of the war. Books on the development of Civil War battlefield parks tend to focus on politics and on veterans' interests in creating those parks, including Timothy B. Smith, *The Golden Age of Battlefield Preservation: The Decade of the 1890s and the Establishment of America's First Five Military Parks* (Knoxville: University of Tennessee Press, 2008); and Timothy B. Smith, *The Untold Story of Shiloh: The Battle and the Battlefield* (Knoxville: University of Tennessee Press, 2006). For a chapter on GAR and United Confederate Veterans' paraphernalia as well as soldiers' home souvenirs, see Marten, *Sing Not War*, chapter 3.

10. Wendy A. Woloson, "The Rise of Consumer Culture in the Age of Jackson," in *A Companion to the Era of Andrew Jackson*, ed. Sean Patrick Adams (Chichester, U.K.: Wiley-Blackwell, 2013), 489–508, quote on 494.

11. Joanna Cohen, "'You Have No Flag Out Yet?': Commercial Connections and Patriotic Emotion in the Civil War North," *Journal of the Civil War Era*, 9 (September 2019): 378–409, quotes on 380.

12. Lawrence A. Kreiser Jr., *Marketing the Blue and Gray: Newspaper Advertising and the American Civil War* (Baton Rouge: Louisiana State University Press, 2019).

13. Joanna Cohen, *Luxurious Citizens: The Politics of Consumption in Nineteenth-Century America* (Philadelphia: University of Pennsylvania Press, 2017).

14. Jackson Lears, *Fables of Abundance: A Cultural History of Advertising in America* (New York: Basic Books, 1994).

15. Joan Cashin, ed., *War Matters: Material Culture in the Civil War Era* (Chapel Hill: University of North Carolina Press, 2018), 7.

J. W. Neighbor, editor of *Neighbor's Home Mail*—which was one of more than two dozen veterans' newspapers published in the 1880s and 1890s—urged veterans to subscribe to and to promote his newspaper as a matter of patriotism and self-interest. (*Neighbor's Home Mail*, December 1880)

All True Soldiers
Defining Veteranhood

Like J. W. Neighbor, S. A. Cunningham, who began publishing the *Confederate Veteran* in 1893, constantly cajoled his readers to resubscribe to his monthly newspaper, to get others to subscribe, and to promote the paper. His survival as a businessman and editor depended on the loyalty of his readers, and to build that loyalty he invited them to join a community of veteran subscribers and their allies to protect their interests and to ensure that their stories would be told. According to Cunningham, the *Confederate Veteran* was "the most important medium that has ever been printed to represent the principles for which you suffered," and he asked "all who believe in the good faith of Confederates" to "rally now to their advocate, and the world will yet honor them more and more in what they did."[1] Like its northern counterparts, the *Confederate Veteran* would help shape the ways in which veterans lived their lives.

The five essays in this section explore various efforts to create and to shape veterans' lives by building communities of veterans that would watch out for their own interests and offer them a platform from which to tell their own stories. Veterans of the Union and Confederate armies were the most recognizable group in the United States for much of the Gilded Age. They had lived the war and no doubt relived it every day of their lives. But, as the essays in this section demonstrate, numerous publishers and entrepreneurs sought to insert themselves into the everyday lives of veterans. The first essay, by the late John Neff, offers the story of the relocation of Libby Prison from Richmond to Chicago. Although the prison was conceived purely as a tourist attraction, the plan quickly descended into controversy. Union veterans who had been imprisoned at Libby or elsewhere initially resisted the idea of making money from their misery, while white southerners insisted it would serve only to revive sectional animosities. Profits appeared to outweigh veterans' desires for those determined to showcase the famed prison. Jonathan S. Jones places the plight of veterans who became addicted to opiates due to the lingering effects of wounds or disease in the context of the patent medicine craze of the late nineteenth century. Dozens of entrepreneurs obliged veterans with dubious but profitable remedies that promised to help them regain lost manhood. Two authors explore the role of the *National Tribune* in shaping a veterans' culture. The *Tribune* helped build veteran communities, argues Kevin Caprice, by offering "premiums" for veterans who mobilized fellow comrades to subscribe to the newspaper; those same premiums—clocks, cufflinks, framed certificates—provided concrete ways for veterans to display evidence of their service. Crompton B. Burton's essay on publisher George Lemon shows the importance of the *Tribune*'s role in making pensions an important economic force in their lives and a vital element of their identity as veterans. Shae Smith Cox shows how the simple action of designing and marketing Confederate-style uniforms helped both the United Confederate Veterans and the United Daughters of the Confederacy fashion a distinctive identity and to instill pride in Confederate veterans and their communities. Finally, Edward J. Harcourt reveals how the wartime memory of Tennessee veterans was determined by the market. Though the proprietor intended his *Military Annals of Tennessee* to be a reconciliationist gesture that would unite veterans of both sides, he soon found his efforts shaped by a public desire to subscribe to the publication dedicated solely to the memory of Confederate veterans.

NOTES

1. *Confederate Veteran* 2 (May 1894): 130.

A Simple Business Speculation

The Selling of a Civil War Prison

JOHN NEFF

In February 1888, William H. Gray, acting for a syndicate of investors, purchased a large warehouse in Richmond, Virginia, near the James River docks. Colonel William H. Palmer, president of the Southern Fertilizer Company, was happy to sell. Such an ordinary real estate transaction should not have attracted much attention, but this one roused the nation. What created the sensation was that this warehouse, twenty-six years earlier, had been known as Libby Prison, in which thousands of Union officers had been incarcerated during the Civil War. Moreover, Gray announced the building would not remain in Richmond, but would be carefully dismantled, shipped to Chicago, and there exactly rebuilt as a southern war prison on the shores of Lake Michigan.

Mark Twain described "that astonishing Chicago" as "a city where they are always rubbing the lamp, and fetching up the genii, and contriving and achieving new impossibilities."[1] In the wake of the Great Fire of 1871, much of the city needed to be rebuilt and reinvented, the ground having been cleared for what became an explosive period of growth. Investment opportunities were everywhere, and speculation on the part of the wealthy was rampant. By 1888, serious talk about competing to be the host city for the World's Columbian Exposition began to occupy city leadership, and provided the context for at least some of that speculation. Purchasing, transporting, and reassembling a notorious Civil War prison in Chicago fit the temperament of the time, in audacity if nothing else.

News of the prison's purchase inspired widespread suspicion. When Gray enthused that the building might be in place, restored fully, in time for the Republican National Convention to be held in Chicago that June, suspicion transformed into conviction—the venture was about reviving the worst of sectional animosities. Josiah Cratty, a member of the original syndicate, made haste to quiet such talk. "It should be understood that there is no idea of waving the 'bloody shirt' in this. It is simply a business speculation for what there is in it." He compared the syndicate's efforts to another Civil War–related enterprise already generating profit in Chicago, an immense panoramic painting of the Battle of Gettysburg. "The Gettysburg panorama people," Cratty asserted, "divided $400,000 in three years, and it still pays 8 per cent on a capital stock of $360,000—so I guess there is a fair chance at any rate of the [Libby Prison] thing taking."[2]

Cratty did not convince anyone. The *Richmond Dispatch* asked, "Is the result of the next presidential election to turn upon the removal of Libby Prison to Chicago?" A Chicago paper was quoted by that city's *Tribune* expressing the same sentiment: "It is absurd to say that the reërection in Chicago will not have the effect of perpetuating paltry sentiments from rabid South-haters. The expectant beneficiaries of the scheme can have the satisfaction of knowing that they are making money by the exhibition of a monument to foster and perpetuate Northern hatred of the South." The *Richmond State* asserted that the removal of Libby "will make a part of the furniture of the Lost Cause a drawing card for a show, while rabbles, for only ten cents, can see the exhibition and go away with a full appreciation of how lost indeed is that cause when its very public buildings are carted off a thousand miles and set up for sport or jeers."[3]

Fearful that Libby's removal to Chicago was designed to highlight southern cruelty to Union prisoners, some argued that northern prisons—Elmira, Point Lookout, or Fort Delaware—should also be brought before the public in some fashion. Rarely, however, were any comparisons made to Chicago's own Civil War prison, Camp Douglas. Illinois's *Mattoon Gazette* argued that "if it be a great and glorious thing to bring Libby prison up here to show how our soldiers were starved down there . . . why not send a few of the remains of camp Douglas down to New Orleans or Richmond to refresh the memories of those who have dead at Oakwood [Cemetery]?" The *Louisville Courier-Journal* also invoked the Richmond cemetery: "the great double circle of unmarked graves at Oakwood show that life to rebel prisoners [at Camp Douglas] was not all pastime, and that death was a familiar visitor." A Chicago paper found it "surprising to note the lack of knowledge that the general public, Chicagoans especially, [have] regarding the old prison, the site of which [was] almost in the heart of the city." The *Louisville Courier-Journal* asked bluntly, "what person in Chicago ever thinks of . . . Camp Douglas?" Part of the answer may be explained by Chicago's extraordinary postwar growth. The population of Chicago in 1890 was ten times that of 1860. By the time Libby arrived in Chicago, relatively few in the city had any connection to Camp Douglas, and most had not arrived until long after it had disappeared in 1865.[4]

In addition to fears of a revival of sectional animosity, the reduction of the human misery associated with the prison to a means of earning a profit troubled many. A Union veteran scorned, "it might serve to collect dimes and dollars as a ghastly circus exhibition to fill the pockets of sharp, unprincipled speculators—men that have conceived the selfish and despicable idea of violating the sanctity of the soldier's sufferings and to many the very spot of their death." He continued: "I trust the good people of Richmond will take measures so that the old prison will not be removed and used for the purpose of filling the pockets of the ghoulish company who planned the nefarious project." A Union veteran wrote to Richmond mayor William C. Carrington that "we consider it an insult to and mockery of our suffering that the very cells hallowed to us by our grief should be thrown open as part of a 10-cent show." Another paper opposed the move: "What would the brick walls of Libby prison amount to without the filth and wretched fare and cruel discipline to which the inmates were subjected? Would these walls still re-echo the groans, curses and prayers of the miserable inmates?" The editorial concluded the "morbid curiosity that would be sated by such an exhibition should not be pandered to."[5]

Significantly, however, many of the critics of the scheme, as it was most often called, attacked the financial dimensions of the project. A Richmond paper noted the city's potential loss of financial revenue from tourism alone. Virginia hotels, merchants, and relic sellers would suffer, as well as the hack drivers who had made good money showing off Libby Prison since the war. "That revenue is henceforth to be turned into the pockets of the white hack-drivers of Chicago and withheld from the pockets of the negro hackmen of Richmond." A more urgent concern was that southern merchants would withdraw their business from Chicago because of the prison. A newspaper editor overheard one southern businessman in the Palmer House: "The day the Libby Prison is opened I cease to buy goods in Chicago. . . . I tell you, sir, the bringing of Libby Prison to Chicago as a show will cost her people millions of dollars in the loss of Southern trade. The war is over, and any city that tries to keep alive the hatreds engendered by it makes a wide mistake." Another paper reported that while southern men "appreciate the fact that nothing is sacred in the eyes of the average Chicago man when there is a dollar in sight, [they] fear in this instance that ten dollars will leave the city where one comes in."[6]

The *Tribune*, easily the most influential paper in Chicago, opposed the move from the beginning. In a number of articles and editorials, the paper proclaimed the reasons Libby had no place in Chicago. First, it would fail financially. "The whole scheme to tear down the building, bring it here and set it up for a public show, to which an admission will be charged, is silly and useless and will be unprofitable." Second, as almost all of the inmates of Libby had been captured from eastern state regiments, no one in Chicago would feel any connection to the place. "If it is intended to bring up personal reminiscences of the war, it will fail in its purpose, as few if any soldiers west of Indiana were confined there. The Western ex-soldiers will care nothing for it." Falling in line with suspicions of sectional and political animosities, the *Tribune* stated that "if it is intended for a display of the 'bloody shirt' it would be more practical to move it to Philadelphia, New York, or Boston, as 95 per cent of Libby prisoners belonged in the East." Finally, if the aim was to evoke the cruelty and harshness of the prison experience, the speculators had better remember that "Chicago has no bitter memories connected with [Libby] and no desire to have the old tobacco warehouse brought here." To these basic elements of the *Tribune*'s attack, the editor added that "the building itself would be a public eyesore . . . and every person with the slightest sense of fitness and propriety would shrink from going near it."[7]

Other Chicago papers were more enthusiastic than the *Tribune*. In March the *Daily Inter Ocean* reported that the syndicate had incorporated as the United States War Relic Association. In a statement outlining the goals of the group, George E. Wright explained the association planned the building to house a museum of relics, "not . . . simply Northern relics, but Federal and Confederate alike—a National museum of the war." Furthermore, "we do not propose to make it a chamber of horrors, but a place of National interest and not sectional." The association had fielded offers from political leaders in Virginia, boasted Wright, including Mayor Carrington and Virginia governor Fitzhugh Lee, who expressed willingness to attend and speak in support of the project at its opening, slated for the first of June 1888. Within days the corporation advertised the opening of its office at 134 Dearborn Street, announcing that "parties owning [Civil War] relics are requested to communicate at the earliest possible date with the agents of the Association."[8]

For a time, however, it seemed that transporting Libby to Illinois might not take place at all. W. H. Gray, having acted as agent for the incorporated investors, turned over the deed to them as well as the obligation of satisfying the three outstanding payments. For this he received $35,000 for his outlay of $23,300. When it came time for the corporation to complete the process of obtaining Libby Prison, however, they inexplicably failed to do so. Although they had boasted that the prison would be rebuilt and open for business by June 1, that date and most of the following summer passed without action by the corporation. For reasons that are not at all apparent, the United States War Relic Association failed to make the second payment due in late August. Had they become persuaded that public opinion ran so strongly against them that the venture would become the financial failure so many predicted? For whatever reason, the default returned the property to Richmond real estate firm Rawlings & Rose, which offered the building and property at public auction. On September 20, 1888, Libby Prison was purchased by Dr. D. D. Bramble of Cincinnati for $11,000. He stated at the time of purchase that his interest in Libby was as an investment only, which he intended to sell at profit, possibly to a syndicate in Richmond.[9]

Before the *Tribune* and other critics could get comfortable with knowing the scheme had failed, a new syndicate in Chicago intervened. Gray approached Charles F. Gunther and, with his endorsement, assembled a room full of potential investors to explain the opportunities still within reach. Within days the new investor group purchased all rights to Libby from Dr. Bramble for $24,000, departed on a junket to Richmond to inspect the property, and confirmed the feasibility of moving the edifice to Chicago. Gunther and his associates incorporated as the Libby Prison War Museum Association on October 6, 1888.[10]

At this point, Charles F. Gunther becomes the central figure in the Libby Prison story. Following the Civil War, he established a confectionary business in Chicago, which survived the 1871 fire to become one of the most profitable businesses in the city. Making caramels and confections provided Gunther enough wealth to indulge his broad interest in history, particularly in owning its artifacts. By the time he become president of the Libby Prison War Museum Association, Gunther had collected avidly, if idiosyncratically, in historical books, manuscripts, art, and artifacts. His favored subjects were early Americana and the American Civil War, and it is the latter with which he planned to fill the halls of Libby Prison. As president of the association, Gunther masterminded the arrangements

Libby Prison, Richmond, Virginia, in April 1865.
(LC-DIG-ppmsca-34911, Library of Congress)

that finally brought the prison to Chicago. He also selected the lot for the rebuilding project, a large property on Wabash Avenue, 284 by 175 feet, for which the association signed a ninety-nine-year lease for $7,500 annually.[11]

By April 1889, the deconstruction of Libby Prison had begun in Richmond. In accord with Gray's original arrangements, the plan had been to dismantle the former warehouse with painstaking care, numbering each brick, post, beam, and rafter. It was an immense undertaking. The building was four stories tall on a sloping lot where the basement walls were visible on the lower side, and this slope was replicated in Chicago. The building measured 132 feet in length and 110 in width, internally divided into thirds by stout brick walls twenty inches thick. Section by section, the disassembled building was packed in separate rail cars, then sealed for transport. The total effort required 132 twenty-ton train cars, transportation over 800 miles, and the materials reassembled according to the numbered plans. At least one of the cars did not make the journey intact. On May 6, one of the freight cars broke an axle near Springdale, Kentucky, spilling its cargo. Papers reported no injuries, but noted nearby residents carrying away bricks and lumber as curiosities. As the project

Exterior view of Libby Prison inside its ornate castle walls on Wabash Avenue in Chicago, 1889. (ICHi-017809, Chicago History Museum)

had proudly maintained the care and exactitude with which the prison would be restored, the loss of these materials threatened that perception. Gunther acted to minimize the damage, telling reporters that only one car had opened, "and maybe a dozen bricks stolen." Later he stated the missing materials "did not amount to anything . . . I do not think we lost ten bricks there."[12]

The association's choice of building on Wabash came at an opportune time, as a vitalization of the long avenue was just beginning. The *Tribune* reported on the avenue's upswing: "Many thriving retail establishments deserted State street last May for Wabash avenue, and the testimony is almost unanimous that the shift was advantageous, and old tenants on the avenue declare that the growth of business is noticeable week by week." Hopeful of a relocation of business and traffic, some predicted it would soon lose its residential qualities altogether. As for a relocated prison in this mercantile environment, "Libby Prison Museum just south of Fourteenth street can also reasonably be expected to draw business to the street, as the museum, besides its unique character, promises to possess permanent attractions."[13] One of the attractions of the street almost certainly became the immense castellated wall that rose around the prison, ornamented with turrets, towers, and portcullis. The quixotic construction was certainly the most unusual architecture on Wabash, but not so that real estate values were harmed.

Finally, on September 21, 1889, the Libby Prison War Museum, tucked inside its immense stone keep, was ready to open for business. Admission was fifty cents, twenty-five cents for children under fifteen. Only the first floor was stocked with war relics on opening day, but the whole of the building was available for tour. Perhaps to defuse the accusation of partisanship, the first room, what had been the prisoner receiving room, was populated mostly by Confederate articles and artifacts, except for two letters—from Abraham Lincoln and Ulysses S. Grant—and the table on which the surrender was signed at Appomattox. To augment the ticket income, the museum began to sell a brochure, souvenirs, and a catalog of the many artifacts on display. Among the souvenirs sold were charms, medals, spoons, and photographic and lithographic images, as well as canes, "rebel" flags, bullets, Confederate money, and even pieces of the prison's flooring. Books like Melvin Grigsby's *The Smoked Yank*, a narrative of life in Andersonville, A. W. Bomberger's *Generals and Battles of the Civil War*, and even Harriet Beecher Stowe's *Uncle Tom's Cabin* sold steadily. The association also entered into an arrangement with Berriman Bros., a Chicago cigar manufacturer, which developed and sold a Libby Prison cigar. In exchange, Berriman Bros. received specially printed tickets that the firm then distributed free to their customers, paying the prison association half price for each cigar ticket collected.[14]

On April 25, 1890, Congress declared Chicago the host of the World's Columbian Exposition, setting in motion three years of furious activity aimed at "achieving new impossibilities." Despite not being associated with the Columbian Exposition, Libby Prison influenced some fair preparations. The relocation of the prison suggested to some the feasibility of transporting other historic buildings. Chicagoans were rumored to be interested in a number of historic relics. One commentator noted that Faneuil Hall was at risk and that Bostonians had better make certain Bunker Hill was well tied down. Others asserted a log cabin once lived in by President Grant, the oldest house in Washington, D.C., and the first settlement established by Columbus in the New World were all possible targets of relic movers. One reporter accused Chicagoans of planning to move Civil War battlefields, perhaps even Gettysburg itself, to the Lake Michigan shoreline. A Chicago group was even alleged to be investigating the feasibility of relocating Rome's Colosseum.[15]

Amid all these rumors, some more fancied than others, a few actual buildings were—like Libby—relocated to Chicago. At Harpers Ferry, the building that had become known as John Brown's Fort needed to be moved to make way for a new railroad right-of-way. Avid investors managed to move it all the way to Illinois where, installed inside a new building a short distance from Libby Prison, it aspired to entice tourists from the fair. Similarly, an entrepreneur purchased a cabin in Coles County, Illinois, that had been the last residence of Abraham Lincoln's father and stepmother. It was dismantled, its components carefully marked for rebuilding, and shipped to Chicago on the hopes of becoming a great attraction at the fair itself. And yet another cabin was retrieved from a Red River plantation in Louisiana that was claimed to have belonged to *the* Uncle Tom, the inspiration for Stowe's eponymous novel. It, too, was dismantled and sent to Chicago. One editor summed up his disdain for all such enterprises thus: "the bow of Ulysses, the iron bow with which Tell shot the apple, and the long bow of the modern myth-maker and equally long bow of the myth-destroyer, are all interesting in their way, but have as little to do with archery as log cabins have to do with history."[16]

In the end, the relocation projects were neither instigated nor accomplished by the Libby Prison War Museum associates, and Gunther's connections to these projects—if any—remains unclear. Those managing the Columbian Exposition had been offered the Lincoln cabin, and perhaps the others as well, but all were rejected as fair exhibits. The *Tribune* reported "that if the owners of these relics wished to pay for the privilege of having them on the [exposition] grounds they might receive some attention."[17]

The Libby Prison War Museum, like the rest of Chicago, profited enormously from the fair. The six months the fair was open, from May 1 to October 30, 1893, the museum proved its popularity as an attraction. According to one report, the association cleared $60,000 profit, $33,000 in the last month of the fair alone. Perhaps 250,000 visitors made their way through the castle walls to explore the prison and museum, a small percentage of the estimated 27 million fairgoers that had made the Columbian Exposition their goal.[18]

After the fair had decamped, leaving behind the ghost town of the White City, Libby Prison continued to operate, seven days a week, focused on its main constituents, tourists and veterans. Despite predictions that veterans—especially those who had been prisoners of war—would want nothing to do with the relocated prison, the former soldiers instead seemed to claim Libby as their own. Veterans of the Grand Army of the Republic (GAR) visited frequently, from Cook County's sixty posts as well as those throughout Illinois and beyond, often while traveling to or from state and national encampments. Chicago played host to the conventions of numerous veterans' associations, particularly the GAR and the Army of the Tennessee. When veterans gathered together in the city, Libby Prison was on everyone's must-see list. The museum also became a special meeting place for the National Association of Union Ex-Prisoners of War, both its local chapter as well visitors from the national association as well. A register was kept near the museum's entrance for former prisoners of war, a giant book with carved wooden spine and covers. In the ten years it was open, its oversized leaves were filled with some 3,600 signatures, Confederate and Union, signatures of men once held in almost every Civil War prison.[19]

Former Libby inmates forged a special relationship with the old building, which had in great part been reassembled to such exacting standards that the traces of their time in the prison was evident. Graffiti provided evidence of habitation, the names and initials still plainly visible on the walls, posts, and joists. Being in the building brought back memories—of hardship and pain, but also of brotherhood, shared misery, and survival. Libby survivors traveled to the old building and found their places, the length of floor they called a bed. Some could identify their places with great detail. One veteran wrote that he slept "in the NW corner of the Chickamauga Room, about 8 or 10 feet from the North wall," and he was able to name two men who slept to his south and four men who slept to his north. Other writers drew maps. When these locations were identified in letters or pointed out to the guides employed by the museum, a small brass rectangle was placed at those spots, which—for seventy-five cents—could be engraved with the prisoner's name, rank, and regiment.[20] All of this constituted tangible proof, validating the stories they had been telling since their incarceration ended.

One group shared a unique experience of the prison. During the war, on February 9, 1864, 109 prisoners escaped from Libby, and although more than half were eventually recaptured and returned to prison, their identity as escapees remained a bond throughout their lives. Once the prison was rebuilt in Chicago, an opportunity presented itself that had not existed before. The Libby Tunnel Association held annual reunions in Libby on the anniversary of their escape. Although scattered throughout the country, as many as possible returned to mark the effort with dinner and grand speeches. They kept the anniversary with admirable con-

Civil War veteran guide
at the Libby Prison War
Museum, Chicago, circa
1900. (ICHi-30989,
Chicago History Museum)

viction. Just before Libby Prison closed its doors for the last time, the
society held their last meeting. In their thirty-fourth year, there were but
thirty-four survivors of the escape.[21] The following year, Libby Prison was
no more.

The point man for many of these arrangements for veterans was Robert C. Knaggs, formerly of the Seventh Michigan Infantry, who was captured and taken prisoner the first day of Gettysburg, July 1, 1863. Transported to Libby, he later joined the escape in 1864. A veteran, a prisoner
of war, and a member of the Libby Tunnel Association, Knaggs was well-
suited to act as the museum's manager virtually from opening to its close.
Almost all of the extant correspondence of the Libby Prison War Museum Association passed through Knaggs's capable hands, and much of
that shows him to be eager to help on a wide array of fronts.

Many of the letters that came to Knaggs's attention sought to foster
business for Libby Prison: offers of advertisements from distant newspapers in exchange for tickets, for example, or requests for lithographs of
the prison that would be displayed publicly in an effort to drum up interest. Other letters sought bookings at the museum, for choral groups, dis-

plays of art, or lecturers. Certainly, there is an element of building revenue through building goodwill, but the effort Knaggs put forth seems much more valuable than additional admission fees or souvenir sales. The connection between most writers, especially veterans, and Knaggs stretched far beyond the prison. The connections were personal. One correspondent wrote Knaggs, at first referring to him as Mr. Knaggs. Knaggs's response does not survive, but the second time this individual wrote Knaggs, his relationship with him had changed. He saluted the manager as "Comrade Knaggs" and closed his letter with "Yours in F. C. & L.," that is, in fraternity, charity, and loyalty, the core values of the GAR. A letter from Milton Russell of Des Moines, Iowa, expressed a bond with Knaggs but not for his place of work: "Now I would like very much to see you when I come to Chicago and I will see you. But to be square and honest with you I don't believe I will ever see the inside of that building again. I don't want to feel ugly and mean as I use to when there."[22] The value of these relationships cannot be easily valued within the calculus of a profit-making amusement attraction.

More poignant still are the letters that came to Libby Prison seeking connections with other veterans. The ten years the museum operated in Chicago were tumultuous years for the military pension system, but in that time pensions expanded and became easier for dependents to obtain. Veterans did, however, need to supply information for eligibility: corroboration of the military service, or the wounds, or the death of a loved one that formed the basis of a claim. Hester Everard's husband, Gardiner, had been an inmate at Libby. He had died ten years after the war from an illness she was sure he contracted while in prison. What she needed were affidavits from someone who knew of his imprisonment. "Will you please see if there is one or two who was in prison at the same time or knew him." Similarly, S. O. Blodgett wrote to inquire about his brother who had died at Libby in 1862. "My mother is now trying to get a pension, and would like the address of any of the men that knew him." One letter struck a little closer to home. May Wickes wrote for her father, who wanted addresses of "the old members of Company H—7th Mich. Infantry," Knaggs's own regiment. "He has applied for a pension and needs witnesses."[23] These transactions were far more significant than anything else Libby Prison ever accomplished.

The outreach performed by Knaggs and the museum extended well beyond veterans. T. E. Daniels, superintendent of the Chicago Waifs' Mission and Training School, wrote to Knaggs asking if he could obtain tickets so his "boys" could visit the museum. They would have to attend in the evening, Daniels wrote, as the morning was devoted to school instruction and the afternoon given to manual training in their shoe factory. "Since we have opened our school . . . we have made the History of Our Country one of the special branches of studies, in order to infuse patriotism into the hearts of our little newsboys." Daniels's charges had taken to the program of study, and "we are anxious to increase their interest which could be done in no better way than by a visit to your Museum." Within the week, Knaggs forwarded to Daniels fifty tickets, who replied, "I cannot thank you too much for your kindness in the matter." Similarly, on the last day the museum was open, newsboys for the *Chicago Tribune* crowded the place on complimentary tickets.[24]

Despite Knaggs's efforts—some of which worked to stimulate the museum's customer base—the earnings of the Libby Prison War Museum gradually declined from its height in 1893. The museum continued to make money, but the revenue was underperforming considering the potential value of the property. The Wabash lot had 284 feet of frontage, leased at a valuation of $455 per foot. Property all along Wabash had increased in value to an estimated $1,000 to $1,200 per foot, and had actually sold as high as $1,600. Faced with this math, the Libby Prison War Museum Association pursued two strategies. The first was to entice greater visitation of the site through the acquisition or staging of new attractions alongside the museum. The second strategy was to pursue using the property in ways that would provide more revenue, ways that would likely not include a future for the prison.[25]

The first new attractions to the Libby Prison property came as a result of the closing of the World's Columbian Exposition. Gunther somehow acquired or appropriated the alleged cabin of Uncle Tom, which was promptly erected on the museum grounds. The Thomas Lincoln cabin, once stored behind the John Brown Fort building, also was delivered to the prison property, but was apparently never rebuilt. Then, in January 1894, the museum acquired an extraordinary Civil War relic, albeit only on loan. "The General," a railroad engine that had been on display in the fair's Transportation Building, was brought to sit alongside Libby Prison. In 1862, "the General" had been the target of a daring raid by Union troops, who stole the engine and fled toward Union-held Chattanooga, wrecking rail lines behind them. Running out of fuel short of their goal, all of the raiders were captured by Confederate troops. Of the twenty-two participants in the raid, eight were executed, eight escaped from custody, and six were eventually exchanged from prison, but not before spending a brief time in Libby Prison. It is unclear whether all of this activity increased revenue. In August, despite an economic downturn, a Chicago paper was able to report that the prison "had been doing a gratifying business this summer," but also noted that the directors of Libby had decided to reduce the admission price to twenty-five cents, "to meet popular demand and the present condition of the average pocketbook."[26]

Under the second strategy, rumor of what might happen to the Wabash property outpaced fact so that it was difficult to discern what Gunther and the association intended. They first announced that the "stockholders of the Libby Prison War Museum" had approached the Chicago Hussars about subleasing the Wabash property. Created in 1888, the Hussars were a civilian equestrian unit that helped ornament the Columbian Exposition's opening ceremonies. The commander of the unit, Captain Edwin L. Brand, thought the property suitable for a large show arena, clubhouse, and underground stables. More was possible if the prison were removed. When asked about the future of the museum, association vice president L. Manasee floated the idea that "the people of Richmond" might want Libby returned, "and if we desire to relinquish it at a nominal figure they would buy it." But there was no thought that they would want the building for its history: "it could be removed and rebuilt for manufacturing or storage purposes." This alternative seemed far-fetched, to say the least. Later, John Ringling of Ringling Brothers Circus confidently declared that "we have just succeeded in getting the Libby Prison site on Wabash," with plans to construct a "large building like Madison Square Garden." The hall would be a permanent base for the circus to perform for two months, and then alternate with "carnivals, exhibitions, and conventions." The next day, Charles Gunther had to announce that "no negotiations whatever" have been entered into with Ringling Brothers, to which John Ringling admitted he was looking at several sites. Finally, a lease was signed to create a skating rink on the Wabash property over the winter, complete with more than 22,000 square feet of ice, a band stand, and spectator seating for five hundred. It was also noted that "Uncle Tom's Cabin will be used as the ladies' retiring room."[27]

Ultimately, Libby Prison would fall victim to another simple business speculation. Neither strategy to improve the income relative to frontage foot had succeeded, but Gunther was inspired by the process. In 1894, rumors had circulated concerning Gunther's continuing pursuit for a great exhibition hall. He had failed to acquire two, the first through collapse and the second—after a brief existence—through fire. Whether or not there was any truth to the assertion that Chicagoans took a flyer at relocating the Roman Colosseum, Gunther determined to build one. His, known as the Coliseum, would be the largest indoor exhibition and meeting facility in the world. The most obvious piece of real estate available was the enormous lot on Wabash currently occupied by Libby Prison. Without much fanfare, the Libby Prison War Museum Association announced the museum's closing.[28]

The final evening in March 1899 was one of music and speech-making. Typical of the association's regard for veterans, all GAR members as well as all United Confederate Veterans were specifically invited. Charles F. Gunther led at the podium. No city paper reprinted his speech, though the *DIO* observed that he asserted that "Chicago did not appreciate the prison," to which the *Tribune* responded that "perhaps the people of this city cared more about this city than the object brought to it." A twenty-four-gun salute ended the ceremony, fired by Chicago's Eighth Illinois Volunteer Infantry Regiment, Illinois's only–African American military unit.[29]

Overall, the papers had little response to the closure of the museum. The *Daily Chicago News* reported that the building would be disassembled as carefully as it had been in Richmond, given the possibility that it might be reassembled once again. The wrecking company had already been contracted by that point, however, and Gunther, in his closing remarks, set such hopes aside by stating flatly that "it was unlikely that [the prison] would ever be reconstructed." Oddly, the *Chicago Tribune*, which had never supported the enterprise, took advantage of the museum's demise by arranging for tens of thousands of tickets to be printed that it then distributed free of charge at the paper's many branch offices. The initial printing of eighty-five thousand tickets went quickly, and the paper would later claim to have printed and distributed as many as two hundred thousand tickets by the time Libby closed its doors.[30]

The following day, workers crated the museum collection for storage. The papers had claimed the wreckers would sell bricks from the building to relic hunters. Gunther stated he thought each brick would sell for twenty-five cents, at least (at four hundred thousand bricks, not an insignificant sum). But just three weeks after closing, the wreckers placed advertisements in Chicago papers: "For Sale—Yellow Pine Joists, 3x12; flooring; girders; posts; rubble stone[,] coping, sills; [planed] curbing, ornamental stone, brick, etc.: cash. Libby Prison 1500 Wabash av."[31]

As Libby Prison closed, Robert C. Knaggs, manager, veteran, and Libby inmate, signed the Prisoner of War Register kept near the front door, the last name in the book. The prison had stood behind its castle walls on Wabash Avenue from September 21, 1889, to its closing on March 28,

1899. The warehouse had been built around 1850. It was used as an improvised prison for almost four years, and twenty-four years later was a prison again, at least in name, for another ten. In between it served as a tobacco warehouse, a chandlery and grocery, and a fertilizer factory. In its fiftieth year it was totally demolished, sold for scrap, and what could not be sold was discarded. No trace remains of the 3,500 brass plates that once identified a prisoner's place, a floor "studded . . . with memorials of the days when the building was a living thing."[32] Ultimately, there was no sentiment in Gunther and his partners that could not be outweighed by the promise of profit, no emotions that could not be ventured in a simple business speculation.

NOTES

1. Mark Twain, *Life on the Mississippi*, in *Mississippi Writings* (New York: Library of America, 1982), 585.

2. "Libby Prison, Chicago," *Chicago Tribune* (hereafter *CT*), February 5, 1888, part 2, p. 9.

3. "Libby Prison," *Richmond (Va.) Dispatch* (hereafter *RD*), February 14, 1888, 2; "Libby Prison Sure to Come," *CT*, February 26, 1888, 24; "Libby a Museum," *Richmond State* quoted in *Anderson Court House (S.C.) Intelligencer*, March 8, 1888, 2.

4. "Libby Prison in Chicago," *Manning (S.C.) Times*, October 2, 1889, 2; *Alexandria (Va.) Gazette*, June 5, 1889, 2; "Preparing for More Pensions," *Mattoon (Ill.) Gazette*, August 2, 1889, 8; *Louisville Courier-Journal*, June 12, 1889; "Theatrical Gossip," *Daily Inter Ocean (Chicago)* (hereafter *DIO*), December 6, 1891, 20. Camp Douglas, in which 26,000 men were incarcerated, was dismantled in 1865 and the land absorbed by the expanding city (Dennis Kelly, *A History of Camp Douglas, Illinois, Union Prison Camp, 1861–1865* [Washington, D.C.: Department of the Interior, National Park Service, Southeast Region, 1989], 155–56).

5. "A Soldier's Protest," *New York Times*, February 15, 1888, 2; "Against the Removal of Libby," *CT*, March 1, 1888, 9; *Helena (Mont.) Weekly Herald*, February 9, 1888, 6.

6. "Libby Prison," *RD*, February 14, 1888, 2; "The Libby Prison Show," *CT*, May 6, 1889, 10; "Libby May Hoodoo Chicago," *New York Herald*, May 31, 1889, Newspaper Scrapbook, 6, Charles F. Gunther Papers, 1600–1920, Chicago History Museum.

7. "The Libby Prison Folly," *CT*, April 7, 1888, 4. For similar statements, see *CT*, May 25, 1888, 4; *CT*, October 27, 1888, 4; "The Libby Prison Show," *CT*, May 6, 1889, 10. Chicago once had its own Civil War prison, Camp Douglas, in which 26,000 men were incarcerated.

8. "Chicago Gets Libby Prison," *DIO*, March 1, 1888, 7; "Chicago Secures

Libby Prison," *Fort Worth Daily Gazette*, March 3, 1888, 3; "Libby Prison," *CT*, March 4, 1888, 6.

9. *CT*, August 30, 1888, 4; "Libby Prison Will Not Come to Chicago," *CT*, September 21, 1888, 5; advertisement, *RD*, September 15, 1888, 4.

10. "The Libby Prison Project," *Chicago Daily News*, October 3, 1888, 1; "The Libby Prison Museum," *CT*, October 3, 1888, 9; "New Incorporations," *DIO*, October 7, 1888. 3.

11. *The Biographical Dictionary and Portrait Gallery of Representative Men of Chicago, Milwaukee and the World's Columbian Exposition* (Chicago: American Biographical Pub. Co., 1892), 310–15; Biographical Sketch, Miscellaneous folder, Charles F. Gunther Papers; "Some Important Deals," *CT*, February 10, 1889, 6.

12. "Libby Prison, Chicago," *CT*, February 5, 1888, 9; "Libby Prison Located in Kentucky," *CT*, May 7, 1889, 1; "At Home and Abroad," *Frank Leslie's Illustrated Newspaper*, May 18, 1889, 263; "Sectionalism Not Intended," *CT*, June 1, 1889, 3.

13. "The Wabash Avenue Outlook," *CT*, June 30, 1889, 27.

14. "A Visit to Old Libby," *CT*, September 29, 1889, 29; account books "July 27, 1892–Sep. 2, 1893," and "May 2, 1895–Dec. 30, 1897," and Berriman Bros. to Libby Prison War Museum Association, July 1, 1890, Correspondence, July–October 1890 folder, all in Libby Prison War Museum Association Records, 1889–1898, Chicago History Museum.

15. "If She Wants It, She'll Get It," *CT*, April 3, 1890, 4; "Better Keep Your Eye on It," *CT*, April 8, 1890, 4; "Grant's Cabin as an Exhibit," *CT*, August 27, 1891, 8; "Not Likely to Come to Chicago," *CT*, May 18, 1891, 1; "Fair Gossip," *CT*, April 25, 1890, 2; "Chicago Cutlets," *CT*, November 29, 1891, 13; "The Colosseum for Chicago," *CT*, May 22, 1891, 4.

16. "John Brown's Fort to Be Torn Down," *CT*, October 21, 1889, 9; "Relics of Abraham Lincoln," *Chicago Herald*, August 13, 1891, 9; "Tires of Lincoln Cabin," *CT*, June 12, 1897, 13; "Log Cabins, Obelisks, Etc.," *Chicago Herald*, August 23, 1891, 20.

17. "Grant's Cabin as an Exhibit," *CT*, August 27, 1891, 8.

18. "Plans for a New Hussars' Armory," *CT*, March 4, 1895, 3. No significant financial records of the Libby Prison War Museum, or any of Gunther's businesses, have apparently survived.

19. Prisoner of War Register, Libby Prison War Museum Association Records. Originally, additional rosters for non-prisoner soldiers and civilians were also kept but have seemingly since been lost ("A Private View of Libby," *Chicago Times*, September 12, 1889, Newspaper Scrapbook, 2, Charles F. Gunther Papers).

20. Thos. E. Rose to Robert C. Knaggs (hereafter RCK), Jan. 9, 1890; George W. Corliss to RCK, March 27, 1890; Albert Wallber to RCK, January 18, 1890; E. P. Rogers to RCK, December 23, 1889; Adolf Lange to RCK, December 27, 1889, all in Correspondence, Libby Prison War Museum Association Records.

21. "Tunnel Prisoners to Meet," *CT*, February 5, 1898, 13. Even though the

prison was still standing when the next anniversary came around, February 9, 1899, no reunion seems to have been held.

22. Geo. F. Crouch to museum, September 24, 1889; A. B. Hewett to C. F. Gunther, September 12, 1889; R. C. Morgan to RCK, October 2, 1889; C. M. Rawlings to RCK, June 17 and June 30, 1890; Milton Russell to RCK, January 23, 1890, all in Correspondence, Libby Prison War Museum Association Records.

23. Hester Everard to RCK, August 2, 1890; S. O. Blodgett to [RCK], December 6, 1889; May Wickes to RCK, March 6, 1890, all in Correspondence, Libby Prison War Museum Association Records.

24. T. E. Daniels to [RCK], February 20 and 28, 1890, in Correspondence, Libby Prison War Museum Association Records; "Newsboys at Libby Prison," *CT*, March 28, 1899, 2.

25. "Some Important Deals," *CT*, February 10, 1889, 6; "Plans for a New Hussar's Armory," *CT*, March 4, 1895, 3.

26. *DIO*, August 12, 1894, 24; "'The General,' in Libby Prison," *CT*, Jan. 7, 1894, 5; William Pittenger, *Danger and Suffering: A History of the Andrews Railroad Raid into Georgia in 1862* (New York: War Publishing Co., 1887), 375–77; *CT*, August 12, 1894, 8.

27. "Plans for a New Hussars' Armory," *CT*, March 4, 1895, 3; "New Carnival Hall for Chicago," *CT*, October 5, 1895, 6; "Local Items," *CT*, October 6, 1895, 5; "Ice Rink at Libby Prison," *CT*, November 23, 1895, 3; *DIO*, November 24, 1895, 41.

28. "Coliseum Building May Be Erected on Libby Prison Site," *CT*, October 16, 1898; "Plans for Coliseum," *DIO*, December 22, 1898, 5.

29. "Days of Libby Prison End," *DIO*, March 29, 1899, 3; "Days of Libby Prison Ended," *CT*, March 29, 1899, 13; W. T. Goode, *The "Eighth Illinois"* (Chicago: Blakely Printing Co., 1899).

30. "Tribune Opens the Door," *CT*, March 14, 1899, 5; "Many Will See War Museum," *CT*, March 15, 1899, 7; "Libby Is Visited by 14,000," *CT*, March 17, 1899, 8.

31. *DIO*, April 17, 1899, 11.

32. "Tribune Opens the Door," *CT*, March 14, 1899, 5; William W. Ellsworth, "Forty-Eight Hours in Chicago," *Christian Union* 47 (February 11, 1893): 267.

Buying and Selling Health and Manhood

Civil War Veterans and Opiate Addiction "Cures"

JONATHAN S. JONES

Tucked away in the correspondence pages of an obscure Kentucky medical journal is the remarkable story of a Civil War veteran who tried to buy back his health and manhood. Like countless other physically debilitated veterans, "Mr. J.T.B." had fallen on hard times by 1880, the year his case appeared in a physician's letter to the editors of the *Louisville Medical News.* J.T.B. contracted chronic diarrhea during the Civil War, like most soldiers at one point or another in their army days. Stricken by an especially severe bout of diarrhea in April 1862, J.T.B. began taking opium pills, a common Civil War–era antidiarrheal. Opium seemed to do the trick, stopping the diarrhea by "plugging up" the bowels, as one nineteenth-century physician put it. But relief came at terrible cost. Opiates are addictive, and J.T.B. soon contracted the "opium habit."[1]

As the years passed, eighteen in all, J.T.B. resolved to quit the opium, and for good reason. Long-term opium abuse took a terrible physical toll on his body, including fatigue, emaciation, and impotence. A deeply stigmatized condition, opiate addiction also branded J.T.B. as weak in body and willpower, and thus unmanly. Hoping to ameliorate these disastrous consequences, J.T.B. likely tried to quit the opium cold turkey through sheer willpower, enduring hellish withdrawal symptoms along the way. These attempts, however, failed again and again. Growing desperate to quit, J.T.B. eventually became willing to try any means of ridding himself of addiction, even those of dubious effectiveness. One fateful day, the veteran chanced upon an advertisement for a patent medicine claiming to cure opiate addiction without the pains of withdrawal. Perhaps he discovered this "cure" in a newspaper classified advertisement, or a pamphlet lying on a pharmacy counter. With great hopefulness at the possibility of simply buying his escape from addiction, J.T.B. mailed the confidential order form and a check to the patent medicine company. When the cure arrived, the addicted veteran gleefully took his first swig of liquid freedom. He was, unfortunately, sorely disappointed to find that the patent medicine "cure" failed to relieve his cravings for opium. Still, there were other brands on the market. Hoping one of these might help him yet, J.T.B. tried again and again, ultimately experimenting with a slew of patent opiate addiction cures that failed one after another. By 1880, when J.T.B. finally came under the care of a physician, who resorted to the equally addictive drug coca to treat the veteran's addiction to opium, the beleaguered old soldier had spent some $1,800 on opium and the patent medicines he hoped would free him from it.[2]

Astonishingly, Mr. J.T.B.'s story was relatively common during the Gilded Age. While the amount he spent might have been extreme, many Civil War veterans shared J.T.B.'s experience with opiate addiction and patent medicine addiction cures. One desperate veteran even outspent J.T.B., spending $2,500—equivalent to nearly $63,000 in 2020—on "all the so-called 'cures' and 'antidotes'" but felt "worse than ever" after the remedies failed. This essay investigates the buying and selling of patent medicine remedies for opiate addiction by Civil War veterans during the Gilded Age. During and after the war, countless veterans became addicted to medicinal opiates, standard remedies for chronic pain and a wide spectrum of ailments in the nineteenth century. Opiate addiction caused terrible physical suffering and harsh social consequences for veterans, undermining men's health and masculinity, leaving them unable to work and excluded from military entitlements, and, all too often, culminated in grisly, fatal overdoses. As addicted veterans like J.T.B. sought ways to avoid these outcomes, patent medicine proprietors, many of whom were themselves veterans, spotted a bonanza. Responding to a growing demand among veterans for opiate addiction remedies, Gilded Age entrepreneurs invented patent medicine "antidotes" and "cures" for the "opium habit" and marketed the products widely to veterans in newspapers, magazines, and pamphlets. Out of desperation, many old soldiers swapped their money for the patent medicines, hoping to buy freedom from opiate addiction and thereby restore health and redeem manhood.[3]

Investigating this phenomenon shines new light on the intimate health and economic effects of the Civil War for veterans. The war dramatically altered the financial and commercial landscape of the United States, changes that historians have thoroughly investigated at the macro scale. Similarly, recent studies have illuminated various aspects of the war's health fallout in harrowing detail. But historians know surprisingly little about the intersection of the Civil War's economic and health consequences for individual veterans, aside from the pensions and soldiers' homes that supported many ailing Civil War veterans. "Less explored than pensions," as James Marten recently noted, "are the ways in which military service shaped the economic well-being of survivors, especially those who were disabled. It seems clear that the war may have affected the economic prospects of veterans negatively, but few historians have provided empirical evidence."[4] This essay helps fill this lacuna, while also complicating the story.

On the one hand, opiate addiction cost some veterans dearly. The various expenses of opiate addiction—ranging from the costs of opiates and patent addiction cures to lost pensions and wages—proved a severe financial burden for addicted veterans. On the other hand, the postwar epidemic of opiate addiction among Civil War veterans created new commercial opportunities for savvy, if unscrupulous, patent medicine proprietors, the most successful of whom were themselves Civil War veterans who drew on their wartime experiences when developing their cures for opiate addiction. Ultimately, I suggest, the Civil War had a mercurial financial legacy for individual veterans, as illustrated by the patent medicine trade, which enriched some old soldiers at the expense of others.

Patent medicines were pharmaceutical remedies marketed to Americans as do-it-yourself treatments for all manner of medical ailments. Ironically, although called "patent medicines," the remedies were rarely patented, because to do so required proprietors to disclose their products' secret, often dangerous ingredients. Many of the most popular nineteenth-century brands—like Mrs. Winslow's Soothing Syrup and Dr. M'Munn's Elixir of Opium—contained opiates, a fact that was widely known in the Civil War era. For this reason, patent medicines occasionally came under fire in the press as the culprits behind accidental opiate overdoses. Yet despite their dangers, patent medicines were a popular avenue for self-medication, often standing in for physicians. Because patent medicines contained opiates, they were sometimes efficacious against pain, diarrhea, and coughing, which fostered consumers' confidence in patent remedies, driving up sales. As historian Jackson Lears argues, many nineteenth-century consumers also genuinely believed proprietors' claims that patent medicines could "magically" transform one's health and well-being.[5]

While robust in the prewar decades, the patent medicine industry reached dizzying new heights in the Civil War's wake. On the eve of the war in 1859, patent medicine sales in the United States stood at about $3.5 million. During the Gilded Age—the golden age of patent medicines—new nostrums flooded the medical marketplace. Little to no regulation of medical products or services meant that enterprising proprietors could advertise patent medicine as cures for practically any ailment under the sun. By 1900, sick Americans could choose from nearly six thousand brands, and the patent medicine sector had matured into a $74 million-per-year industry.[6]

The Civil War directly contributed to the meteoric Gilded Age rise of patent medicines. Alongside other factors in the mid-nineteenth century—increased commercialization in American health care, the expansion of print media and advertising, and decreased shipping and postal costs—the Civil War's long-lasting health consequences set the stage for the unprecedented postwar growth of the patent medicine industry. Most importantly, the war spawned a new demographic of sick and suffering soldiers to purchase patent medicines, and an influx of novel ailments to treat. The rise of patent medicine opiate addiction cures best illustrates this trend.[7]

The success of opiate addiction cures in the postwar decades was, in large part, due to the health fallout of the Civil War. The war sparked an epidemic of opiate addiction among disabled veterans. Many addicted veterans sought out medical treatments for addiction, becoming a niche market for novel addiction remedies. Indeed, before the Civil War created this consumer base, patent opiate addiction cures were universally commercial failures. In 1859 New York City businessman Henry Zell invented Dr. Zell's Temperance Powder, a remedy that he claimed could "set drunkards against liquor, opium and other narcotics." The product was the first patent medicine for opium addiction in U.S. history. To cure their husbands' addictions, long-suffering wives could, Zell suggested, slip the powders into their unsuspecting husbands' tea. Hoping to rustle up sales for the product, Zell placed at least a dozen advertisements in the *New-York Daily Tribune*, the *New York Herald*, and the *New York Sun* between October and December 1859. Although antebellum New Yorkers were no strangers to opiate addiction—as evidenced by sporadic, panicked reports about the "evil" of "opium eating" in the city's newspapers—Zell's Temperance Powders flopped, likely due to insufficient demand. Zell retooled his patent medicine in the winter of 1859–60, dropping the reference to opiate addiction from advertisements, instead marketing the medicine solely as an alcohol-abuse deterrent.[8] As it turned out, Zell's visionary product was just ahead of its time. But within a decade of its commercial failure, the Civil War stimulated enough demand among veterans to sustain a legion of products like Zell's Temperance Powders.

Veterans suffering from service-related ailments often required long-term medical care in their postwar lives. Opium, morphine, and laudanum were standard medical therapies for a wide spectrum of disabilities, ranging from painful gunshot wounds and amputations to debilitating rheumatism and chronic diarrhea. Ailing old soldiers thus ran the risk of developing opiate addictions through doctors' prescriptions or self-medication. This was Mr. J.T.B.'s story, and thousands of veterans became addicted under similar circumstances. Thus, the Civil War, by igniting an epidemic of opiate addiction among veterans, created demand for a new wave of patent medicine opiate addiction cures.[9]

Beginning in the late 1860, the remedies proliferated, as entrepreneurs developed scores of brands to meet the demand of Civil War veterans for opiate addiction remedies. Veterans' opiate addiction and the rise of patent addiction cures grew hand in hand. Indeed, as the physician and addiction expert J. B. Mattison lamented in 1886, proof of the alarming increase of opiate addiction in the postwar decades "could easily be given by citing the number of individuals engaged in vending the various nostrums, each of which, it is asserted, has the only true claim to merit as the one genuine, sovereign cure for this phase of human ill."[10] Like opiate addiction among veterans, the cures knew no regional lines and were eventually bought and sold in every corner of the United States by both Union and Confederate veterans. Of course, disabled old soldiers were not the only Gilded Age Americans to suffer from opiate addiction, nor to purchase patent addiction cures, which had broad appeal among addicted Americans. The plight of addicted veterans, however, inspired the development of the most successful Gilded Age patent medicine opiate addiction cures.

Samuel B. Collins, a La Porte, Indiana, bricklayer-turned-patent-medicine-magnate, launched the first commercially successful patent opiate addiction remedy in the Civil War's immediate aftermath. Collins was himself a Union veteran—having served in the 48th and 109th Indiana infantry regiments—meaning he would have likely witnessed firsthand how sick and wounded Civil War veterans were treated with opiates, often becoming addicted in the process. Sensing a commercial opportunity, Collins invented the Painless Opium Antidote in 1868, the first patent medicine opiate addiction cure brought to market after the Civil War. Veterans were early adopters of Collins's antidote, contributing significantly to the product's commercial success. One veteran the

Flyer advertising Samuel B. Collins's Painless Opium Antidote featuring an exterior view of his "laboratory" in LaPorte, Indiana, 1873. (U.S. National Library of Medicine, NLM ID A013239)

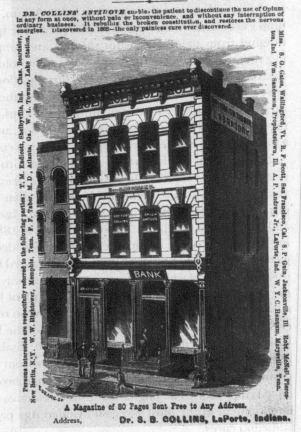

THERIAKI !
Painless Cure for the Opium and Liquor Habits.

DR. COLLINS' ANTIDOTE enables the patient to discontinue the use of Opium in any form at once, without pain or inconvenience, and without any interruption of ordinary business. It rebuilds the broken constitution, and restores the nervous energies. Discovered in 1868—the only painless cure ever discovered.

Persons interested are respectfully referred to the following parties: T. M. Endicott, Shelbyville, Ind. Chas. Beardsley, New Berlin, N.Y. W. W. Hightower, Memphis, Tenn. F. F. Taber, M. D., Atlanta, Ga. W. L. Towner, Lake Station, Ind.

Miss. S. G. Gates, Wallingford, Vt. R. F. Scott, San Francisco, Cal. S. P. Guin, Jacksonville, Ill. A. P. Andrew, Jr., LaPorte, Ind. Robt. McNeil, Pierceton, Ind. Wm. Sanderson, Prophetstown, Ill. W. F. C. Hasgum, Marysville, Tenn.

BANK

A Magazine of 80 Pages Sent Free to Any Address.

Address,   Dr. S. B. COLLINS, LaPorte, Indiana.

Fourth Michigan Infantry, Joseph Darrow, began taking the remedy in April 1869. By November "he was pronounced cured," according to the local justice of the peace, whose affidavit featured heavily in Collins's early advertisements.[11]

Embarking on a nationwide advertising blitz, Collins placed classifieds in scores of newspapers and magazines during the Gilded Age. Postcards and flyers advertising the Painless Opium Antidote also circulated widely. Within a few years, sales of the product skyrocketed, indicated by Collins's prolific advertising. One could hardly open the back pages of any major Gilded Age newspaper without encountering one of Collins's advertisements, like the classified he placed in nearly every 1879 issue of *Frank Leslie's Illustrated Newspaper*, forty-nine times altogether. After catching readers' eyes with his various short-form advertisements, Collins invited would-be customers to correspond with him, replying to inquiries with a pamphlet loaded with testimonials for the Painless Opium Antidote, including many written by formerly addicted veterans like Darrow.

Collins's pamphlets were nearly as prolific as his newspaper advertisements. *Theriaki*, Collins's main pamphlet—the title being a French term for opium eaters—flew off the press, going through several editions under various subtitles during the 1860s, 1870s, and 1880s. It informed customers how to obtain and use the Painless Opium Antidote. Collins instructed readers to write him, describing their regular dose of opiates, symptoms, constitution, and the duration of their addiction. This information supposedly allowed Collins's laboratory to concoct a dose of the antidote tailored specifically to each patient. Customers typically paid about twenty-five dollars for a month's supply of the medicine—the minimum order Collins sold—which came in a specially sealed bottle wrapped in an unmarked package. In return for this steep fee, the antidote would bring about what Collins claimed was "a certain and a perfect cure accomplished without pain and without inconvenience" in the privacy of customers' homes. While his business records are no longer extant, Collins evidently made a fortune from sales of his remedy, indicated by the palatial Victorian residence he built in La Porte and his regular donations to local institutions like the Grand Army of the Republic (GAR). This windfall stemmed largely from the desperation of addicted veterans, whose suffering proved a financial boon for the cunning Collins.[12]

By the mid-1870s, Collins faced stiff competition from a host of similar products. The most successful of the lot was Leslie Keeley's Double Chloride of Gold, widely known as the "Gold Cure," although it contained no gold. Keeley worked as a contract surgeon for the U.S. Army during the Civil War. Observing addicted soldiers, Keeley became convinced that addiction to alcohol and opiates was a disease of the body, rather than simply a personal failure, the predominant contemporary belief. With this medicalized approach to addiction as an intellectual foundation, Keeley concocted patent medicines that, he claimed, treated the physical causes of alcohol and opiate addiction. He achieved unparalleled commercial success with the Gold Cure, even surpassing that of Collins. Advertising nationwide in periodicals, pamphlets, and songs he commissioned, Keeley sold the Gold Cure to a half-million Americans between 1880 and 1920. Keeley eventually turned his Gold Cure into a temperance-style

Members of the Veterans' Keeley League, based at the National Home for Disabled Volunteer Soldiers Leavenworth, Kansas, branch (*The Keeley Institutes of the United States, Canada, and Other Countries* ([Dwight?, Ill.]: Leslie E. Keeley Co., [1895?]), 17)

movement by developing a kind of social club, the Keeley League. The league became the key element in Keeley's success, enabling the Gold Cure to eclipse Collins's Painless Opium Antidote. Scores of franchised "Keeley Institutes" sprang up around the country, where customers received in-patient treatment with the Gold Cure in conjunction with an early version of group therapy. Even the U.S. military bought into the movement. In 1892, the National Home for Disabled Volunteer Soldiers (NHDVS) founded a Keeley League to treat opiate and alcohol-addicted veterans in Leavenworth, Kansas. By 1894, thirty opiate-addicted veterans had received the Gold Cure at the Leavenworth facility on the government's dime. Veteran Gold Cure devotees also founded Keeley Leagues at several NHDVS branches, receiving praise and support from NHDVS officials.[13]

By the 1880s, Americans had only to skim the classifieds of their favorite newspaper to spot advertisements for various brands of patent medicine addiction cures. The *Chicago Tribune* for example, hawked not only Collins's Painless Opium Antidote and Keeley's Gold Cure, but also remedies invented by the city's own Clesson Pratt, H. H. Kane of New York

City, W. B. Squire of Indiana, Carlos Bruisard of Cincinnati, and Mark M. Thompson of Chicago, whose Bichloride of Gold blatantly aped Keeley's Gold Cure. Americans could choose among no fewer than thirty addiction cures by 1900. Such widespread advertising suggests that the cures appealed to a great number of people. Indeed, a wide demographic spectrum of Gilded Age Americans suffered from opiate addiction and resorted to patent remedies.[14]

Yet veterans stood out among consumers of opiate addiction cures, not only inspiring the development of the products in the Civil War's wake, but also consistently representing an important segment of consumers. Many brands explicitly targeted veterans through advertisements in periodicals like the *National Tribune*, the unofficial mouthpiece of the GAR. Medical products in high demand among aging and disabled veterans—including wheelchairs, and prosthetics—were some of the *National Tribune*'s most consistently advertised products, and opiate addiction cures were among the most prominent. The periodical's first advertisement for an opiate addiction cure appeared in May 1883. F. E. March of Quincy, Michigan, promised to cure veterans of the opium and morphine habits in under a month, with "no pay till cured." March's classified ran alongside others hawking a cure for hemorrhoids, a book of addresses of ex-army surgeons, and the services of a pension lawyer, all items of great interest to old, ailing soldiers.[15]

The *National Tribune* ran hundreds of advertisements for patent opiate addiction cures between 1883 and 1911. A host of proprietors used the newspaper to target veterans, including Keeley, H. H. Kane, M. C. Benham, the Humane Remedy Co., and several others. J. Stephens of Lebanon, Ohio singlehandedly placed at least 120 advertisements for his brand of addiction cures during the 1880s and 1890s. Another Ohio vendor, H. C. Keith of Toledo, dared veterans to test the effectiveness of his remedy, offering a handsome $1,000 payout for any case of opiate addiction he could not cure. In many issues of the *National Tribune*, veterans could spot advertisements for several competing brands on the same page. *Confederate Veteran*, a magazine for ex-Confederates, also sported advertisements for various opiate addiction cures. In one typical advertisement, the Wilson Chemical Company of Dublin, Texas, sought to sway addicted Confederate veterans with endorsements from "physicians, ministers and soldiers."[16] Like newspapers, pamphlets hawking addiction cures were replete with testimonials written by Civil War veterans, underscoring how patent medicine proprietors specifically targeted addicted veterans.

Classified advertisement for the
Wilson Chemical Company's
addiction "cure." (*Confederate Veteran*
5, no. 1 [January 1897]: 46)

Testimonials provide a unique window into the phenomenon of opiate addiction among Civil War veterans, illuminating what they thought about opiate addiction, how they experienced its physical and social consequences, and the strategies they used to ward off negative outcomes of addiction. William H. Chappell, a veteran of the Third and Twenty-Sixth Alabama Infantry regiments, furnished Samuel B. Collins with a roughly three-page narrative testimonial in March 1874. Hoping to catch the eye of veterans with similar stories, Collins titled Chappell's account "The Experience of one Redeemed—His Gratitude Expressed" and printed it in an 1874 promotional pamphlet for the Painless Opium Antidote.[17] Many of the elements in Chappell's narrative also appeared in other veterans' testimonials, including the origin of veterans' opiate addictions, the dire physical and social consequences they suffered for their addictions, and the utility of patent medicines as a tool to counteract addiction and its consequences.

Severely wounded at the Battle of Nashville in December 1864, Chappell suffered through a painful amputation of his left leg above the knee. Army surgeons gave Chappell opium to mitigate the pain. "The use of those remedies" during his five-month convalescence at the hospital saved his life, Chappell wrote, but was "followed by the most unhappy results." His amputation did not fully heal but continued to eject "specula of bone" for three years. Suffering from intense, chronic pain, Chappell "could get no relief save by using opium." By the time the final bone fragment at last worked its way out of his flesh, as Chappell tortuously described, "my system was completely under the influence of the drug, so that without it, I *could not* attend to any business."[18] When the wound healed, Chappell attempted to discontinue the opium, believing he no longer needed it to manage the pain. But after years of swallowing thirty grains of opium and morphine pills daily, Chappell found himself unable to quit. Each time he attempted, his will was overpowered by excruciating withdrawal symptoms.

Opium thus become to Chappell "a tyrant . . . binding me in chains, from which, it seemed to me, no human power could free me." He dreaded his bleak prospects: facing the unbearable pains of withdrawal, or risking a fatal overdose from the ever-increasing dose needed to counteract his body's mounting tolerance of opiates. For the next eight years, Chappell tried repeatedly to quit opiates, failing each time, until a chance encounter in 1874 changed his fortunes. Out of sympathy for Chappell's condition, according to the narrative, a friendly pharmacist passed along a copy of Samuel B. Collins's latest pamphlet for the Painless Opium Antidote. "From the moment of reading your magazine, and the numerous testimonials therein," Chappell testified, "I felt the Lord . . . was about to save me from that terrible fate" of fatally overdosing. The Lord and Collins, that is. As Chappell explained in the narrative's climax, "Deliverance has come, thank God; and to your opium antidote." Chappell purchased a two-month supply of the antidote by mail for fifty dollars, which cured him "from the thralldom of that enemy which well nigh proved my ruin." Chappell concluded his testimonial by urging other veterans to waste no time in purchasing Collins's Painless Opium Antidote, pointedly expressing his desire that Collins share his story. As Chappell phrased it, "write this testimony (yea, a more impressive one if possible), in *letters of fire and hand it in the heavens for a world to read.*"[19]

Scores of Civil War veterans shared similar testimonials on behalf of their favorite addiction cures, mirroring the plot and narrative elements of Chappell's account. Naturally, veterans' accounts were likely edited by proprietors, who employed testimonials to lend veracity to claims of their products' effectiveness. Indeed, Collins solicited testimonials from veterans and other satisfied customers, and he likely added narrative flourishes to these accounts. But for his part, Collins also swore that accounts like Chappell's were bona fide, even offering a five-hundred-dollar reward payable to any critic who could prove that he published fraudulent testimonials. Naturally, because testimonials were created to serve a specific purpose—to sell patent medicines by testifying to their efficacy—historians thus cannot take veterans' claims about the therapeutic utility of opiate addiction "cures" made in the testimonials at face value. However, by filtering out the overt salesmanship inherent in testimonials, these exceptional sources nonetheless reveal much about veterans' experiences with opiate addiction and the reasons that motivated them to purchase patent opiate addiction cures. Many of the details in testimonials are corroborated in veterans' military service records, lending plausibility to their accounts. For example, Chappell's service record indicates that he spent time as a hospital steward during the Civil War, a position that would have likely given him unfettered access to opiates at the hospital, facilitating his addiction.[20]

Taken together, testimonials illuminate common aspects of veterans' experiences with opiate addiction. First and foremost, they reveal the terrible physical toll of opiate addiction, including fatigue, severe weight loss, impotence, and heightened sensitivity to pain. As an Illinois veteran, J. M. Richards, wrote on behalf of Keeley's Gold Cure in 1881: "I felt that to die and go to hell would involve less torment than that I was suffering every day. I was emaciated, pallid, weak in body, and my strength of will and energy of mind were all gone." A former Union surgeon, John J. Patterson, suffered a similar experience, as he testified on behalf of Collins's Painless Opium Antidote. "My wife would get up at all hours of the night and use the syringe on me," Patterson reported. "My health was so poor that I was confined to my room, and at last to my bed. I could not eat until I used the morphine. My nervous system was a total wreck . . . I was a walking skeleton; no appetite; low spirits."[21]

Alongside the physical manifestations of opiate addiction, a close reading of veterans' testimonials also illuminates the social risks of addiction for veterans, particularly the threat it posed to manhood. First, the abuse of painkilling opiates signaled that veterans were unwilling to endure painful war wounds stoically, as was expected of men of the Civil War generation. The physical emaciation, fatigue, and inability to work stemming from opiate addiction also violated Gilded Age expectations that men possess robust, able bodies and serve as family breadwinners. Perhaps most damning of all, the inability to quit the "opium habit" through willpower alone signaled that addicted veterans lacked self-control. Indeed, as Chappell explained in his testimonial, opium waged "a direct attack upon the *will*," rendering addicted men incapable of resisting cravings, try as they might. Encapsulating the stigma and gendering of opiate addiction, veteran addicts frequently described their condition as a kind of "slavery," the opposite of manly self-mastery. According to Chappell, addicts like himself were "slaves to that most pernicious of all drugs—opium; and who like myself are fully conscious of the evil effects it will ultimately bring unless abandoned." Descriptions of "slavery" to opiates suggest that addicted veterans believed they suffered a loss of self-control and, by extension, manhood.[22] Self-control over one's body and actions was a hallmark of masculinity during the Gilded Age. The inability to refrain from taking opiates was antithetical to self-mastery, to the detriment of addicted veterans' sense of manhood.

Opiate addiction also proved a severe financial burden for many addicted veterans, who had to consume opiates daily in order to remain functional. Most immediately, the cost of the drugs themselves often proved burdensome, especially as tolerance to opiates built up over the years, forcing veterans to consume ever-higher dosages. In 1875, an addicted New York veteran reported spending an average of $10 per month on laudanum since 1865, totaling $1,200 in a decade of addiction. This large expense would have overwhelmed many men's budgets, considering that the average New York farmer earned just $36.50 a month in 1875. Such an expense also surpassed many veterans' meager pensions, even without considering the ancillary costs of addiction, like lost wages and pensions. Many veterans became physically debilitated by prolonged opiate abuse, leaving them unable to work. John J. Patterson, the former Union surgeon, wrote in his testimonial for Collins's Painless Opium Antidote that years of morphine addiction left him too weak to practice medicine, robbing Patterson and his wife of their main income source. Union veterans losing risked their pensions by becoming addicted, which the U.S. Pension Bureau considered to be a "vicious habit," and addicted Confederate veterans faced similar restrictions on entitlements. Some were discharged from soldiers' homes because of their condition. Considering the severe physical, social, and financial toll of opiate addiction, veterans had ample reason to seek medical remedies for addiction.[23]

Patent medicine cures promised veterans a solution for the myriad costs of opiate addiction. Testimonials indicate that veterans adopted patent addiction cures as tools to restore their bodies to good health and to redeem their manhood by curing addiction. Not only could patent medicines potentially cure one's addiction and relieve its financial and physical burdens, veterans believed, but the remedies also offered a path for reclaiming manhood. Many veterans who authored testimonials invited public scrutiny by signing their names. Freely admitting their addiction, exposing their suffering to the public eye, stood in contrast to most opiate addicts, whose drug use remained a closely guarded "concealed practice," as one Gilded Age physician explained.[24] But by confessing their opiate addictions in a testimonial form, while also narrating their delivery from opiates, veterans framed addiction as an experience of the past from which they had been redeemed. They were enslaved to opium no more, but were, rather, freed from addiction and thereby restored to health and manhood.

By publicly proclaiming freedom from opiate slavery, formerly addicted veterans hoped that testimonials would raise their manly stature in the eyes of their readers. Some veterans even invited skeptics to correspond with them. A. W. Henley, a former Confederate surgeon, confessed plainly that in the Confederate service he "took Opium, and

Opium wound and bound me up with chords that God only knows how often I tried to break, and as many times failed." But Woolley's American Opium Cure gave him "a new lease on life, and to-day am in perfect health, rejoicing in perfect freedom" from opium slavery. Texas veteran Byron McKeen likewise praised Collins's Painless Opium Antidote for rejuvenating his body and manhood. "To-day, I am one week old, and feel like a new human being—no longer a slave to that miserable Opium," McKeen proclaimed. He had even gained weight to boot. Joseph C. Darrow admitted to becoming "addicted" to "the habit of using Morphine" in 1863, which he deeply regretted. But his self-control was restored by Collins's antidote, and an observer noted that "Since Nov. 15th [1869] he [Darrow] has had Morphine at his command, with no necessity or desire to use it."[25] Such descriptions revealed how addicted veterans had not only been cured of opiate addiction, but also regained physical and mental virility, self-control, and, by extension, their manhood.

Such narratives were evidently quite effective, generating substantial sales of patent medicine addiction cures among veteran and nonveteran consumers for decades after the Civil War. In fact, the commercial success of the cures triggered a backlash among physicians, who competed with patent medicine sellers in the medical marketplace for profit and prestige. As patent opiate addiction cures proliferated during the Gilded Age, so too did physicians' attacks on the products and their proprietors. Most critics focused on the secret ingredients of opiate addiction cures, which almost universally contained opiates, according to late nineteenth- and early-twentieth-century chemical analysis. Ironically, the opium and morphine content of the remedies likely masked addicted customers' cravings for opiates, alleviating the worst symptoms of withdrawal, and thus fooling consumers into thinking that they had been emancipated from opium slavery. But in the eyes of critics, "cures" that contained opiates did not actually cure addiction at all, but merely bilked gullible consumers while prolonging addiction. Skeptical physicians and muckraking journalists, determined to expose patent addiction cures as medical frauds, published dozens of exposés in the Gilded Age and Progressive Era. Eventually, during the first decade of the twentieth century, the efforts of antipatent medicine crusaders turned U.S. legislators and much of the public against "nostrum makers" like Samuel B. Collins. Federal legislation, particularly the landmark 1906 Pure Food and Drug Act, largely ended the Gilded Age patent medicine craze, and with it the opiate addiction cure industry.[26]

Yet demand among addicted veterans, who sometimes spent thousands of dollars on patent addiction cures, sustained the patent medicine opiate addiction cure industry for decades before its twentieth-century demise. Desperate to rid themselves of opiate addiction and reverse its catastrophic consequences for health and manhood, addicted veterans inspired the development of patent medicine addiction cures in the Civil War's wake and fueled the industry's dramatic growth in the Gilded Age. The buying and selling of patent medicine opiate addiction cures by Civil War veterans ultimately provides a unique window into the phenomenon of opiate addiction among veterans, as well as the Civil War's financial and health effects on individual veterans.

NOTES

1. *Louisville Medical News: A Weekly Journal of Medicine and Surgery* 9–10 (August 7, 1880): 63–64; Thompson McGown, *A Practical Treatise on the Most Common Diseases of the South* (Philadelphia: Grigg, Elliot and Co., 1849), 349.

2. *Louisville Medical News* (August 7, 1880), 63–64.

3. Leslie E. Keeley, *The Morphine Eater: Or, From Bondage to Freedom* (Dwight, Ill.: C. L. Palmer & Co., 1881), 120, 166.

4. James Marten, "Civil War Veterans," in *A Companion to the U.S. Civil War*, ed. Aaron Sheehan-Dean (West Sussex, U.K.: John Wiley & Sons, 2014), 608–28, quote on 619.

5. John C. Burnham, *Health Care in America: A History* (Baltimore, Md.: Johns Hopkins University Press, 2015), 81–83; for example, "Suicide of the Murderer Macdonald," *Harper's Weekly*, May 26, 1860, 326–27; Diane Miller Sommerville, *Aberration of the Mind: Suicide and Suffering in the Civil War-Era South* (Chapel Hill: University of North Carolina Press, 2018), 221–25; T. J. Jackson Lears, *Fables of Abundance: A Cultural History of Advertising in America* (New York: Basic Books, 1994), 44.

6. Burnham, *Health Care in America*, 114; David G. Schuster, "The Rise of a Modern Concept of 'Health,'" in *A Companion to the Gilded Age and Progressive Era*, ed. Christopher McKnight Nichols and Nancy C. Unger (West Sussex, U.K.: John Wiley & Sons, 2017), 255–67, quote on 261; Burnham, *Health Care in America*, 83.

7. Burnham, *Health Care in America*, 80–83; James Harvey Young, *The Toadstool Millionaires: A Social History of Patent Medicines in American before Federal Regulation* (Princeton, N.J.: Princeton University Press, 2961), chapter 7.

8. An example advertisement is in the *New York Herald*, October 30, 1859; Jonathan S. Jones, "The 'Worst Species of Inebriety': Opiate Addiction in Antebellum New York City," *Gotham: A Blog for Scholars of New York City History*, March 12,

2019, https://www.gothamcenter.org/blog/the-worst-species-of-inebriety
-opiate-addiction-in-antebellum-new-york-city.

9. Jonathan S. Jones, "Opium Slavery: Civil War Veterans and Opiate Addiction," *Journal of the Civil War Era* 10, no. 2 (June 2020): 185–212.

10. J. B. Mattison, "'Opium Antidotes,' and Their Vendors," *Journal of the American Medical Association* 7, no. 21 (November 20, 1886): 568.

11. S. B. Collins, *Theriaki: A Magazine Devoted to the Interests of Opium Eaters* 1, no. 1 (July 1872): 54.

12. S. B. Collins, *Theriaki: An Annual Devoted to the Interests of Opium Eaters* (La Porte, Ind.: La Porte Chronicle Steam Print, 1878), 78–85; Keeley, *Morphine Eater*, 164; Collins, *Theriaki* (1878), 7–8; Jonathan S. Jones, "Opium Slavery: Veterans and Addiction in the American Civil War Era" (PhD diss., Binghamton University, 2020), 341–48.

13. James Marten, *Sing Not War: The Lives of Union and Confederate Veterans in Gilded Age America* (Chapel Hill: University of North Carolina Press, 2011), 114–20; *The Keeley Institutes of the United States, Canada, and other countries . . .* ([Dwight?, Ill.]: Leslie E. Keeley Co., [1895?]), 10; Jones, "Opium Slavery: Veterans and Addiction," 323–28, 349–51.

14. *Chicago Daily Tribune*, February 8, 1880, 5; *Chicago Daily Tribune*, March 26, 1884, 8; *Chicago Daily Tribune*, February 29, 1880, 5; *Chicago Daily Tribune*, April 16, 1899, 6; *Chicago Daily Tribune*, September 14, 1893, 8. Veterans represented a minority among opiate-addicted Americans. David T. Courtwright, *Dark Paradise: A History of Opiate Addiction in America*, rev. ed. (Cambridge, Mass.: Harvard University Press, 2001), 9, 26–27, 36, 54–55.

15. *National Tribune* (Washington, D.C.), May 24, 1883, 8.

16. Examples are *National Tribune*, March 26, 1885, 7; February 18, 1887, 7; August 14, 1887, 7; November 30, 1893, 2; August 22, 1907, 7; the Stephens figure calculated through a keyword search for the term "J. Stephens" in the full-text issues of the *National Tribune* via the Library of Congress Chronicling America database, https://chroniclingamerica.loc.gov (accessed January 17, 2019); *Confederate Veteran* 5, no. 1 (January 1897), 46.

17. S. B. Collins, *Positive Cure for the Opium Habit* (San Francisco: Alta California Book and Job Printing House, 1874), 22–26.

18. Chappell quoted in ibid., 23, original emphasis.

19. Chappell quoted in ibid., 24–25, original emphasis.

20. S.B. Collins, *Theriaki and Their Last Dose* (Chicago: Evening Journal Print, 1870), 11; William H. Chappell, Civil War Service Records, folder 3, https://www.fold3.com/image/20/6869761.

21. Keeley, *Morphine Eater*, 121, 166; Richards and Patterson quoted in S. B. Collins, *Theriaki: A Treatise on the Habitual Use of Narcotic Poisons* (La Porte, Ind.: S. B. Collins, 1887[?]), 25–26.

22. On opiate addiction and manhood, see Jones, "Opium Slavery: Civil War Veterans"; Collins, *Positive Cure for the Opium Habit*, 23, original emphasis; B. M.

Wooley, *The Opium Habit and Its Cure* (Atlanta: Atlanta Constitution Press, 1879), 30; Keeley, *Morphine Eater*, 163.

23. "An Opium-Eater's Cure," *Galaxy: A Magazine of Entertaining Reading* (January 1875): 127; *History of Wages in the United States from Colonial Times to 1928. Revision of Bulletin No. 499 with Supplement, 1929–1933 (p. 523)* (Washington, D.C.: Government Printing Office, 1934), 225; Jones, "Opium Slavery: Civil War Veterans."

24. H. R. Hopkins, "The Intoxicant Habit," *Transactions of the Medical Society of the State of New York for the Year 1887*, 204.

25. Woolley, *Opium Habit and Its Cure*, 17; Collins, *Theriaki* 1, no. 1 (July 1872): 53–4.

26. An example is Mattison, "'Opium Antidotes,' and Their Vendors," 568; Young, *Toadstool Millionaires*, chapters 13–14.

Premium Veteranhood

Union Veterans and Manhood in Post–Civil War America, 1879–1900

KEVIN R. CAPRICE

"The war of the rebellion was a glorious exhibition of American manhood," the *National Tribune* proclaimed in 1892. Three years later, in 1895, the *Tribune* went further, declaring that Union veterans embodied "the very best manhood this country is capable of producing" and that the Union veteran was "the best man that all our methods for making good men could develop." By the early to mid-1890s, the editors of the *Tribune*, in their estimation, had fully connected veteranhood with manhood, a term that, in this context, suggested honor, bravery, and self-reliance. But it had not always been that way. Even these articles, both titled "Slandering American Manhood," were in response to negative pieces on veterans in the *New York Herald* and the *New York Evening Post*. These, and other "soldier-hating" papers, lobbed insults against "virtually all the survivors of the war," claiming that all veterans were beggars who abused the pension system. Further, antiveteran papers deemed aging former soldiers "shirks, cowards, and bounty-jumpers," in other words, not true men.[1] This battle was nothing new. The *Tribune* had defended the manhood of Union veterans since its inception.

Following the American Civil War, Union veterans expected to be welcomed home as paragons of manhood, having physically asserted their dominance over the South and preserved the Union. Once home, however, these men learned that the boundaries of masculinity were changing. By the late 1860s and early 1870s, the domain of manliness was shifting from the battleground to the boardroom. Older conceptions of manhood did not disappear, but more and more it seemed financial success made men. Far removed from this domain, many veterans were physically broken and financially broke, lagging behind their neighbors who had remained home and enjoyed the booming wartime economy. During the transition from soldier to citizen, veterans learned that the one aspect of their manhood they sacrificed nearly everything to secure, soldierly glory, was falling out of favor.

Underlying the discussion of manhood and manliness was a core question that veterans were facing after the war: where was the veteran's place in a postwar society? Terms like manhood, which Gail Bederman describes as "a *historical, ideological process*" through which "men claim certain kinds of authority," and manliness, a similar term that denoted "honor, high-mindedness, and strength stemming from this powerful self-mastery," provided a vocabulary for veterans experiencing a feeling of placelessness that is not uncommon for soldiers returning from war. Men who had not gone through the war, or veterans who had easily blended back into civil society, seemed to command a level of authority and respect that veterans who struggled to return to civilian life could not achieve. For these veterans, claiming that manhood was under attack expressed their feeling that they were being squeezed out of society. The new question for these men, then, was how to find a place in a community that seemed unwelcoming.[2]

The *National Tribune*, founded by George Lemon in 1877, sought to answer that question. By the late 1870s, it had developed a marketing campaign that offered a "Premium List" of goods that could serve the dual purpose of selling newspapers and aiding veterans in feeling like proper late nineteenth-century men. Between 1879 and 1900, the *Tribune* featured these "premiums"—various mass-produced items, likely of questionable quality—primarily as rewards that readers could earn by selling subscriptions to the *National Tribune*. Through the *Tribune*'s Premium List, advertisers could specifically target the veteran's feeling of isolation from the norms of society. Just as the standards of manliness shifted during this period, so too did the items on the Premium List. When veterans struggled to find work, advertisers pitched items that highlighted conformity with the middle- to upper-class, nonmilitaristic, monetary ideals of postbellum manliness. As veterans aged, and came to rebel against such civilian conceptions of manhood, advertisers added items that highlighted the value of a veteran's martial achievement. The Premium List, then, developed according to the needs and demands of its customers, or at least to how the editors of the *Tribune* imagined those needs and demands, allowing insight into how consumerism and the *Tribune* promised veterans a better, manlier, life. In many ways, the consumerism found in the *Tribune* was an early example of the twentieth-century shift noted by

Jackson Lears in his work *Fables of Abundance*, with ads taking on a bureaucratic nature and pushing the benefits of industriousness and factorylike efficiency. As veterans went through various life stages and identities, the one constant was their role as consumer, and consumerism's ability to bolster their confidence in their place in the world.[3]

Though the *National Tribune* pitched its Premium List as a benefit to readers, it was above all a strategy to increase subscriptions. The first premium made available by the *Tribune*, the National Tribune Clock, came as a free gift for any reader who signed up a club of ten new subscribers. New items were added to and removed from the list, and the eventual totality of the list includes more items than can be fully unpacked here. But a close reading of representative items, and the frequency and content of the ads for those items, reveals a method behind the *Tribune*'s marketing strategy. The goal of the *Tribune* was to find the product that excited the veteran enough to hit the streets and sign up new readers.

Few records exist of the men who earned these premiums, but what remains indicates they were eager to sell subscriptions in order to earn their rewards. William H. Victor proudly wrote to the *Tribune* that, after signing up twenty subscribers, he felt he had done his duty. On certain occasions, the *Tribune* would reward its best sellers with a mention in the paper. One example, titled "Chat about Clubs," praised men such as William O'Connor, who sent in ten additional subscribers that week, "making seventy-five in all, and says he is good for as many more." Others, such as Chase H. Allison and A. W. Pepper, enrolled twenty subscribers. It is possible that these men were more enthusiastic than if they were to merely purchase the items, due in part to the fact that they had to work hard to receive their rewards, replicating the contemporary mores of industrious manliness. Considering that many veterans struggled to find their way back into civilian life, working to earn rewards and help the *Tribune* may have given veterans a sense of purpose and comfort in a world that was looking less and less like the one they left when they enlisted.[4]

It should be noted that the *Tribune* was not the first nor the only publication to offer premiums—although few premium campaigns reached the level to which the *Tribune*'s grew. For example, the *Kentucky Farmer*, published in Louisville, offered a similar premium campaign in 1885. With a similarly homogenous reader base, it offered a watch engraved with an image of a ten-point buck on the casing, appealing to readers' identity. Unlike the *Kentucky Farmer*, however, the *Tribune*'s Premium List exploded, growing to include dozens of offerings, and filling multiple pages in each publication. The *Tribune* tapped into existing social net-

works in the Union veteran community through large fraternal organizations such as the GAR, a luxury few other papers possessed. Knowing its current readers and the connection those readers had to others
who would likely enjoy its paper, the *Tribune* pounced on the opportunity
to mix advertising with wish fulfillment, gaining new subscribers in the
process.

The *Tribune* was also not the first publication to target these veterans
as consumers. During the war, when these men were still soldiers, advertisers deployed the specific demands of combat. *Harper's Weekly*, for example, often contained advertisements for "Army Watches" and "Watches
for Soldiers," along with other goods pitched through a military lens;
the watches were "durable" and American made. These ads identified
the perceived needs of soldiers just as they would later identify the perceived needs of aging veterans, but veterans, over their lifetime, evolved
as a group in a way that active soldiers, in just four years, could not. Still,
uniform groups allow advertisers distinctive opportunities. Because it
was primarily Union veterans reading the *Tribune*, the Premium List's
growth and evolution provide a unique window into the role consumerism played in the veterans' attempt to cope with their insecure place as
men in a changing world.[5]

Manhood in the nineteenth century was fraught with contradiction
and confusion. As Lorien Foote notes in her study of masculinity in the
Union army, those "attributes some men deemed essential to manhood—
such as moral character or physical prowess—others disdained." In a period of already turbulent masculinity, Union veterans found themselves
stuck precariously in the middle. Many lacked the physicality that defined
the masculinity of men Foote termed "roughs": "those from the very bottom of the economic ladder whose manly identities seemed to be centered on violence and drink," having wrecked their bodies, in one way or
another, while preserving the nation. But many, especially those veterans
struggling to find work, also lacked the capital of upper-class manliness,
having sacrificed prime earning years in the booming wartime economy
to defend the Union.[6]

Several scholars of the post–Civil War period have noted that veterans
had a fraught relationship with civilian culture upon returning home.
Historian Caroline E. Janney finds that, amid the turmoil surrounding
veterans in the postbellum period, "the northern public increasingly ste-
reotyped veterans as grasping pensioners, alcoholic dependents, or even
wayward tramps." James Marten writes that "in the North, as veterans' papers came to argue, at least some veterans were ignored or even treated

with contempt." That Union veterans had such difficult relations with their peaceful counterparts is likely due to Marten's other point, that the "meaning of Gilded Age manhood ultimately came to exclude martial abilities," and that in fact "military service could hinder the development of manhood."[7] Veterans were a people without a clear place in the postwar society, making them especially susceptible to advertisers willing to exploit those concerns.

While the value of one's wartime record waned, the value of one's ability to earn a wage waxed. In the world veterans inhabited, Americans, especially northerners, came to appreciate the monetary value of time. In his landmark "Time, Work-Discipline, and Industrial Capitalism," E. P. Thompson explains how this phenomenon occurred. The essay traces the cultural and manufacturing changes that coincided with the transition to industrial capitalism in eighteenth-century England, and their role in transforming how people understood time. It argues that during this period, people went from a "task-orientation" understanding of time, where people structured their day around the tasks they needed to complete, to a new "time-discipline," which measured labor through hours worked. Though some aspects of Thompson's work have been criticized since its publication in 1967, his claim that industrialization chained the worker to the clock has held true.[8]

In the United States, time discipline appeared somewhat later. In *Keeping Watch: A History of American Time*, Michael O'Malley finds that "in antebellum America, time had been resolutely linked to social discipline and control. Politicians warned against idle hands, ministers urged their parishioners to 'redeem the time,' schoolbook homilies reminded children of the busy bee and industrious ant." The fighting of the Civil War served to further the development of time-discipline, at least in soldiers. Alexis McCrossen argues that while the Civil War "did not introduce a new consciousness of time," it certainly "accelerated the halting and slow embrace of clock time that had begun a century earlier."[9]

As clock time matured in the minds of Americans, so too did the monetary value of time. Timepieces and time itself came to evoke a sense of industriousness and money. McCrossen finds that "timepieces aurally and visually saturated public spaces not only with indications of the time, but with messages about the cosmic and national importance of time itself." Time's value grew as its application became more and more connected to industry. Time was for working. As industrialism took hold in America, which it did with increasing speed during the late nineteenth century, and wage labor grew, time quite literally became money.[10]

The connection between industry and time helps explain the popularity of the National Tribune Clock. Beginning in 1879, advertisements for the clock became a regular feature in the *Tribune*'s Premium List. The clock itself was quite plain; it was nickel plated, the face lacked ornament aside from the standard Roman numerals, and it stood on two simple metal legs. But to the *Tribune* and its readers, it was beautiful. The clocks proved a useful marketing tool, primarily because they served two functions: first, they helped the owner manage work and scheduling, and second, ownership of a clock demonstrated to the world that the owner's time was valuable. Advertisements in the *Tribune* reinforced these two functions by focusing on the accuracy and beauty of the clocks.

An accurate clock could keep a worker from being late and losing his job, which was just the message the *Tribune* offered in its clock testimonials. When Mr. H. A. Case of Troy, Pennsylvania, wrote that "Your clock . . . keeps correct time, runs to a charm," he was testifying not only about the quality of the clock but also to its utility. Reviews like Case's proliferated in each *Tribune* issue. In addition to applauding the accuracy of the clock, testimonials praised its ornamental role in places of business. If the accuracy of a clock accounted for its practical value, the beauty of a clock conveyed its value as a status symbol. Two reviews in the *Tribune* provided insight as to why the clock's appearance was so important, with F. Edgar Foote, Esq., bragging that his clock was "the admiration of all beholders." A. B. Lee wrote similarly that his clock "is hanging in my office, and is admired by all who see it." The *Tribune* made it a point that it was important that people *see* that veterans had clocks, and transfer the industrious implications clocks carried with them onto their owners.[11]

In 1882, the editors of the *Tribune* added a new timekeeping device to the Premium List: the Waterbury Pocket Watch, available for anyone sending in fifteen subscribers. With this new item came a new advertising strategy: make the connection between timepieces and industry explicit. The *Tribune* began combining visual sketches with short narratives to drive home the importance of a good timepiece. The men in the sketches were not clearly veterans, but the message was nonetheless clear: every successful man had a watch. One ad from 1883 read, "He missed the train and an important engagement, and all because his old silver repeater was one minute slow." The ad closed simply, "Moral: Send to The National Tribune for a Waterbury Watch." In the attached image, the unfortunately late man races after a train, while a railroad worker holds out his watch, displaying the proper time. One is gainfully employed, while the other is watching his future rumble down the tracks, and all due to a lost minute.

Advertisements unambiguously contrasted the type of men who owned watches and the type who did not. "Waterbury watches . . . are now carried by railroad men, school-teachers, business men, mechanics, farmers," one ad noted. Other testimonials followed the same script. "Every working man . . . ought to have a Waterbury watch," wrote Daniel Maloney, who also noted that "it is both ornamental and, decidedly, useful."[12]

Maloney was correct; watches were more than purely ornamental. O'Malley found that during the nineteenth century, "even more than now, owning a watch made everyday tasks easier." As more and more American men found themselves employed by other men, watches indeed helped men get to their trains, their desks, and their appointments on time, all activities that would help them stay employed. One ad in the *Tribune* made an explicit connection between time and money, asserting that "you cannot have a Waterbury watch any too soon. You want money, you say, worse than anything else? Well, time is money, and if you have a reliable time-piece, you can readily dispose of your time so as to convert it into money." Watches helped domesticate and monetize the time that was rapidly ruling the lives of nineteenth-century Americans. It was no surprise, then, when the *Tribune* announced that "the favorite premium of The Tribune list is, and has always been, the Waterbury watch."[13] As the *Tribune* sold it, veterans had no choice but to be molded by the society they inhabited, and to look to the Premium List for the tools they needed.

Not long after the Waterbury became the "favorite" reward, a subtle shift began in the *Tribune*'s Premium List. The change was signified in the Waterbury itself, when in 1885 it was rebranded "the G.A.R. Watch," sported on its back "an artistic representation of the G.A.R. badge," and could be earned by the veteran who sent in ten new subscribers.[14] Though smaller items dealing directly with veteranhood had previously appeared on the Premium List, they were often short lived or lightly advertised. Never before had a product so symbolic of industrial manhood been directly connected with martial glory. For these veterans, manhood, just as the Waterbury Watch, appeared to be changing. Increasingly, the veteran's place in manly society marked him as a veteran.

With the "new and improved" GAR Watch in 1885, deemed "much handsomer than its predecessor," the importance of making veteranhood visible began to take precedence over emphasizing a veteran's ability to earn a wage.[15] Prior to the GAR Watch, the *Tribune* Premium List pushed industry through working, and owning items that showed others you were a worker. The ability to earn money was paramount. Attempt-

An advertisement for the GAR Watch from an 1885 issue of the *Tribune,* the beginning of the campaign to directly pair veteranhood and industriousness. (*National Tribune,* December 17, 1885)

ing to connect veterans with industriousness played into the developing middle- and upper-class conceptions of what it meant to be a man. But that middle- to upper-class manhood was seemingly disconnected from martial valor. If anything, highlighting the militaristic side of men risked bringing to mind the violence typically associated with the roughs of the lower classes, an undesirable section of society.

But times were changing, as were Northern perceptions of the Civil War and of the men who fought in it—and for the better. Public interest in the war was recovering from the nadir of the 1870s. The GAR, too, was growing, as was its political pull. From its low of 25,000 comrades in the 1870s, the GAR's membership steadily increased in the 1880s, reaching 409,489 by 1890. Whether it was due to the rebounding economy, the distance from the horrors of war, or the coming of age of a new generation, interest in the Civil War was on the rise, and veterans seemingly had more to gain by making themselves known, through various items of veteran memorabilia, than they had previously.[16]

As interest in the Civil War grew, its veterans were aging. Bell Irvin Wiley estimates that the average age of the Union soldier in 1865 was a little over twenty-six. By the mid-1880s, then, the average veteran was in his midforties. Twenty years after the war, generational changes were occurring. The new generation of men entering their prime during the late nineteenth century began placing a higher value on a more physical masculinity, which would develop through the 1890s, and culminate in Theodore Roosevelt's famous "Strenuous Life" speech in 1899. As historian Gail Bederman observes, "By the 1890s, strenuous exercise and team sports had come to be seen as crucial to the development of powerful manhood." Masculinity was on the verge of achieving a full revolution to once again emphasize physical domination, glorified in sports such as football and boxing. And though veterans themselves could no longer toe the line, they could at least remind others that, in their prime, they were fighters too.[17]

If the new GAR Watch of 1885 represented the *Tribune*'s push toward reclaiming a martial version of masculinity, the veteran subscribers had already hinted that they were willing customers. Two years prior, in 1883, the *Tribune* added to the Premium List a simple "G.A.R. Sleeve Button," which could be earned by sending in six new subscribers. Intended to have a limited run, the veterans proved such eager buyers that the *Tribune* made the buttons a permanent staple of the list. "The sales of our Grand Army sleeve buttons have been so large during the last two months," the *Tribune* announced, "that we have decided to continue them on our regular premium list." By 1885, the buttons had become "All the Rage," with "Thousands of Comrades Wearing Them." When providing a quick description of the button, the Tribune gushed that it was "one of the most handsome, useful, and valuable pieces of jewelry that has yet been devised."[18]

While a sleeve button might be useful in its ability to keep a sleeve closed, it also served the secondary purpose of alerting the public that the wearer was a Union veteran. The Grand Army of the Republic was a household name in the Gilded Age, and a passerby would have been able to associate those initials with the organization of Union veterans. Overwhelming demand for the button exposed veterans' desire to reclaim their past. Having identified the high demand, the editors of the *Tribune* gave customers what they wanted.

In the fall of 1891, veteran-themed jewelry began to flood the Premium List. The "'Same Canteen' Charm," meant to evoke the image of men sharing water from the same canteen, was advertised as "an old friend . . . which needs no introduction," and could be had for six new subscribers. Another offering, a charm engraved with the GAR insignia, was deemed "just the thing for veterans." Elsewhere on the list, a Grand Army badge combined various symbols that connected a veteran's service to the Union he had helped to preserve. The badge featured "double eagles" as well as "two rolled gold cannon lying upon a pile of enameled cannon-balls" on top of "the United States flag. . . . Attached to the flag is the star containing the various military emblems, so well known to our readers that we will not endeavor to describe them."[19] This charm, requiring seven new subscribers, was to be worn on a veteran's breast, sure to meet the eye of anyone with whom the veteran engaged. Each of these offerings had clear messaging. The canteen showed the importance of shared service, of soldiers standing shoulder to shoulder. The GAR charm embraced a similar shared service but accentuated the importance of veterans standing with one another in the present, rather than the past. Finally, the Grand Army badge made visible the nation and the values for which they had fought. This jewelry represented the meaning of veteranhood at its best.

The piece of jewelry that achieved prominence above the others, deemed "Our Specialty" by the *Tribune*, was the GAR ring, which could be had after sending in ten new subscribers and an additional two dollars and fifty cents. The *Tribune* stated its purpose in no uncertain terms: "Thousands of veterans have been asking for a Ring that would identify them with that great and glorious host of men whose fame will never die, and who fought and suffered for their country in her time of need. . . . We can imagine

1861 G.A.R. 1866

GRAND ARMY RING.

The National Tribune Gem.

[COPYRIGHTED.]

Thousands of veterans have been asking for a Ring that would identify them with that great and glorious host of men whose fame will never die, and who fought and suffered for their country in her time of need. We have made arrangements with one of the greatest firms of ring-makers in the world to manufacture exclusively for us a SOLID GOLD RING set with a PRECIOUS STONE, upon which that emblem of glory, the Grand Army Button, should be reproduced in solid gold. Months of time and a great amount of money have been spent in creating this gem in exact accordance with our order. Now we offer to our subscribers only this Grand Army emblem. We can imagine no distinction greater than that conferred by wearing this ring. In the generations to come tales will be told of the ancestor whose sufferings and privations contributed to the glory of the fiercest war recorded in the world's history. The accompanying cut but poorly shows the details of this elegant ornament. The shank and the head in which the stone is set are solid gold, standard U.S. Assay (this quality being the best to use in rings). The onyx is cut and polished by experts expressly for this ring, and the solid gold button shown on the front is cut in a die, just as gold dollars are made. The shank or ring part is highly ornamented, as shown in the cut. We call this ring "THE NATIONAL TRIBUNE GEM." Any subscriber may purchase any number of rings for himself and his friends. Every veteran attending the great Reunion at Washington this Fall should wear a G.A.R. ring. This ring is for sale, delivery guaranteed, for $6. Sent as a premium for a Club of 10 subscribers and $2.50 added money.

An 1892 pitch for the Grand Army Ring, explicitly noting a demand from veterans for a way to render their past service visible to others. (*National Tribune*, May 12, 1892)

no distinction greater than that conferred by wearing this ring." Because it was so easy to wear and so noticeable, earning—and wearing—the ring would show others you were among the men who saved the country in its darkest hour, an identity becoming more and more desirable in its own right.[20]

Parallel with the growth in GAR jewelry was the development of certain displayable images that served as signposts of veteranhood. Rather than being pinned to one's body, or slipped over one's finger, these signposts were hung on walls in the homes or offices of veterans. The most popular of these signposts was the GAR Record, a free gift for veterans sending in clubs of fifteen new subscribers. As described by the *Tribune*, "The Grand Army of the Republic Record is a beautiful work of art . . . and is intended to furnish every comrade of the Grand Army with an attractive and permanent means of preserving a record of his military services during the war of the rebellion."[21]

Recipients of these signposts were given explicit instructions on how to get the most out of their GAR Record. "It is worthy to occupy a prominent place" one ad read, "upon the walls of office, library, or parlor." Once hung, "it brings forcibly to the mind of the observer the dangers encountered, the hardships endured, and the bravery exhibited by the grand army of 'boys in blue.'" Just as in the description of the GAR Ring, the *Tribune* explicitly stated the intended purpose of the GAR Record: to *force* anyone who saw it in its "prominent place" to remember the sacrifices veterans made to preserve the Union. The text included terms associated with masculinity, such as bravery, to drive the point home: those who had served had proven their manhood through past patriotic service; they had nothing to prove in the present.[22]

The GAR Record became a prominent feature of the Premium List and reemerged several times during the Premium List's run. A later advertisement provided a more in-depth description of the record: "In the center is a blank for the military record of the owner, to be attested by the officers of his Post. Around this are spirited pictures of war scenes. . . . A vignette of Lincoln on the left hand and a representation of the G.A.R. badge on the right are real artistic gems." These images further connected the veteran's service with other images of American manhood. Battle scenes were displayed prominently, rejecting the notion that physically dominant men could only be roughs. Indeed, these scenes glorified the danger involved in battle. The image of Lincoln, the ultimate martyr for his country, shows the full sacrifice men risked when they enlisted. The GAR badge tied the actions of yesterday with the pride of today. In the middle of all of this was a description of their personal contributions—the proof of their courage. Items such as these, and the prominence they achieved among the offered premiums, help to exemplify the way idealized manhood was shifting in the minds of veterans. By the late nineteenth century, former soldiers decreasingly felt that they had to escape their past identity as soldiers to be seen as men. Instead, they reclaimed the manhood they had gained by taking up arms in their country's time of greatest need.[23]

Acknowledging the shift away from ads for objects of industry and toward ads for objects of visibility is not to suggest such a shift was immediate or even total. The GAR Watch was still a watch, after all. An 1887 article asked "Are You Making Money?" and followed by asserting that "there is no reason why you should not make large sums of money if you are able to work." Advertisements for watches did not disappear either. "Every man . . . ought to have a watch, because that enables him to save time and accomplish his work in the best manner," advised an 1885 ad. Similar ads continued into the 1890s. But though it was not instantaneous nor complete, the shift in messaging from the *Tribune* was clear: a veteran's place in the world was as a veteran, not just as a worker.[24]

In its final five years, the Premium List continued to feature new items, but the importance of the veteran identity never waned. In 1896, the editors of the *Tribune* made one final marketing push, the National Tribune Library, featuring books such as *Statistics of the War, Lincoln's Words,* and *Pension Statistics.* Each of these titles was advertised as having two purposes: to preserve the legacy of the Civil War and to protect the dignity of its veterans. Publications like *Statistics of the War* and *Pension Statistics* had easily referenced data for both purposes, with the former even featuring a ready-made rebuttal to certain aspects of the Lost Cause narrative of the war. With the help of these books, the *Tribune* asserted, veterans could defend their own dignity and the true history of the war.[25] That books were the primary offering at this time should come as no surprise; the veteran's mind may have been sharp, but his body was breaking down.

By the 1890s, veterans were entering old age, as the 1891 "Vets Getting Too Old" article admitted. In a letter to William W. Clarke from the same year, Henry Twelvetrees painted a bleak picture of their E. A. Kimball Post, located in New York City. Twelvetrees informed Clarke that "our numbers are getting smaller and smaller every year." The post had "lost 5 members this year." By the mid- to late 1890s, more and more veterans were "mustering out." As the veteran population shrank, so too did the readership of the *Tribune,* and likewise the profits that helped fund the

Premium List. An April 26, 1900, an announcement warned that all premiums were to be withdrawn on June 15, 1900. On June 21, 1900, the *Tribune* printed a notice that it had "a limited stock of these goods leftover. While they last we will supply them at the following low cash prices." And so ended the Premium List.[26]

The *National Tribune*'s Premium List was a particular form of post–Civil War era commerce. Often couched in the language of masculinity, the premiums offer the two sides of consumerism that help to suggest what these men wanted during this period, or at the very least what the *Tribune* thought and hoped these men wanted. It exposes a transitionary period in veterans' understanding of their place in society between 1879 and 1900, and the items that were pitched as being necessary during that transition. Beginning in 1879, veterans showed a readiness to see their place as civilians, finding their way in the new economy, and the National Tribune Clock could help them navigate a laborer's life. By 1885, however, renewed public interest in the Civil War encouraged veterans to buck the previous desire to look forward, rather than backward, and a demand emerged for symbols that made veteranhood respectable, even exemplary.

For those reading the *Tribune*, and those engaged with the Premium List, this version of consumerism became a part of their veteran experience. The items themselves certainly helped to shape how veterans understood themselves and their service, but the veterans' tastes also helped to shape what came onto and stayed on the list. The *National Tribune* was not alone in its attempt to make money from veterans and to monetize veteranhood itself, but it is a telling example of the confluence of supply and demand that consumerism creates. Veteranhood did not develop in a vacuum, nor did it develop by only looking backward; the veterans actively curated their identity, in this case through the items they earned, by trying to define for themselves where they fit in the world that followed the Civil War.

NOTES

1. "Slandering American Manhood," *National Tribune* (Washington, D.C.), July 28, 1892; "Slandering American Manhood," *National Tribune*, May 16, 1895; "Slandering American Manhood," *National Tribune*, July 28, 1892.

2. Gail Bederman, *Manliness and Civilization: A Cultural History of Gender and Race in the United States, 1880–1917* (Chicago: University of Chicago Press, 1995), 7, 12, original emphasis; Lorien Foote, *The Gentlemen and the Roughs:*

Manhood, Honor, and Violence in the Union Army (New York: New York University Press, 2010); Judy Hilkey, *Character Is Capital: Success Manuals and Manhood in the Gilded Age* (Chapel Hill: University of North Carolina Press, 1997).

3. Jackson Lears, *Fables of Abundance: A Cultural History of Advertising in America* (New York: Basic Books, 1994).

4. "One of the Hundred Thousand," *National Tribune*, October 19, 1882; "Chat About Clubs," *National Tribune*, October 19, 1882; Bederman, *Manliness and Civilization*, 13.

5. "200,000 Elegant Gifts!," *Rochester (N.Y.) Democrat and Chronicle*, February 1, 1885; "American Watches for Soldiers," *Harper's Weekly*, April 4, 1863; "Army Watches," *Harper's Weekly*, April 4, 1863.

6. Foote, *The Gentlemen and the Roughs*, 5, 6; Theda Skocpol, "America's First Social Security System: The Expansion of Benefits for Civil War Veterans," *Political Science Quarterly* 108 (Spring 1993): 96.

7. Caroline E. Janney, *Remembering the Civil War: Reunion and the Limits of Reconciliation* (Chapel Hill: University of North Carolina Press, 2013), 104; Brian Matthew Jordan, *Marching Home: Union Veterans and their Unending Civil War* (New York: W. W. Norton, 2014), 7; James Marten, *Sing Not War: The Lives of Union and Confederate Veterans in Gilded Age America* (Chapel Hill: University of North Carolina Press, 2011), 19, 26–27.

8. E. P. Thompson, "Time, Work-Discipline, and Industrial Capitalism," *Past and Present* 38 (December 1967), 90; Paul Glennie and Nigel Thrift, "Reworking E. P. Thompson's 'Time, Work-Discipline and Industrial Capitalism,'" *Time and Society* 5, no. 3 (1996): 275–99; and Michael O'Malley, "Time, Work and Task Orientation: A Critique of American Historiography," *Time and Society* 1, no. 3 (1992): 341–58.

9. Michael O'Malley, *Keeping Watch: A History of American Time* (Washington, D.C.: Smithsonian Institution Press, 1996), 178; Alexis McCrossen, *Marking Modern Time: A History of Clocks, Watches, and Other Timekeepers in American Life* (Chicago: University of Chicago Press, 2013), 59.

10. McCrossen, *Marking Modern Time*, 7–8.

11. Ibid., 12–13; H. A. Case, "Compliments for Our Clock," *National Tribune*, February 1, 1879; Woster Mandeville, "Our Paper and Clock," *National Tribune*, July 1, 1879. Wendy A. Woloson, *In Hock: Pawning in America from Independence through the Great Depression* (Chicago: University of Chicago Press, 2012), 107; W. E. Pratt, Henry Sillet, and George H. Blackburn, "More Clock Compliments," *National Tribune*, March 1, 1879; F. Edgar Foote, "More Clock Compliments," *National Tribune*, March 1, 1879; A. B. Lee, "More Clock Compliments," *National Tribune*, March 1, 1879.

12. "He Missed the Train," *National Tribune*, October 4, 1883; "Now Is Your Chance," *National Tribune*, July 12, 1883; Daniel Maloney, "Read These Letters," *National Tribune*, December 27, 1883.

13. "Read These Letters," *National Tribune*, December 27, 1883; "The Waterbury, Right Again," *National Tribune*, July 31, 1884; "The Waterbury Watch," *National Tribune*, November 15, 1883.

14. "A G.A.R. Watch," *National Tribune*, February 19, 1885.

15. "The National Tribune's G.A.R. Watch," *National Tribune*, April 23, 1885.

16. Stuart McConnell, "Who Joined the Grand Army? Three Case Studies in the Construction of Union Veteranhood, 1866–1900," in *Toward a Social History of the American Civil War: Exploratory Essays*, ed. Maris A. Vinovskis (New York: Cambridge University Press, 1990), 139–70, 142; Janney, *Remembering the Civil War*, 109.

17. Bell Irvin Wiley, *The Life of Billy Yank: The Common Soldier of the Union* (Indianapolis: Bobbs-Merrill, 1952), 303; Bederman, *Manliness and Civilization*, 15.

18. "G.A.R. Sleeve Buttons," *National Tribune*, November 15, 1883; "All the Rage," *National Tribune*, October 15, 1885.

19. "'The Same Canteen' Charm," *National Tribune*, October 22, 1891; "Fall Novelties in Fine Rolled Gold," *National Tribune*, October 22, 1891.

20. "Our Specialty the G.A.R. Ring," *National Tribune*, December 8, 1892; "1861 G.A.R. 1866 Grand Army Ring," *National Tribune*, May 12, 1892.

21. "Grand Army of the Republic Record," *National Tribune*, November 15, 1883.

22. Ibid.

23. "G.A.R. Record," *National Tribune*, October 15, 1885.

24. "Are You Making Money?," *National Tribune*, February 24, 1887; "Carrying the Time O' Day," *National Tribune*, December 31, 1885.

25. "The National Tribune Library," *National Tribune*, January 30, 1896.

26. "Vets Getting Too Old," *National Tribune*, June 4, 1891; Henry Twelvetrees to William W. Clarke, August 13, 1896, William W. Clarke Collection, 1855–1896, American Historical Manuscript Collection, Patricia D. Klingenstein Library, New York Historical Society; "All Premiums to Be Withdrawn," *National Tribune*, April 26, 1900; "Cash Prices," *National Tribune*, June 21, 1900; "Prospectus of the National Tribune," *National Tribune*, November 25, 1897; "Secure a Handsome Premium Free," *National Tribune*, November 29, 1906.

"Let Every Comrade Lend Us a Hand"

George E. Lemon and the National Tribune

CROMPTON B. BURTON

The *National Tribune* represented many things to many people during its publication over the last three decades of the nineteenth century. For old soldiers like William Decker of Austin, Missouri, and hundreds of thousands of Union Army veterans just like him, the newspaper's articles and editorials proved relentlessly supportive in advocating for legislation that advanced their pension claims. For other survivors of the Civil War, like Captain Grenville Sparrow, formerly of the Seventeenth Maine Volunteer Infantry, the journal's reminiscences and memorials provided a vital connection to comrades likewise seeking to transition back to civilian life. And, for Republican candidates for political office in America's Gilded Age like Benjamin Harrison, the periodical's veteran-first perspectives helped generate indispensable support that contributed to narrow margins of victory at the polls.

For its founder, George E. Lemon, the *National Tribune* evolved from an advertising organ for his practice as a pension attorney into the foundation for a wildly successful business empire built on a simple concept: that today's informed readers were very likely tomorrow's pension claimants. It was his entrepreneurial genius to recognize the particular needs of both audiences and how to serve them while cleverly creating a self-sustaining pool of potential clients with ongoing recruitment efforts on behalf of the Grand Army of the Republic (GAR).

The *Tribune* was one of dozens of periodicals published by veterans, often by veteran organizations. Less than a decade after Appomattox, more than forty such journals were competing for a share of a very crowded newspaper and magazine marketplace.[1]

Chief among the organizations driving the early introduction of a *national* veteran press was the GAR, founded in 1866 by former U.S. Army surgeon Dr. Benjamin Franklin Stephenson. Establishing the group's first two local posts in Decatur and Springfield, Illinois, he later sought eastern members at a mass rally in Pittsburgh. Membership grew to the point that the Grand Army soon sponsored its first convention or "national encampment" in Indianapolis, where it adopted the *Great Republic* as its official organ.[2]

The *Great Republic,* paranoid to the point of seeing resurgent Confederate plots around almost every corner, proved short lived, ceasing publication in 1867. It was quickly followed by William Oland Bourne's *Soldier's Friend* in 1868 and the official *Grand Army Journal* of William T. Collins. Neither editor could help stem the flow of GAR members rejecting the organization's convoluted membership policies. Total membership in the Grand Army of the Republic stood at just 26,899 by 1876, less than 2 percent of the Union veteran population.[3]

GAR-sponsored publications with a national audience remained only marginally viable, but local independent journals enjoyed relative prosperity. Across the North, newspapers such as New Hampshire's weekly *Veteran's Advocate* attracted loyal and enthusiastic followers from among the survivors of the conflict. The *Advocate*, published by Ira Evans, a former drummer in the Twelfth New Hampshire, actively encouraged a return to the campaign and the battlefield, if only in the mind's eye, inviting submissions of recollections and strange-but-true incidents. "Let us fill up the pipe," Evans offered. "And while engaged in a good, solid smoke, we will chat of the days that are gone."[4]

Unlike Evans or Collins, however, George Lemon was not immediately interested in sentimental journeys back to the days of tramping across the Virginia countryside. He was among the growing number of attorneys and agents specializing in facilitation of pension claims on behalf of veterans. So numerous had such legal advocates become by 1862 that the pension act of that year was forced to devote significant language to their regulation. By war's end, when Lemon founded his own pension practice, whole columns of classifieds in newspapers like the *Chicago Tribune* were choked with advertisements for war claims offices and agencies providing service for no advance fee and completely free of charge unless a claim was successfully prosecuted against the government.

By the 1870s, the process to submit an application required such inordinate amounts of time, travel, and funds that veterans were often hard-pressed to pursue claims on their own. The bureaucracy of the Bureau of Pensions (now the Veterans Administration) was so daunting that, as one old soldier from Indiana complained, it had required only a few minutes for physicians to declare him fit for active duty at enlistment, but more than a decade "for pension examiners to determine that he was physically unable to support himself."[5]

Paid a set amount for each veteran's claim he pursued, Lemon assisted his clients in sorting through a tangle of eligibility requirements and attended to such details as the completion of multiple forms, collection of affidavits from supporting witnesses, and arrangements for qualifying physical examinations. The claims agent often corrected faulty paperwork and even offered to replace lost discharge papers or to help men get on the pension list despite mustering into the army under false pretenses, such as using an assumed name. Attorneys and agents were aware of the urgency of the situation, since many of their clients suffered in circumstances of "anguish, insolvency, and destitution."[6]

Lemon was himself both a veteran and a pensioner. In 1862, the recent graduate of Troy University (later Rensselaer Polytechnic Institute) received a captain's commission in the 125th New York Volunteer Infantry. He was captured and paroled at Harpers Ferry in September 1862 and went on to serve in the field with distinction before suffering severe wounds at Bristoe Station a year later. Reassigned to administrative duties in Washington during his convalescence, he stayed on in the capital after the surrender, earned his law degree, passed the bar, and became intimately familiar with disability statutes while pursuing his own claim and those of friends under the Pension Act of 1862.

In this he was far from alone. Pension applications soared in the decade immediately after the close of the war. In the fiscal year ending June 30, 1875, the Bureau of Pensions received thousands of claims, reports, and supporting materials documenting service and medical treatment. The pension rolls contained the names of more than a hundred thousand army invalids and an equal number of widows and other dependents. Those numbers would double in the decade to come. It is little wonder that Lemon and others like him quickly identified the representation of veteran or family interests in these claims as the source for lucrative law practices.[7]

While representing a small number of veterans in their pension claims, Lemon eventually took a post in the U.S. Treasury Department and added patent work to his legal portfolio. The pension and patent practice soon began to generate sufficient income to launch his newspaper on October 1, 1877. He was clear in announcing that his journal would be "devoted to the interests of soldiers and sailors of the late war, and all pensioners of the United States." He declared, "Our interests and the interests of soldiers are mutual. By helping us, you help yourselves."[8]

Moreover, these interests were definitely designed to help George E. Lemon, counselor-at-law and solicitor of claims. On page 8 of the first issue of the *National Tribune,* Lemon described the "Five Great Measures" to be the object of the new enterprise. The first "Great Measure . . . vital to the interests of all who fought in the late war" was passage of legislation to equalize bounties and to standardize the payments awarded to volunteers who enlisted or were wounded at various stages of the war. He also sought consideration for their widows, minor children, and parents, as well as an amendment to existing law that would enable pension payments to begin not at the date of application, but rather at the date of death or of discharge due to disability. The newspaper would further pursue the extension of pension law to include veterans of the Mexican War and the War of 1812 and their widows. The fifth measure advocated the passage of "amendments by Congress to remedy innumerable defects in the existing pension laws."[9]

Toward that end, in just the second issue of the *Tribune,* Lemon brought sharp focus to the matter of "arrearages," an issue that had already seen significant discussion among veterans and legislators. The position advocated by Lemon and other claims agents called not for adjustment of service or disability requirements for receiving a pension or even the rates of compensation. Instead, it argued for allowing veterans or their widows who had applied for pensions prior to July 1, 1880, to receive an extra payment dating to the original date of discharge (the so-called arrearage). He made the case seem a simple choice. The adoption of a bill to establish arrears payments "needs no argument to convince a person familiar with the pension laws of the justice and necessity of the passage of some such measures."[10]

Ultimately, Lemon proved an especially persuasive advocate for arrears legislation. On May 1, 1878, he proposed a "fearless war upon all measures that in our judgement tend to delay, diminish, or defeat the speedy settlement of just claims." He sought support from his subscribers and fellow veterans: "We need to feel that there is a host behind us cheering us on, co-operating with our efforts. We want to be able to say to members of Congress, to these officials, that we express the views, wishes, and feelings of hundreds of thousands of the voters of the country."[11]

For Lemon, signs of support came not only from the robust numbers of ex-soldiers subscribing to his newspaper, but also from the growing influence of the pension lobby. On June 19, 1878, just six weeks after Lemon's emotional appeal to his readers, the House of Representatives approved a bill introducing arrears legislation before sending it on to the Senate, where it was referred to committee.

In his report for the Bureau of Pensions for 1878, Commissioner James A. Bentley noted the palpable power surge in the pension lobby. He documented a year's worth of activities by claims agents, citing aggressive canvassing efforts that invited both valid and fraudulent claims cases. According to Bentley, attorneys and their firms routinely "advertised and drummed" for business coast to coast, utilizing "sheets issued in the form of periodical newspapers purported to be published in the interest of the soldiers, the columns of which contained matter in which apparent anxiety for the soldier's welfare and appeals to their love of gain were cunningly intermingled."[12]

Bentley was no doubt referring to Lemon and the *Tribune*, among others, and as if to validate the characterization of his journal, the claims-agent-turned-editor escalated his advocacy efforts as the Senate vote on the bill approached. His January 1, 1879, editorial confirmed Bentley's analysis. "We advocate not only the interests of the living soldier," he claimed, "but we speak for the widows and orphans, the aged father and mother of him who laid down in death in the woods of Shiloh, or on the banks of the Potomac." Not content to merely tug at heartstrings, Lemon called his readers to action, exhorting them to remember, "that you, and each of you, must work to secure this desired action. Both by pen and by speech to your Congressman as well as 'all in authority', constantly demand a recognition of what justice and patriotism would allow you, and you are sure to triumph." Lemon reminded readers that "some Congressmen, if they are lukewarm as to your rights are ever anxious for your votes."[13]

In the end, the Arrears Act passed the Senate with ease, and President Rutherford B. Hayes, himself a veteran, signed it into law on January 25, 1879. The cascade of paperwork that accompanied the promise of lump-sum payments was predictable. In the twenty-one days following enactment of the arrears bill, 2,301 claims were received at the Pension Bureau, representing an average of more than one hundred per day. To that point, the average number of claims received per day had been thirty-four. Requests for claims forms or "blanks" exceeded 140 per day, more than ten times the previous rate, and in the five months between the bill's passage and the end of the fiscal year, more than a hundred thousand total claims were submitted, almost double that of any previous twelve-month period.[14]

These statistics fail to adequately capture the very real personal and practical benefits that accrued to veterans for the one-dollar cost of a year's subscription to the *National Tribune*. Letters to the editor early in 1880 expressed heartfelt appreciation for timely tips in pursing pension claims, glimmers of hope for future employment, expressions of energy and motivation to launch spinoff organizations dedicated to the relief of old soldiers and sailors, and the maintenance of an active political agenda serving the interests of Union Army veterans. One telling testimonial came from contributor William Decker, who wrote, "I received my pension which was $892.20. I hereby state that I am perfectly satisfied with the manner in which you conducted my business and am under many obligations to you."[15]

Well-publicized advocacy was good for business, although not always positive press, and Lemon drew his share of criticism. While not known for resorting to the promotional methods of unsavory competitors—such as trolling waterfronts and alleyways for desperate veterans—he was at various times derided in newspapers as "that millionaire pension agent" and profiteer cornering the "old soldier racket." Yet the detractors were outnumbered by thousands of satisfied customers like Decker, who believed the captain took "more pleasure in the joy which his endeavors bestowed upon many a bereaved house than in the accumulation of wealth which came from the conduct of his business."[16] His faithful service earned him their loyalty and gratitude and ample reward in a pension trade emerging as the lead service sector of the increasingly commercialized postwar veteran marketplace

In 1880, new claims and petitions for arrearages poured into the Bureau of Pensions at a rate exceeding the total of the five previous years combined. In the last month before the deadline, the bureau received 44,532 new applications. Lemon's tireless advocacy was not lost on the GAR's national leadership. At the 1881 national encampment, immediate steps were taken to create a permanent committee to formally take up the task of lobbying for future pension reform.[17]

A lesser entrepreneur than George Lemon might have been content to settle for profits created by the waves of potential pensioners now clamoring for the services of his law firm. But, ever the canny businessman, he looked beyond pension applications to observe that the Grand Army of the Republic was on the move and picking up momentum in support of veterans and their interests. Membership in the organization jumped from 44,802 at the close of 1879 to 60,678 in 1881. This explosive growth was sustained over the next three years, and by 1884, membership swelled by more than 185,000 veterans.[18]

The fall of 1881 seemed a propitious time to convert the *Tribune* to a weekly publication. In the November 5 issue, Lemon presented a prospectus in support of the journal's new format. Of special note was the announcement that "attention will also be given to the various organizations of ex-soldiers and sailors and particularly to the Grand Army of the Republic throughout the United States." It was Lemon's "intention to make the *National Tribune* such a complete journal of instruction, information, and amusement no ex-soldier or sailor, no claimant for pension or bounty, no person interested in whatever pertains to the late war, no loyal man, woman, or child can afford to do without it." Seeking to cultivate new readers, potential clients, and vocal activists, his more aggressive publication schedule was the call to arms for the next campaign: to transform the once moribund GAR into a formidable political force for agitation of further pension reform.[19]

Lemon believed GAR membership could be doubled within the year and, in typical fashion, he set out to make it happen. Recognizing the potential popularity of GAR news, he devoted a column in the *Tribune* to the activities of the organization so that by the time of the National Encampment of 1882, Lemon was prepared to declare his newspaper the de facto official organ of the Grand Army. To ensure support for his ambitious bid to dominate the veteran audience, his representatives placed an edition of the *Tribune* in the hands of every delegate attending the group's June encampment in Baltimore.

Lemon proved a relentless and resourceful recruiter, teaming effectively with the commander of the GAR, Paul Vandervoort. By late in 1882, Vandervoort noted that announcements of new Grand Army post charters were appearing in the *Tribune*. At the same time, new subscriptions were pouring in at the rate of a thousand each week.[20]

This dramatic increase in subscriptions was due largely to aggressive strategies to boost circulation. Encouraging competition among existing readers to enlist new ones, Lemon and the *Tribune* rewarded enterprise and interest with such premiums as Waterbury watches (later rebranded as the GAR Watch), thirteen dozen of which were distributed in the previous month alone. For truly outstanding initiative, the "getter-up" of a club of ten new subscribers could for a mere $1.50 receive the 320-page *Roster of Regimental Surgeons and Assistant Surgeons during the War of the Re-*

bellion, an indispensable reference guide for anyone seeking to assemble the paperwork required for a successful pension claim. The newspaper's circulation soared.[21]

Just how closely Vandervoort and Lemon were collaborating in their efforts to revitalize the Grand Army to mutual benefit was never more apparent than in an interview with the GAR commander in December 1882. Offering "Kind Words for the Tribune," Vandervoort praised the paper for its unique and unequalled appeal to the veteran audience and applauded its instrumental role in helping establish new posts for the GAR. The "Kind Words" also featured content designed to provide post organizers with the necessary fundamentals to recruit, market, and maintain their new chapters. It even included tips on how to enlist women's auxiliary societies in identifying new members. As Vandervoort explained, "women are much better at seeking out soldiers who are really in need of assistance than we are."[22]

Lemon maintained early on that his mission was driven not by any specific partisan agenda but rather by devotion only to the interests of his veteran constituency. Despite these claims, however, during the presidential campaign of 1884 the journal assumed a decidedly Republican tone. Whether advocating for veterans to assume active roles in their state and national conventions to ensure soldier candidates on each and every ticket or helping to hammer pension-friendly planks into party platforms, Lemon and his *Tribune* remained solidly in opposition to Democratic candidate Grover Cleveland.

Such sustained anti-Cleveland efforts were maintained on multiple fronts even as Lemon aggressively conducted his business operations. Despite the demands of his political lobbying and agitation, he never lost sight of his competition for the veteran dollar. On the eve of Congress passing legislation raising the fees claims agents could charge clients from ten dollars to twenty-five dollars, in June 1884 Lemon bought out rival N. W. Fitzgerald. The transaction yielded forty thousand new pension cases and access to the twenty thousand subscribers to the *Tribune's* popular competitor, Fitzgerald's *Citizen Soldier.*[23]

After Cleveland narrowly defeated James G. Blaine to become the first Democratic president since James Buchanan, Lemon devoted his energies to the two causes closest to his heart and his pocketbook. By 1885, collaborative efforts to boost the fortunes of the GAR had brought the number of posts nationwide to more than five thousand, with a total membership of 269,684 veterans. And, during a January hearing before the House of Representatives, Lemon testified to a circulation for the

Tribune of 112,000 and the routine practice of distributing "200,000 or 250,000" sample copies. His testimony also included a reference to the fact that he had, on multiple occasions, mailed as many as a half million copies of a single issue during the early fall of 1884.[24]

President Cleveland found himself continually at odds with Lemon and his readership. Routine rejections of private claims brought before him by members of Congress on behalf of disabled constituents, bitter dismissals of veterans from civil service posts, and the veto of the Dependent Pension Bill that might have awarded honorably discharged veterans pensions no matter the cause of their disability, drew howls of protest from increasingly restive echelons of ex-soldiers. And when, in June 1887 Cleveland endorsed a War Department proposal to return captured Confederate battle flags to their southern owners, a "tornado of wrath from the indignant North struck the White House with the suddenness and power of a fierce Texas 'norther' beating upon a settler's cabin."[25]

Cleveland truly believed his "graceful act" was in harmony with what he perceived to be a growing spirit of reconciliation among Union and Confederate veterans. He miscalculated badly. An overwhelmingly negative reaction swiftly came from "those who decided Cleveland had erred egregiously," and the *National Tribune* was the perfect platform from which outraged veterans vented their "red hot" resentment and indignation over the ill-advised executive order. The June 23, 1887, issue of the *Tribune* featured patriotic banners, stinging editorials, and strident calls from governors and old soldiers alike to rescind the order. Thus chastened, Cleveland backtracked in the face of Union veterans rallying around Confederate battle flags, but the misstep would haunt him throughout the next presidential campaign.[26]

Even as Cleveland stumbled through an aborted invitation to the GAR's annual encampment of 1887 in St. Louis, rumors filled the Republican press. Word was George Lemon was at it again, selling the party's National Committee two hundred thousand editions of the *Tribune* to fuel its efforts to encourage voters to "holler" for their "old beloved colonel," Benjamin Harrison, the former senator from Indiana.[27]

In opposing Cleveland and his policies of limiting pension approvals while turning out veteran office holders, Lemon shamelessly boosted Harrison. "We are opposed to the re-election of Grover Cleveland as President of the United States solely because we are concerned that such re-election would be very prejudicial to the best interests of the veterans of the Union," he declared. "The only test applied to any public man is his disposition toward the unrequited saviors of the Nation. When subjected to this test, Mr. Cleveland is found deserving of opposition of every veteran in the country."[28]

In yet another tightly contested election, Harrison prevailed and with great energy and vigor successfully guided the Dependent Pension Act to passage in 1890, not only making good on a campaign promise but once again opening the floodgates for claims agents. In allowing disabled veterans a pension regardless of whether that infirmity was a result of their military service, Harrison "put away the apothecary's scale for weighing the nation's obligations to veterans and their dependents." The result was that by 1893 more than one million men were on the rolls of the pension office, receiving payments amounting to more than 40 percent of the government's annual revenue.[29]

By the time President Harrison signed the legislation into law, letters to the editor in the columns of the *Tribune* had evolved into an "Our Correspondents" section. In anticipation of the confusion accompanying the provisions of the new pension law, the entrepreneurial Lemon seized on the opportunity to once again reinvent the level of service provided subscribers. He invited questions pertaining to individual challenges and circumstances, saving his readers the cost of counsel and cast his editors as ombudsmen. The *Tribune* assisted widows—sometimes via postcards—in understanding eligibility after a second marriage, advised veterans about deadlines, and offered hints on how those who had enlisted under assumed names might file a successful claim. The *Tribune* staff sought to live up to Lemon's claim that his journal was "the only champion the soldiers have among the great papers of the country."[30]

With its role in securing the passage of measures that would ultimately pay out more than $1 billion in veterans' pensions, a weekly newspaper circulation of well over a hundred thousand, and no small role in boosting the 1890 membership of the GAR to 351,244, it is tempting to quantify the impact of the *National Tribune* on strictly statistical and financial terms. However, this overlooks a significant feature of the newspaper that delivered emotional benefit to subscribers such as Captain Grenville Sparrow of the Seventeenth Maine, a veteran who survived the war without a scratch, but was hardly untouched by his experience with the Red Diamond Regiment (nicknamed for the distinctive patches on the soldiers' caps identifying them as members of Major General Philip Kearny's division).[31]

Sparrow and the Seventeenth Maine saw hard service at Gettysburg and in the Wilderness, which left indelible marks on those who survived the close combat of the Wheatfield and Brock Road. Eager to maintain a connection to his comrades and their shared experience, he devoured the *Tribune*, carefully clipping more than three hundred articles, placing them in a leather-bound scrapbook, and creating a meticulous index. Sparrow was among those ex-soldiers described by David Blight as men who "burrowed into their memories and, in many ways, buried their imaginations in their war experiences." "They relived and remade those experiences," writes Blight, and "they reassembled the chaos and loss inherent to war into an order they could now control."[32]

George Lemon knew that his journal offered a rallying point for men such as Grenville Sparrow: survivors of the conflict consumed with a burning desire to preserve the memory of their bold and daring deeds. Immediately after making the *Tribune* a weekly edition in 1881, Lemon invited veterans to submit narratives of their Civil War experience. By August 1883, a section tagged "Fighting Them Over: What Our Veterans Have to Say About Their Old Campaigns" had become a popular feature.[33]

Typical of these early entries was the submission of Ben Naylor, a veteran of the 183rd Pennsylvania who appealed for someone to document the hard-fought battle of Deep Bottom, which had been eclipsed by such well-chronicled struggles as the Battle of Gettysburg. So voluminous did such correspondence become that Lemon surrendered the role of managing editor of the paper to John McElroy in 1884. A veteran of the Sixteenth Illinois Cavalry and Andersonville survivor, McElroy had held a similar position at the *Toledo (Ohio) Blade*. He proved as entrepreneurial as Lemon. Under McElroy's guidance and relentless promotion, "Fighting Them Over" grew to become one of the *Tribune's* signature features, made all the more popular because its submissions came not just from officers—the source of the overwhelming majority of contributions to the popular *Battles and Leaders* series in the *Century* magazine—but from enlisted men such as Naylor.[34]

Blight observes that the burst of correspondence more than two decades after the war ended can be explained by understanding veteran interest in how their experience would be perceived in the future. "Veterans of all ranks also craved recognition: they wanted their sacrifice, their place in the drama acknowledged," he writes. He also concludes that "many old soldiers were genuinely concerned 'to get the story right'—or to 'correct errors,' as they frequently said—because they believed that accuracy about the war determined how future generations would understand what happened and who was responsible for victory and defeat."[35]

Ben Naylor's plea notwithstanding, by far the topic visited by veterans most often in the pages of the *National Tribune* was the epic struggle between the Army of the Potomac and the Army of Northern Virginia at Gettysburg. More than eight hundred submissions were eventually received, with survivors arguing over everything from "who fired the first shot" of the engagement to "who saved Little Round Top."[36]

They did so without George Lemon officiating their differences. His health broken by tireless advocacy for Union army veterans and their families and his toils to maintain an active pension practice and multifaceted publishing concern, Lemon sought recovery in the sunny climate of San Diego, arriving there by private railroad car late in 1896. Initially, he seemed to rally, but on December 18 he died at the age of just fifty-three. Attended by the local GAR post, his body was escorted back to the Santa Fe depot and placed on a train to Washington for eventual interment at historic Rock Creek Cemetery.

Less than two weeks later, Lemon's will was placed in probate. A bachelor, Lemon left assets originally estimated to be worth more than $1 million (equivalent to more than $30 million today), but on further investigation executors discovered stacks of U.S. government bonds in a safe deposit vault that made the overall value of the estate considerably higher. The greatest benefit passed to the family of the late U.S. senator, General John A. Logan. A further stipulation in the will was the surprising provision ordering the immediate suspension of the *Tribune's* publication. The directive was never carried out, and the newspaper was eventually purchased by McElroy and partners R. W. Shoppell and Byron Andrews, with publication continuing without interruption.[37]

The enduring legacy of Captain George E. Lemon extends well beyond mere speculation over the size of his estate. Commentators and historians alike have been divided on the question of whether Lemon truly achieved his greater goal of mobilizing ex-soldiers into a cohesive political force.

Eugene Virgil Smalley, a journalist and Republican political pundit, rejected the notion of Lemon building a veteran voting bloc in a July 1884 *Century* article. Arguing at the time that there was no cohesive "soldier vote" available to boost the fortunes of one party or another, he did allow that "Congressmen are afraid there may be, and the Washington claim agents keep up the fiction that there is."[38]

William Henry Glasson, weighing in years later, at a time when many veterans were still carried on the rolls of the Pension Bureau, disagreed. "In more than one presidential campaign, the pension vote has played an extremely important part," he claimed. "Many have been the politicians who have sought to ride into power on the strength of lavish pension promises held out to the old soldiers as an inducement to secure their votes."[39]

There was certainly the *perception* that ex-soldiers could potentially influence political campaigns. In this, Lemon and his *National Tribune* undeniably played a pivotal role by tirelessly advocating for pension reform and leveraging the strategic revival of the Grand Army of the Republic to energize and sustain a veterans' movement marked by old soldiers awakening to "a consciousness of their power." Their sense of urgency was heightened by the feeling of loss from years given over to hard service and the struggle to reenter civilian society. As historian James Marten observes, "a generous pension system would help them recover some of that lost potential. And they believed it entirely appropriate that they shape the political system through lobbying and advocacy which, in turn helped to change the nature of politics in Gilded Age America and beyond."[40]

Standing squarely in the ranks of comrades demanding compensation for their sacrifice was George E. Lemon. For more than three decades he built a mutually rewarding relationship with veterans that was both transactional and transformational. In working tirelessly to sharpen the country's sense of obligation to old soldiers, he left a bold imprint on how the U.S. government cared for those eloquently remembered in President Abraham Lincoln's second inaugural address. Both literally and figuratively, Lincoln called for the country to "bind up the nation's wounds; to care for him who have borne the battle, and for his widow and orphan."[41]

In furnishing aid for emotionally and financially impoverished survivors, Lemon proved himself to be something more than a compassionate crusader. He was at the same time an innovative entrepreneur who deployed creative circulation schemes to cultivate thousands of future clients. He was a resourceful capitalist willing to invest heavily in the pension claimant and periodical market. He was an aggressive recruiter for the Grand Army of the Republic, an organization whose growth likewise contributed to the viability of his legal practice and publishing interests. He was a savvy lobbyist and political operative capable of mobilizing the GAR to shepherd advantageous legislation through Congress.

Indeed, for the price of either a subscription to the *Tribune* or the cost of a claims agent retainer or, better yet, both, Lemon was prepared to provide emotional and financial succor to the war's heroes who "lived on for more than 30 years to struggle against disease and pain." Celebrated by his contemporaries as a "sincere, earnest, effective champion of the cause of the veterans," he is as well remembered as an energetic and ambitious man of business gifted with the singular ability to early on recognize that his own financial interests were inextricably tied to those of his future readers and clients.[42]

NOTES

1. Wallace Evan Davies, *Patriotism on Parade: The Story of Veterans and Hereditary Organizations in America, 1783–1900* (Cambridge, Mass.: Harvard University Press, 1955), 105.

2. Stuart McConnell, *Glorious Contentment: The Grand Army of the Republic, 1865–1900* (Chapel Hill: University of North Carolina Press, 1992), 24–25.

3. Ibid., 32–33; Theda Skocpol, "America's First Social Security System," in *The Civil War Veteran: A Historical Reader*, ed. Larry M. Logue and Michael Barton (New York: New York University Press, 2007), 179–99, 185.

4. Brian Jordan, *Marching Home: Union Veterans and their unending Civil War* (New York: Liveright, 2014) 76.

5. Ibid., 152.

6. Ibid., 157.

7. Claire Prechtel-Kluskens, "'A Reasonable Degree of Promptitude': Civil War Pension Application Processing, 1861–1885," *Prologue Magazine* 42 (June 28, 2015), http://www.archives.gov/publications/prologue/2010/spring/civilwarpension.

8. *National Tribune* (Washington, D.C.), October 1, 1877.

9. Ibid.

10. *National Tribune*, November 1, 1877.

11. *National Tribune*, May 1, 1878.

12. William H. Glasson, *Federal Military Pensions in the United States* (New York: Oxford University Press, 1918), 149–50.

13. *National Tribune*, January 1, 1879.

14. John William Oliver, "History of the Civil War Military Pensions, 1866–1885," *Bulletin of the University of Wisconsin* 4 (1915–18): 70.

15. *National Tribune*, January 1, 1880.

16. *Manitowoc (Wisc.) Pilot*, January 7, 1897; *Mineral Point (Wisc.) Tribune*, May 28, 1896; *National Tribune*, December 24, 1896.

17. McConnell, *Glorious Contentment*, 148.

18. Mary R. Dearing, *Veterans in Politics: The Story of the G.A.R.* (Baton Rouge: Louisiana State University Press, 1952), 269; Davies, *Patriotism on Parade*, 35.

19. *National Tribune*, November 5, 1881.

20. Dearing, *Veterans in Politics*, 271.

21. *National Tribune*, November 2 and November 9, 1882.

22. *National Tribune*, December 21, 1882.

23. Dearing, *Veterans in Politics*, 287.

24. Robert Burns Beath, *History of the Grand Army of the Republic* (New York: Press of William McDonald, 1888), 296; Glasson, *Federal Military Pensions*, 185.

25. *National Tribune*, June 23, 1887

26. Alyn Brodsky, *Grover Cleveland: A Study in Character* (New York: St. Martin's, 2000), 190; *National Tribune*, June 23, 1887.

27. Dearing, *Veterans in Politics*, 386, 372.

28. *National Tribune*, September 27, 1888.

29. Kathleen L. Gorman, "Civil War Pensions," in *Essential Civil War Curriculum*, Virginia Center for Civil War Studies at Virginia Tech, May 2012, https://www.essentialcivilwarcurriculum.com/assets/files/pdf/ECWC%20TOPIC%20 Pensions%20Essay%20.pdf; Charles W. Calhoun, *Minority Victory: Gilded Age Politics and the Front Porch Campaign of 1888* (Lawrence: University of Kansas Press, 2008), 185.

30. *National Tribune*, June 18, 1891.

31. Glasson, *Federal Military Pensions*, 238; McConnell, *Glorious Contentment*, 54.

32. David Blight, *Race and Reunion: The Civil War in American Memory* (Cambridge, Mass.: Harvard University Press, 2001), 182.

33. *National Tribune*, August 9, 1883.

34. *National Tribune*, October 18, 1883.

35. Blight, *Race and Reunion*, 186.

36. Richard A. Sauers, ed., *Fighting Them Over: How the Veterans Remembered Gettysburg in the Pages of the National Tribune* (Baltimore, Md.: Butternut and Blue, 1998), i, ii.

37. *New York Times*, December 29, 1896; *CPI Inflation Calculator*, December 3, 2018, http://www.in2013dollars.com/1896-dollars-in-2018?amount=1000000.

38. Eugene Virgil Smalley, "The United States Pension Office," *Century*, July 1884, 427.

39. Glasson, *Federal Military Pensions*, 262, 265.

40. McConnell, *Glorious Contentment*, 147; James Marten, "Those Who Have Borne the Battle: Civil War Veterans, Pension Advocacy, and Politics," *Marquette Law Review* 93, no. 4 (Summer 2010): 1407–13, quote on 1413.

41. E. B. Long with Barbara Long, *The Civil War Day by Day: An Almanac 1861–1865* (Garden City, N.Y.: Doubleday, 1971), 647.

42. *National Tribune*, December 31, 1896.

Outfitting the Lost Cause

The Re-creation of Southern Identity through Confederate Veterans' Uniforms, 1865 to the 1920s

SHAE SMITH COX

In April 1901, the *Confederate Veteran* announced that J. F. Shipp, quarter-master general of the United Confederate Veterans (UCV), had designed the Confederate veteran uniform down to its buttons. In his report to the organization's adjutant general and chief of staff, General George Moorman, Shipp reported that he considered "the most important matter for the consideration and execution by this department" to be to "formulate and promulgate a regulation uniform in compliance with the resolution adopted at the annual meeting." He believed that "formulating an appropriate uniform for an association such as ours required much reflection and investigation."[1]

The UCV had formed in New Orleans in 1889, and as the nineteenth century gave way to the twentieth, Confederate veterans strove to create a cohesive narrative of Confederate involvement during the Civil War. This narrative relied heavily on material culture.[2] Uniforms were deemed central to displaying Confederate identity, prompting the United Confederate Veterans and United Daughters of the Confederacy (UDC) to design uniforms intended for veterans, not soldiers. At reunions, monument dedications, and other functions, the old soldiers would don Confederate veterans' uniforms, providing a homogenous appearance and suggesting a coherent wartime identity. What they could not have expected, however, was the degree to which these new uniforms would simultaneously hearken to an imagined Confederate past and serve to knit the nation back together through their production, marketing, and display at joint Blue-Gray reunions.

In the immediate aftermath of Appomattox, the U.S. government had forbidden Confederate soldiers from wearing their uniforms.[3] But by the late nineteenth century, the moratorium on wartime uniforms was less frequently enforced. Meetings, monument commemorations, and reunions were safe places for veterans to gather with comrades to commiserate or reminisce about their losses, whether of battles or of friends, and about their time in the service. It also allowed them to be seen in their uniforms. Meetings became special occasions with some pageantry, especially in the South, that allowed veterans to gather dressed in their wartime and then eventually their veterans' uniforms. Because meetings were private gatherings of veterans, wartime uniforms were more acceptable there than they would have been at a more public event. The informal but pageant-heavy last tour of former Confederate president Jefferson Davis in 1886 provided an opportunity for Lieutenant General James Longstreet, who had angered former rebels by becoming a Republican during Reconstruction, to appear in his Confederate uniform and sit at Davis's side. As reported in the *Idaho Avalanche*, participants insisted that such a meeting "means no disrespect to any other section of the country, nor is there evidence of disloyalty in the display," adding that their only wishes were to reunite with "old comrades and the revival of never-fading memories."[4] Uniforms were a key tangible element at such gatherings for their evocation of nostalgia. The Davis gathering, however, perpetuated a subversive concept: it allowed veterans to reenvision the war as a glorious endeavor and fabricate a vision of the Old South for southerners to romanticize and elevate.

Discussions about whether it was acceptable to wear battle-worn uniforms to reunions or having new uniforms made for veterans began to play out in newspapers and in organizational meetings. The functional notion of manufacturing new veterans' uniforms concerned the quality and fit of the old uniforms because more than thirty years had elapsed since the fighting ended. Rather than a single, cohesive design, a variety of uniforms were used across the Confederacy during the war for several reasons but including manufacturing issues and supply availability. Further, after four years of war with limited replacements, uniforms had holes from wear and tear, bullets, or moths. The practical solution was to suggest the preservation of the wartime uniforms and the creation of new veterans' uniforms.

Both northern and southern manufacturers of veteran uniforms capitalized on these sentiments, but they were able to do so only because of the creation and consumption of wartime uniforms. Complaints of poor-fitting uniforms and the measurements collected from soldiers during the war aided the growth of the readymade clothing industry, the standardization of sizes, and the rise of department stores. This contribution, coupled with a shift toward a national consumer culture, meant that by the beginning of the twentieth century the market for readymade clothing was twice that for custom clothing. The increase in technology and in consumption forced clothing manufacturers and retailers to compete with one another. The ability to produce, and for the consumer to afford, fashionable attire, especially suits, grew swiftly during the Gilded Age.[5] Uniform manufacturers such as M. C. Lilley and Levy Brothers sold more than just reunion outfits: they sold former Confederate veterans the tools necessary to construct an identity by crafting a cohesive look during the reunion period, which in turn transformed the value and the meaning of the uniforms they peddled. The companies who produced these items filled a consumer need by making and selling new Confederate veteran uniforms. But the veterans and manufacturers were not alone in this endeavor. From the Gilded Age through the Progressive Era, women joined in the conversation through domesticity, consumer culture, and reform activities.[6] At the end of the nineteenth century, the UDC proved essential in shaping Confederate identity in part by funding the manufacturing of Confederate veterans' uniforms.

Uniforms proved especially crucial to the United Confederate Veterans' identity because of the importance of uniforms to wartime Confederates. The Confederate government spent more than $1 million on clothing and uniforms for troops in 1861. This figure does not account for the twenty-one dollars per person—later a twenty-five-dollar stipend every six months—purportedly received by each volunteer who used his own clothes or had them furnished by his community. This raises the question of how the new nation could afford to spend so much to outfit its soldiers. The answer was that it could not. The decision makers for the Confederate government were elite planters. Accustomed to being in debt, the planters failed to carefully consider the consequences of accruing more debt by outfitting troops for war, because their general assumption was that the war would be short. Plantation economics, however, was no way to run a new country, and the planners' commitment to indebtedness cost them dearly. The Confederacy was willing to go into debt at the beginning of the war for uniforms because those garments fit in with the region's perceptions of justice and glory; consequently, the soldiers' gallant appearance became entrenched in their identity, causing an inflated since of self, and appearance became a central focus of the war.[7]

Because of the prohibition on wearing rebel uniforms in public after the war, if the uniforms were salvageable and if they had the money to purchase new clothes, many veterans packed away their uniforms when they returned home.[8] As veterans' events became more commonplace after Reconstruction, some Confederates unpacked their trunks and once again donned the gray. By the 1880s and 1890s they began publicly appearing in uniforms at reunions with Union veterans.[9] But many Union veterans continued to condemn the sight of what they perceived as traitorous rags. At the unveiling of the memorial to the New South advocate Henry W. Grady at Atlanta in 1892, Confederate veterans marched in their wartime uniforms and with their flag beside Union veterans and, in doing so, "gave such offence" to Grand Army of the Republic commander John Palmer. White southerners seemed surprised that the uniforms disturbed Commander Palmer, which led the Georgia veterans to set aside their wartime uniforms for a short while.[10] In addition, leading UCV commanders put in place strict guidelines for attire at important events. For the Ninth Annual Reunion of the United Confederate Veterans, to "keep pace with the growing sentiment," organizers asked veterans to wear "a simple and inexpensive suit, or sack only, of Confederate gray, with a dark hat."[11] Instances such as this and the size and condition of wartime uniforms provided reasons for Quartermaster J. F. Shipp to design the Confederate veteran uniform and created a market for uniform manufacturers.

Shipp intended the veterans' uniforms to represent the varying arms of service and rank in the Confederate army "to perpetuate a true type of our uniform as a part of the history of the Confederate States of America." The Confederate uniform of 1861 "was the pride and glory of the young Confederacy" and "is now revered by all survivors, and is respected by the American people." For uniformity, Shipp "selected the same shade, weight, and grade of goods for all uniforms—namely, No. 1238, Charlottesville Woolen Mills" because its "regulation shade, can be worn at receptions, funerals, and other occasions, as well as reunions" and that all orders "outside of the cloth" should be referred to him. Shipp claimed that the "quality of goods is first-class, and free from shoddy materials," which had been a problem in the North during the war. He suggested that it would even "serve as a proper uniform at death."[12] This report demonstrates the significance white southerners attached to the Confederate uniform, discussing the importance of securing "the regulation uniform" for regional reunions, as if these men were still in the army.[13] The ability to construct all new uniforms in one pattern and one shade of gray for veterans to wear at reunions, instead of the varying colors of gray and butternut that the rebels actually wore, became an opportunity for the UCV and the UDC to recast the Confederacy as united, both during the war and in memory.

UCV quartermaster Shipp thoroughly investigated uniforms worn by the branches of the Confederate military, seeking the ideal representation. His *Information and Design for Uniform and Dress of the United Confederate Veteran Association* pamphlet details how the ideal UCV uniform should appear and specifically cites the Confederate General Orders Nine from June 6, 1861. Shipp did not follow the order verbatim but "sought to observe enough of the main features to make this uniform appropriate, representative and historical." Along with all of the specifics of what the veterans' uniforms should look like, the pamphlet includes the "List and Price of Material and Other Paraphernalia for U.C.V. Uniforms." The 54-inch-wide No. 1238 "Confederate gray cloth" sold for $1.90 a yard. This section lists all of the decorations that could appear on the uniform depending on rank and specifications of the UCV camp.

The UCV chose the Charlottesville (Virginia) Woolen Mills as the official supplier of cloth for veterans' uniforms for a variety of reasons. The mill was known for its uniform fabrics, some winning awards at the Chicago and St. Louis Expositions. From 1899 and for the next thirty years, West Point cadets were clothed in Charlottesville Mill fabrics.[14] Veterans were directed to order No. 1238 from Charlottesville Woolen Mills and all other fabric through Shipp in Chattanooga, Tennessee. Payment was expected with the order. Although Shipp offered to have uniforms made if sent specific measurements, at $15.50 per suit, he recommended that veterans order the material and have uniforms "made by local tailors, so they may be fitted."[15]

Examples of UCV uniforms are in archives and museums across the country. The American Civil War Museum in Richmond, for example, houses one manufactured for Virginian John W. Jewett. His five-button front, cadet-gray wool cloth coat features a gold-embroidered general's insignia on the collar and gold-colored UCV buttons. Another similar piece in its collection is a veteran's coat much like Jewett's, though the gold embroidery represents a lieutenant colonel and the inside pocket contains the label "Only Lexington Suitings bear this label, The Burton-Pierce Co. Boston–New York–Chicago."[16] Established in 1885, this company is mentioned multiple times with advertisements in the *Men's Wear* retailers' newspaper. Their advertisements display a number of styles, including those worn by the Confederate veterans. They boast that "we guarantee every suit to be all wool, indigo dyed in the wool high tensile strength, identical in shade with every other suit," which was exactly what the UCV and UDC wanted—even if it came from a northern manufacturer.[17]

One complete uniform in the North Carolina History Museum in Raleigh is of particular interest because of its label. The coat is blue-gray with a tan lining, gold North Carolina state buttons, a cream collar with matching cuffs, and gold "chicken guts" on the sleeves. The inside of the collar is black crushed velvet and a black label with gold writing reads, "The M.C. Lilley & Co. Columbus, O. Military & Society Goods." The curator believes that the coat was worn during the war and relined for post-war events, which would account for the sprucing on the coat. The pants are the same blue-gray with the higher-cut waist popular during the Civil War. Established in 1865, M. C. Lilley and Co. exclusively manufactured uniforms and equipment for active-duty military, fraternal organizations, and eventually veterans from both the Union and the Confederacy.[18]

Union veterans, too, could purchase veterans' uniforms. In 1887, M. C. Lilley and Co. published an illustrated *Grand Army of the Republic Price List of Uniforms* for distribution to Grand Army of the Republic (GAR) members. These uniforms consisted of a coat, vest, shirt, pants, and hat, made to each man's measurements. The double-breasted coat listed as the official uniform of the GAR started at $9.25, with higher-quality cloth fetching more. The single-breasted option ranged from $7 to $14.50 and pants from $4.25 to $10.20. The coats and vests were equipped with GAR regulation buttons. A basic complete outfit cost about $25. That is the equivalent of about $681.84 in 2020, and these totals do not include sashes, swords, guns, pins, or extra buttons.[19]

While M. C. Lilley and Co. produced no pamphlet for the UCV, the company did advertise in the *Confederate Veteran*, the UCV's most widely read publication. The *Confederate Veteran* published reminisces of war, news about new monuments, and announcements about upcoming reunions and acceptable attire there, but founder and editor Sumner A. Cunningham noted that the magazine was "designed to publish advertisements."[20] By printing stories glorifying the service of the Confederate veterans in their splendid or tattered gray, the *Confederate Veteran* kept alive a vision of Confederate glory, and through advertisements for veterans' uniforms the magazine assisted in selling altered memories that fit this new narrative. Advertisements for new Confederate veteran uniforms began in 1907. The news sections and advertisements for reunions stated that "efforts are being made to induce all who attend to secure uniforms" but did not tell the veterans how to obtain the uniforms.[21] The first advertisement for Pettibone Uniforms produced by the Pettibone Brothers

Manufacturing Company in Cincinnati appeared in the February 1907 issue. The ad featured an illustration of a veteran in full garb resting his arm on a cannon and one of a pin featuring a crossed U.S. flag and Confederate flag. The ad invited readers to mention the *Confederate Veteran* ad when ordering. This company also manufactured items for the Grand Army of the Republic.[22]

It was important to have a UCV uniform in spring 1907 because the annual UCV reunion in Richmond, the former Confederate capital, was set for that May 30 to June 3. The year likewise commemorated what would have been Robert E. Lee's one hundredth birthday, and the veterans wanted the reunion to be a spectacle. The M. C. Lilley and Co. in Columbus, Ohio, purchased its first advertisement in the magazine in March of 1907, offering catalogs on the promise that "we are official manufacturers of uniforms and goods you need."[23] With every subsequent issue of the *Confederate Veteran*, the uniform advertisements became more and more frequent. In 1910 Levy's Brothers from Louisville, Kentucky, began advertising uniforms in the magazine. The Levy's Special included a regulation UCV coat, trousers, and buttons for $8, and even offered "special terms for outfitting whole camps." Once Levy Brothers began advertising with pricing, Pettibone began doing the same, with "prices from $7.50 Up."[24]

The special collections library at Western Kentucky University has several veterans' uniforms, including a set from local Judge Jeptha Crawford Johnson, who served in the Thirty-Seventh Arkansas Infantry Company B, rising to the rank of lieutenant colonel. It is a simple gray coat, with tan lining, and a variety of UCV and eagle gold buttons with stars on the collar to match his rank. Belonging to the same collection is a complete Confederate veteran uniform set with a coat, vest, and pants of the same description. This archive also has an ornate M. C. Lilley and Co. United Sons of Confederate Veterans (USCV) uniform coat with the same blue-gray exterior, but this coat is double-breasted with gold USCV buttons.[25]

At the Kentucky Historical Society in Frankfort is a circa-1910 Levy Brothers UCV coat, identifiable by the "Levy Bros./Louisville" label in the interior breast pocket. It is the same blue-gray wool as the others, with brass UCV buttons on the right cuff.[26] Although Kentucky remained loyal to the Union during the Civil War, the Kentucky UCV applied to have the annual reunion and parade meet in Louisville for the summer of 1905. Levy Brothers provided "goods sold to the Reunion Committee" and requested payment for these items in an invoice addressed to Captain John H. Leathers, "$5.00 for the suit and $.90 for the hat." A June letter to William Haldeman from Levy Brothers requested that he peti-

Companies from states not part of the Confederacy produced and marketed uniforms to Confederate veterans, including M. C. Lilley of Columbus, Ohio, and Levy Brothers of Louisville, Kentucky. (*Confederate Veteran* 18 [May 1910]: 51)

tion the UCV Executive Committee to reconsider the route of the parade because "about fifty retail merchants doing business on Market Street" asked the chairman "to have the parade pass their doors," claiming that their request was motivated not by potential profits but by their desire "merely to see the parade." He added that "you no doubt are aware that the main reason this body is brought to Louisville is to benefit our retail as well as our wholesale trade" and that the merchants "have given liberally to your cause and will decorate appropriately in order to make our houses attractive."[27] The Retail Merchants' Association in Louisville purchased a subscription from the UCV for $2,000.[28] This transaction benefited the merchants and their bottom line, helped defray the UCV's costs for the reunion, and promoted the efforts of the Lost Cause by providing a place for Confederate veterans, in veterans' uniforms, to publicly present themselves.

The physical process of obtaining these new uniforms embodies an even deeper contradiction because northern clothiers manufactured many of them. For a profit, northerners helped Confederate veterans remake white, rebel, martial manhood and peddle their interpretation of the war represented by pristine new veteran uniforms to the rest of the country. The narrative that "former" Confederates simply wanted to remember their sacrifice during the time of joint struggle and forget that they fought for slavery was wrapped in a blue-gray uniform coat and sold for eight dollars. Cheaper veterans' uniforms meant that more people could and would purchase their way into this exclusive club. While veterans and memorial societies bought the new uniforms and promoted uniformity, the rest of the country consumed the narrative that a staged "heritage" was more important than the truth. For the companies that manufactured veterans' uniforms, their overall goal was not to perpetuate the memory of one organization or the other but to make a profit from both the GAR's and UCV's sympathetic leanings toward their respective causes. Through monetary transactions, manufacturers simply provided the tools necessary for each group to create a cohesive sectional memory, one blue or gray uniform at a time.

The United Daughters of the Confederacy supported obtaining new uniforms not only to assist veterans but also to solidify their own narrative of the South's involvement in the Civil War. Veterans' uniforms provided tangible evidence for the women's carefully crafted memory of just, respectable Confederate veterans and their role in aiding them. In his 1902 welcoming speech for the annual UDC convention, Governor D. Clinch Heyward of South Carolina addressed the group, recounting Confederate women's sacrifice during the war. When the factories were "inadequate to the emergency, the handloom was made to supply the deficiency" and their "fairy fingers . . . boldly seized and made the coarse garments of the soldier." He continued that "through you and through your works the suffering, the courage, the patriotism and the glory of the Confederate soldiers shall endure forevermore" because "southern women . . . refused to let time teach forgetfulness," adding that there are "no truer historians than the women of the Confederacy" and that the "old, faded uniforms, precious heirlooms now in every Southern home, can find no more loving custodians than the daughters of the men who wore the gray."[29]

The UDC convention minutes deploy similar memorialistic rhetoric, noting that "it is a pretty idea and if practical a worthy thing" to provide veterans with new uniforms of Confederate gray. These women considered it their duty to care for veterans because they were the "last living links binding us to the old South, the land of chivalry, poetry and romance, and to those old times, of which it may truly be said, that 'Knight-hood was in flower.'" To them, chivalry transcended factual history, and they believed that the era of the Civil War produced "men and women who lived up to their creed of truth, justice, honor, valor and love of country."[30] The opportunity to provide veterans with uniforms allowed the women to replace tattered uniforms and memories with the glori-fied heroism of the Confederacy, thus permitting them to remake their memories and adopt a heritage prettier than the reality. Replacement uniforms fostered the notion central to the Lost Cause that the Confed-eracy's had been motivated by pure and noble intentions. Veterans' uni-forms helped adherents recast the memory of the Civil War, effectively acting as costumes in a propaganda play.

Confederate societies put considerable thought and effort into how to get new uniforms, how much they cost, and who would pay for them. The UDC went into fund-raising mode, and as early as the late 1890s, in-dividual chapters began purchasing new uniforms for local veterans. The Martha Reid Chapter in Jacksonville, Florida, gave its veterans "hand-some new uniforms of the dear old Confederate gray, and they were greeted with enthusiasm" when they appeared at a Confederate monu-ment unveiling.[31] Some chapters convinced the state to pay for veterans' uniforms, the General George Burgwyn Anderson Chapter from North Carolina claiming that "because of four years of splendid service and self-sacrifice to the Commonwealth" that soldiers gave, North Carolin-ians owed it "to their dignity and self-respect to clothe them in new and suitable garments."[32] It became a point of pride at both regional and na-tional UDC meetings for chapters to boast of purchasing new uniforms for their respective veterans. When recounting the yearly financial re-port, the speaker asked each chapter "What have you done to aid and support Veterans?"[33] The representatives of several chapters confidently replied that they furnished uniforms to a number of veterans for the up-coming reunions, therefore fulfilling their duty and furthering the "true" memory of the Civil War.[34]

At the 1913–14 national UDC meeting, the Florida division reported an "extreme financial depression of the past several months" that made it difficult to contribute to the monument funds. Instead, the members fo-cused their finances on their "benevolent work of love and duty" to the soldiers, boasting of "supplying the men with uniforms and many little amenities of life not otherwise possible for them," totaling the "contribu-tions for Confederate work of all kinds" to nearly $7,000.[35] The UDC did not profit from uniforms to their veterans, but the women's efforts ensured a cohesive image of Confederate identity. The monetary transaction benefited an ideological battle.

The veterans' uniform became a popular sight at Confederate monument unveilings and parades, but it remained controversial at joint national reunions held with the Grand Army of the Republic and the United Confederate Veterans. While the GAR wore its own version of a veterans' uniform, a Union blue suit, to veterans' celebrations, and would be willing to attend a joint gathering, some officers did not want to see Confederate veterans in uniform. Only during the fifty-year anniversaries of Civil War battles in the early 1910s did Union feelings begin to relax toward seeing former Confederates in their new veterans' uniforms.

In February 1913, "a group of Confederate veterans, their tanned and wrinkled faces sometimes quivering with emotion," petitioned the commissioners organizing the fiftieth anniversary of the Battle of Gettysburg "for the privilege of wearing their old gray uniforms at the reunion in July." A Union veteran on the Gettysburg reunion commission, Colonel Charles Burrows, had introduced a resolution "that no military uniforms be worn at the celebration by survivors of either army" in order to prevent fractures at the reunion. At the same meeting, a Texas veteran, Major General Felix H. Robertson, "begged for the privilege of carrying the old Texas battleflags in the celebration," to which "Union hands applauded." Robertson claimed no ill intentions, simply stating that the "reunion is not to celebrate a victory," but to "celebrate peace." After hearing their pleas, Burrows withdrew his resolution prohibiting uniforms and flags at the reunion.[36]

While the prospect of Confederate veterans wearing their uniforms to national reunions, such as Gettysburg in 1913, caused a stir with a few northern representatives on the committee, the issue was quickly settled. When addressing the assembled delegates of the Gettysburg committee, Governor John Tener of Pennsylvania "assured them that all veterans will be welcome and nobody will look at their clothes"—they could wear the garments in which they felt comfortable. He stated that "we shall go there as survivors of a war which no human power had been able to avert" and that the "victors in blue will greet with open arms the vanquished in gray, who fought there for a cause they believed was right, and they fought well." Confederate C. Irvine Walker concurred. "We shall go to Gettysburg, not to battle but to seal a lasting peace wearing our gray and bearing the banners which we so gallantly followed on that gory field" he

Confederate veterans attend the fiftieth reunion of Gettysburg in 1913 wearing the uniforms purchased from companies such as M. C. Lilley and Levy Brothers. (GNMP-T-2692, Gettysburg National Military Park)

claimed, adding that former Confederates were "willing to bury forever the bitterness of the past."[37]

Most Union veterans did not share Colonel Charles Burrows's distaste when they saw Confederate gray commingled with Union blue. In a letter to Dr. Samuel Eastman, Colonel J. A. Watrous, a retired Union veteran, stated that "speaking for myself, I would vote to have them coming in their old uniforms or new uniforms in gray and bring along their voices" to indulge in a Rebel yell. He said he wanted to "see the uniform and hear the yell when it will not scare the life out of me as they used to do [during the war]." Still other newspapers, many southern, published articles admonishing the GAR veterans on the committee who fostered the "surviving hatred and rancor" of those who fought on the other side fifty years later. Lobbying for veterans to wear uniforms, another newspaper posited that the objectors may have "missed the meaning of the semi-centennial celebration" because it was not meant to be a gathering of just North or South "but of American citizens, with one flag, one nation and one history, and common memories of the most momentous struggle in

the annals of human liberty."[38] Many critics equated denying veterans the
right to wear their uniforms with denying them their rights to nostalgia
and sentimentality.

At the fiftieth anniversary of Gettysburg, aged men in regulation GAR
and UCV veteran uniforms stepped off trains, talked together, and walked
to their respective tents. They shook hands across a hedge, giving the
public a glimpse of "true peace." Reading descriptions in local newspapers of "veterans in Blue and Gray, arm in arm," hobbling over the Gettysburg battlefield fostered the illusion that the country had healed. Specifically in northern newspapers, photographs and descriptions of regiments
resuming "old positions" as "the thin gray line advanced and as the Union
veterans awaited them at the 'High Water Mark' and other points" played
out in people's imaginations when they read that the groups, "emotion
stirring in the breast of each veteran," shared "tears, hand-clasps, and
embraces."[39] Those stories and photographs with Confederate veterans in gray entered homes across the country through newspapers and
validated the notion that Confederates in gray veterans' uniforms were
harmless because they just wanted to remember their struggle and their
heritage of noble fighting, overlooking the fact that they had engaged in
war to protect slavery.

Confederate veterans' uniforms proved crucial in both buying and
selling Civil War memory in the early twentieth century on two seemingly incompatible fronts. As was the intention of Confederate memorial
groups, the new uniforms helped foster the Lost Cause. Through their
campaign to outfit veterans in the new uniforms, UCV and the UDC attempted to rewrite the "true history" of the Civil War forging an idealized memory of homogenous regimental regalia that had never existed
during the war. Perhaps surprisingly, the uniforms simultaneously helped
peddle reconciliation. Both northern and southern clothing companies
manufactured and marketed the uniforms to veterans of the blue and the
gray across the nation. Perhaps most importantly, seeing older uniformed
Confederate veterans at Blue-Gray reunions helped soften the attitudes
of Union veterans and other loyal northerners toward the former rebels.
The new veterans' uniforms proved not a relic of a divided past, but a tangible representation of both a reconciled nation and a burgeoning Lost
Cause.

NOTES

1. "Uniforms for Confederate Veterans," *Confederate Veteran* (hereafter *CV*), 9 (April 1901): 133.

2. United Confederate Veterans website, http://confederatewave.org/wave /united_confederate_veterans.phtml.

3. In April 1865, Lincoln's attorney general James Speed interpreted General Robert E. Lee's surrender terms, adding the stipulation that "wearing the rebel uniform by officers in the Federal lines is considered incompatible with the agreement, and will be regarded as an act of hostility" and that "they have as much right to bear the traitor's flag through the streets of a loyal city as to wear the traitor's garb." Speed stated that "the stipulation of surrender permits no such thing" because both Confederate uniforms and flags represented treason and hostility. (U.S. War Department, *The War of the Rebellion: A Compilation of the Official Records of the Union and Confederate Armies*, 127 vols., index, and atlas [Washington, D.C.: Government Printing Office, 1880–1901], ser. 1, 3(46): 918–20.) This moratorium affected the acceptability of ex-Confederates to wear their wartime uniforms for years to come and assisted in influencing the need for Confederate veteran uniform production.

4. *Idaho Avalanche* (Silver City, Idaho), May 22, 1886.

5. Adam D. Mendelsohn, *The Rag Race: How Jews Sewed Their Wary to Success in America and the British Empire* (New York: New York University Press, 2015), 192–93.

6. Kristin L. Hoganson, *Consumers' Imperium: The Global Production of American Domesticity, 1865–1920* (Chapel Hill: University of North Carolina Press, 2007), 8.

7. James A. Matthews, *Statutes at Large of the Provisional Government of the Confederate States of America* (Richmond, Va.: Confederate States of America), 58.

8. *Philadelphia Inquirer*, June 17, 1865. Members of the Union army were encouraged to save their uniforms so they could be brought out for future generations in order to display the soldiers' "fidelity to his country."

9. Elaine Frantz Parsons, "Midnight Rangers: Costumes and Performance in the Reconstruction-Era Ku Klux Klan," *Journal of American History* 92, no. 3 (December 2005): 811–36, 814.

10. *Salt Lake Weekly Tribune*, December 15, 1892.

11. *Watchman and Southron* (Sumpter, S.C.), March 22, 1899.

12. "Uniforms for Confederate Veterans," *CV* 9 (April 1901): 133.

13. The *Weekly Register* (Point Pleasant, Va.), September 17, 1901; *Opelousas (La.) Courier*, February 15, 1902.

14. Harry Edward Poindexter, "A History of the Charlottesville Woolen Mills, 1820–1939" (MA thesis, University of Virginia, 1955), 112–14.

15. *Information and Design for Uniform and Dress of the United Confederate Veteran Association*, Charlottesville Woolen Mills Pamphlet, Collection 55-0, United

Confederate Veterans' Papers, folder 13, box 8, Louisiana Research Collection, Howard-Tilton Memorial Library, Tulane University.

16. Collections 1982.010 and 1984.003, United Confederate Veterans coat, American Civil War Museum, Richmond, Va.

17. *Men's Wear: The Retailers' Newspaper* (Fairchild Company, N.Y.) 22, no. 7 (February 6, 1907): 82 and 120.

18. Collection H.19XX.330.95 and Xx330.95, Capt. W. H. S. Burgwyn, 35th N.C., North Carolina History Museum, Raleigh.

19. M. C. Lilley and Company, *Grand Army of the Republic Price List of Uniforms, Caps, Swords, Belts, Banners, and Flags* (Columbus, Oh., 1887), 1–36. Other manufacturers such as L. Gansman & Brothers in Lancaster, Augusta Thomas and Company in Philadelphia, and Gusky's in Pittsburgh, advertised and made GAR uniforms starting at six dollars, but the M. C. Lilley price book was complete and available. *Lancaster (Pa.) Daily Intelligencer*, May 30, 1889; *National Tribune* (Washington, D.C.), July 11, 1889; *Pittsburgh (Pa.) Dispatch*, May 29, 1889.

20. *CV* 1 (January 1893): 1.

21. "Confederation News," *CV* 14 (January 1906): 151.

22. "Pettibone Uniforms," *CV* 15 (February 1907): 99.

23. "Confederate Veterans' and Sons of Confederate Veterans' Uniforms," *CV* 15 (March 1907): 147.

24. Pettibone Uniform advertisements, *CV* 18 (January and April 1910): 50, 194.

25. Collections 3180, 2791, Manuscripts and Folklife Archives, Department of Library Special Collections, Western Kentucky University.

26. Collection 1972.3.13, Kentucky Historical Society, https://kyhistory .pastperfectonline.com/webobject/D1050FDF-A915-4BAF-9C51 -710895323013.

27. Levy Brothers Company invoice and letter, May 12, 1905, June 7, 1905, United Confederate Veterans Records, 1899–1905, Mss. BC U58b, folder 6, Filson Historical Society, Louisville, Kentucky.

28. R. E. Hughes, Secretary of the Finance Committee, to John Leathers, President of the UCV, April 20, 1905, United Confederate Veterans Records, 1899–1905, Mss. BC U58b, folder 6, 227, Filson Historical Society.

29. *Minutes of the Annual Meeting of the United Daughters of the Confederacy* (Opelika: Alabama Post Publishing Company), vol. 9–11, 1902–1904, 5–7, HathiTrust Digital Library.

30. *Minutes of Organization: And of 1st and 2nd Annual Conventions, United Daughters of the Confederacy, North Carolina Division* (North Carolina: The Daughters, 1898), 7, HathiTrust Digital Library.

31. *Minutes of the Fifth Annual Meeting of the United Daughters of the Confederacy, November 9–12, 1898* (Nashville, Tenn.: Press of Foster & Webb, Printers, 1899), 27.

32. *United Daughters of the Confederacy. North Carolina Division. Minutes of the 10th, 11th, 12th, and 13th Annual Convention of the United Daughters of the Confederacy: North Carolina Division* (Raleigh, N.C.: Capital Printing Co., 1909), vol. *1906–1909*, 51, HathiTrust Digital Library.

33. *United Daughters of the Confederacy. North Carolina Division. Minutes of the 14th, 15th, 16th, and 17th Annual Convention of the United Daughters of the Confederacy: North Carolina Division* (Raleigh, N.C.: Capital Printing Co., 1913), vol. *1910–1913*, 133, HathiTrust Digital Library.

34. *United Daughters of the Confederacy. North Carolina Division. Minutes of the 18th, 19th, 20th, and 21st annual convention of the United Daughters of the Confederacy: North Carolina Division* (Raleigh, N.C.: Capital Printing Co., 1917), vol. *1914–1917*, HathiTrust Digital Library. As is the case for the majority of volumes, this one contains several pages of chapter financial reports where uniforms and the cost for the grouping are listed in addition to the narrative form of chapters describing their contributions of the year.

35. *United Daughters of the Confederacy. Minutes of the Twentieth Annual Convention of the United Daughters of the Confederacy* (Raleigh, N.C.: Edwards & Broughton Printing Company, 1914), vol. *1913–1914*, 352.

36. *Bridgeton (N.J.) Pioneer*, February 6, 1913; *Charlotte (N.C.) Daily Observer*, January 25, 1913.

37. *Carroll County Democrat* (Huntingdon, Tenn.), January 31, 1913. "Conference of Gettysburg Commission," *CV* 21 (March 1913): 107.

38. "The Boys in Gray at Gettysburg," *CV* 21 (April 1913): 183. *Charlotte (N.C.) Daily Observer*, January 27, 1913. *Richmond (Va.) Times Dispatch*, February 3, 1913.

39. *Seattle Star*, July 1, 1913.

"A Book That We Want to Hand Down to Posterity"

Social Memory by Subscription in the Military Annals of Tennessee

EDWARD JOHN HARCOURT

On the eve of Independence Day 1884, the *Pulaski Citizen* in Giles County, Middle Tennessee, published a notice calling on "all survivors" of Company K, Eleventh Tennessee Cavalry, Confederate States of America (CSA), to meet the following Monday by urgent request of its former commanding officer, Colonel D. W. Holman. Holman, recently assigned as a contributor and subscriptions agent for the *Military Annals of Tennessee* by its editor, J. Berrien Lindsley, was assembling a regimental history for Lindsley's book. Almost twenty years after the conflict, and before Confederate veterans had begun regularly to assemble in reunions, Holman was evidently struggling to recall the finer details of who had served and the circumstances in which some had died. Yet he knew that veterans were keen to record their service to the Confederate cause and eager to shape their own stories as public interest in the history of the war grew. The previous year, in neighboring Giles County, Private Sam R. Watkins had self-published his own account of Confederate service in *Co. Aytch* to local acclaim and modest commercial success. Lacking Watkins's skills as a storyteller, as well as any extant service records on which to rely, Colonel Holman looked instead to crowdsource a history of Company K. "Bring any papers or write out from memory and bring with you," he urged former comrades, "all matters and incidents relating to the . . . acts of the company during the war." Lamenting later, as he completed his research into the regiment, that "very meagre reports have been furnished" with "the rosters, muster-rolls, orders, and reports . . . lost or destroyed," Holman "had to rely on his recollection of events, which, after the lapse of twenty years, has doubtless failed."[1]

Colonel Holman's appeal was just one of many similar efforts, orchestrated by the Nashville educator and antiquarian J. Berrien Lindsley, to assemble the scrappy details of service testimonials from veterans across Tennessee to provide in subscription book form a definitive memorial to those who served in the war. As editor and compiler of the annals, however, Dr. Lindsley found that his vision of the work was far broader than what his audience wanted to subscribe to in post-Reconstruction Tennessee. Lindsley's project was one of reconciliation, attempting to unite veterans of all sides and from all nineteenth-century wars in Tennessee, with the goal of honoring the Volunteer State's full pantheon of martial service. His contributors and subscribers, however, were interested only in a record of Confederate valor, establishing for posterity the comradeship and sacrifices among veterans who wore gray—those who had taken up arms against the United States—while ignoring the claims of those Tennesseans (including more than forty thousand African Americans) who served in Federal blue. Lindsley found that sales of the *Military Annals of Tennessee* started and stopped with the Confederate cause, bequeathing an archival record and shaping thinking about the war that cast long shadows over Tennessee's memorialization of the 1860s.

John Berrien Lindsley—physician, clergyman, and university administrator—was in truth an unlikely editor of a Confederates-only *Military Annals of Tennessee*. Descended from a line of East Coast educators and physicians—his father was a classics professor and briefly president of Princeton College before moving to Nashville in 1824—Lindsley was educated in medicine at the University of Pennsylvania and on his return to Nashville married into the prominent McGavock-Grundy family. Although not a political or military figure, he could not avoid the politics of secession, Federal occupation, emancipation, and Reconstruction that tore Tennessee apart in the 1860s and trod a careful line between loyalty toward the Union and sympathy for the South's plight. Remaining in Nashville throughout the war, he served first as superintendent of Confederate hospitals and then, following Union occupation, ensured that the University of Nashville, of which he was chancellor, remained open throughout the conflict. Although his sympathies were tested on many occasions—particularly when a brother-in-law died in Confederate service and during the intense periods when Union forces took the fight to the people—he never supported the Confederacy; instead he celebrated the demise of the CSA, noting in his diary his "great rejoicings" over Robert E. Lee's surrender and his "mourning" after Lincoln's assassination.[2]

In the early postwar years, Lindsley busied himself with leadership of educational and medical institutions and became a leading advocate for better public sanitation and cleaner government. He had been a founding member of the Tennessee Historical Society in 1849, and by the late 1870s, his long-standing interest in the history of Tennessee had developed into an avocation. In 1878 he resolved to compile a set of annals of Tennessee's history from 1795 to 1878, incorporating volumes on politics; industrial and commercial history; religion, education, literature, and science; and military affairs. With this project, Lindsley typified what one commentator termed a "new historical consciousness." Comparing it to the disruption caused in France by its revolution, and in Germany after the Napoleonic wars, J. B. Henneman of the University of Tennessee identified a "growth of this historical instinct" as "one of the main results of the war." "The *historic* sense," argued J. B. Henneman in the *Sewanee Review*, "has grown in proportion as the *personal* feeling has become blunted." In setting out his prospectus, Lindsley put it this way: "the people or the family which does not honor the noble deeds of those who have gone before, will do none worthy of being honoured by those who come after."[3] What he did not count on, however, was the persistent strength of personal feelings about the war, particularly among Confederates.

Lindsley intended to start his monumental project with the most recent war and work his way back to earlier wars. Believing that the Civil War would become "the great theme in American literature," he was troubled by the "meagreness of authentic information concerning Confederate Tennessee." Believing that Tennesseans "in heroic gallantry and self-devotion were second to none on either side in the long contest," he was also troubled by the "want of records." "How very barren are the records of Confederate Tennessee," he lamented in 1878, "the gap must be filled up from original and living sources . . . without delay." As a man of letters and as an educator, Lindsley held a deep interest in the state's history; moreover, he was a student of history and was interested in the book trade. His record of books read during the war included Bancroft's eight-volume *History of the United States* as well as Clarendon's seven-volume *History of the Rebellion and Civil War in England*. During the war he had arranged for his late father's collected works to be published in three volumes by Lippincott in Philadelphia. These interests suggest that Lindsley had some idea of how to assemble and edit books, though he was a novice at the arts of gathering original sources, marketing, and subscription sales. Although Lindsley's project was not profit driven, his decision to focus initially on the 1860s seems to have been motivated in part by a desire to fund his larger project with the anticipated proceeds of the military annals. He was aware that some war accounts from East Coast publishing houses were commercial successes. Selling books via subscription had become a highly systematized and lucrative industry, with publishers arranging for their books to be presold by canvassing agents carrying salesmen's dummies. The *Century Magazine*'s Civil War series (published serially between 1884–87) was a hit, doubling the magazine's circulation to 225,000 and generating profits in excess of $1 million for the magazine. A handsome four-volume edition of the collected articles, *Battles and Leaders of the Civil War*, sold seventy-five thousand copies through subscription agents.[4]

Lindsley's task was made that much harder because Nashville was on the periphery of the book trade. Louisville, Kentucky, home to the *Southern Bivouac*, and Richmond, Virginia, home to the *Southern Historical Society Papers*, offered Confederate authors more opportunities than Nashville, which became recognized as a publishing center for the Lost Cause only after the 1894 launch of Sumner A. Cunningham's *Confederate Veteran*. The *Southern Bivouac*, launched in 1882, focused on the sacrifices of "the private Confederate soldier" and presaged Lindsley's approach by inviting all veterans to send their "anecdotes and reminiscences." Sam Watkins took the editors at their word and sent along a copy of *Co. Aytch*, inviting the *Bivouac* to print excerpts. In his cover note to the *Bivouac*, Watkins heralded the veteran spirit and called for veterans of the Civil War to be as celebrated as "our forefathers who fought for the broad principles of liberty at the battle of Cowpens, King's Mountain, and Yorktown, over a hundred years ago." Concluding that Confederates were entitled to no less honor than Revolutionary-era veterans, Watkins voiced a grassroots sentiment common among veterans that their sacrifices were at best being forgotten, or, worse, seen as dishonorable or treasonous.[5]

Lindsley evidently shared these views and believed that the state needed a sense of closure following the Civil War. In selling these annals by subscription to memorialize all Tennessee soldiers, he hoped to reconnect the valor and sacrifices of veterans of both sides with Tennessee's proud military heritage and thereby heal the divisions caused by the Civil War. Lindsley intended to use the publishing technologies and marketing techniques of the age to shape the meaning and memory of the late war and to establish what he regarded as Tennessee's unequalled role in the military annals of the nation. Lindsley also proposed to establish a "Tennessee Survivors' Association" for any surviving soldier of the Indian and Mexican wars as well as all soldiers of the Civil War.[6]

Lindsley followed subscription book trade practices. He assembled a circular, prospectus, and specimen pages to show to prospective subscribers; engaged agents in county towns; and called for former regimental offices to effect a "roll call" of former comrades, supplementing these local assemblages with more than 7,500 surviving muster rolls procured—with Secretary Robert T. Lincoln's help—from the War Department in Washington. Lindsley spoke at countless public meetings, publicizing his work through newspaper articles and appealing directly to regimental officers for sources in their possession. One agent, Captain Pol G. Johnson, was happy to devote "the time, labor and expense" involved in soliciting subscribers. "I was not afraid to make this promise for our county, for I knew the troops she furnished and dead she left on the field." Over the next several months, as Lindsley gathered material for the project, leading veterans and newspaper editors called on citizens to provide information and subscribe to the work. "We can furnish testimony if we do not write history," noted one veteran in calling for "facts, dates, names, and incidents." Veterans encouraged each other to step forward and contribute names, details, facts: "boys," one editor put it colloquially, "hurry up if you don't want to be left out."[7]

The book that took its shape from the submissions, however, was not the inclusive volume Lindsley had envisioned. By seeking a subscription base, Lindsley found himself reshaping the project to align with what many took to be the significance of the annals: an opportunity for Tennessee's Confederate veterans alone to record their names and accounts of service. In fact, Lindsley's plan received a rough reception from some former Confederates. Speaking at an 1883 veterans' reunion in Nashville, Lindsley promoted both the annals project and the inclusive Tennessee Survivors' Association. According to an eyewitness who recalled the scene for the *Confederate Veteran* twenty years later, Lindsley explained that the proposed association was "to embrace all surviving soldiers of the State of Tennessee, from its earliest history to the present; [including] all survivors of the Mexican War . . . and all soldiers of the late war who as Tennesseans were in the Confederate army or the Federal army." When Lindsley stopped speaking, recalled the observer, he was met with a "painful silence." Former Confederate general W. H. Jackson then rose and pointedly rebuked Lindsley for suggesting that Federal veterans from Tennessee could be in any association with the Confederate veterans. "'I am always ready to give my hand in friendly grasp and to greet as a soldier and comrade any *Northern* man, from Maine to California, who . . . fought under the flag of the Union; but [and here he raised his hand and brought out his words deliberately and forcefully] *none of your d—— Tennessee Federals for me.*'" The large assembly of veterans, according to this eyewitness, then burst into "a storm of prolonged applause and cheers as one seldom hears."[8]

Chagrined, Lindsley dropped the idea of a survivors' association and stressed in subsequent communications that the first volume in his series on Tennessee history would focus on Confederate veterans alone. In dropping any intention to include Federal veterans in his work, Lindsley capitulated on its inclusiveness and nearly halved the book's potential market. (In the 1890 census, Nashville alone had 927 Confederate veterans and 703 Union veterans, of whom 355 were African Americans; many more Union veterans lived in East Tennessee.) A year later, Lindsley was writing to newspapers to stress that the first volume in his work "will be *entirely* confederate" and incorporating the recollections of "nearly one hundred writers who took part in the war." The *Military Annals of Tennessee* in effect became Tennessee's first Confederate memorial, with contributors supplying details of their service to shape a community memory of the war that was exclusively Confederate in character. It was clear evidence of consumer interest shaping production, with Lindsley's annals becoming what today we might describe as a "social media bubble," providing subscriber-readers with the interpretations they wanted and silencing those with other views.

The bulk of the volume contained potted regimental histories and memorial rolls of men who had died in service. Written either by former officers or local civic leaders, the "histories" ranged from a single page listing the names of those who had fallen to ten-page descriptions of a regiment's muster, organization, engagements, and the odd biographical vignette of the distinguished and the dead. Some contributors invested considerable time in assembling the relevant "facts." Alex W. Campbell of Jackson wrote that he had been obliged to reconstruct a narrative from "fragmentary memoranda and the recollection of its surviving members widely scattered throughout the South and South-west." Others were overwhelmed by the task before them. G. H. Baskette of the Eighteenth Tennessee Infantry wrote of the "insuperable" difficulty of "writing a history in which all of the factors which make up the multiple [*sic*] of fate shall be given proper place and value." An author from the Twelfth Tennessee Infantry wrote that "we regret that the history of a regiment which bore itself so gallantly on so many fields . . . must be written mainly from memory, the only data at hand being an imperfect diary of . . . a private in the regiment."⁹ From such fragmentary recollections were the annals constructed.

Captain Joseph Love provided the history of the Forty-Eighth Tennessee Infantry. After a short description of the unit's organization, he eulogized the late captain of Company E, George W. Gordon, "my ideal of a Christian soldier" who "would call the boys around him at the close of day and ask God's blessing upon those under his command." Like other submissions, this narrative featured themes of heroism, persistence against overwhelming odds, sacrifice, renewal, loss, and nobility in surrender—themes that would come to dominate in the Confederate memory of the war. Captain Love was silent about the terrors of the battlefield, the fears of the ordinary soldier in the line of fire, and the plight of the wounded and dying. He also gave no mention of the regiment's total defeat at the battle of Nashville and the subsequent desertions that depleted the regiment's ranks.[10]

Captain Love and the other regimental historians who contributed generally avoided discussing the war's cause, purpose, and meaning—that, one wrote, was the editor's responsibility. Lindsley devolved this responsibility to Alexander P. Stewart, Confederate lieutenant general of the Army of Tennessee. Stewart's own lengthy piece suggested he was still grappling with both the cause and the consequences of the war. Declaring that "there can be no greater crime against humanity than a needless or an unjust war," Stewart presented an apocalyptic vision of the war's consequences—the overthrow of the Confederate government, the subjugation of the seceded states, the abolition of slavery, black enfranchisement, and the abolition of the right of the minority to secede from a Union in which its interests are not protected. But in narrating the journey from 1789 to 1860, he merely sketched the grievances of southern states over the protective tariff debate of the 1830s and the protection of slavery debates that followed the Mexican War in the 1850s. His argument was underdeveloped on both constitutional and political grounds. Jefferson Davis's two-volume memoir published in 1881 had vigorously asserted the South's constitutional right to secede, defended slavery, and placed blame for the war wholly with the North and the rise of the Republican Party. Stewart's 1886 analysis was much less emphatic, contained no apologia for slavery, and captured the divisions of allegiances in Tennessee much more clearly than he defended the righteousness of the South's cause—a line in keeping with Lindsley's original conception of the work.[11]

Stewart cast emancipation as a disastrous consequence of the war. This followed from Lindsley's reluctant decision to exclude Union veterans from the volume following the criticism his original and inclusive approach had received from Confederates. But Tennessee Unionists did not ignore what they perceived to be a more assertive and coordinated Confederate commemoration. In 1885, while Lindsley was working on the annals, the *Fisk Herald*, organ of the freedmen's college established in 1865, challenged the tendency to valorize the Confederate soldier without reference to the cause for which he fought. "No one finds fault with the Southern people for loving the deeds of their heroic dead," the editor allowed. "They may build monuments to their fallen heroes, ad libitum, but if all admit that the North was right and that the South was wrong, why in the name of candor and moral honesty do they not come out and say so?" Slavery, the writer emphasized, was the cornerstone of the conflict, and by defending old institutions and occluding this fact the Confederate memorialists were "kicking against the pricks."[12]

The publication of the first *Annals* volume in 1886 was no small achievement, with Lindsley dedicating the volume "with reverence and admiration" to the memory of "the heroes, whose valor and blood earned and maintained for Tennessee the glorious name of Volunteer State." It was an extraordinary effort in social commemoration representing a sizable investment in an archival record of the service of Tennesseans who fought on the side of the CSA. Yet the volume carefully picked out the details of Confederate service from the bloody mess of Tennessee's Civil War past. Even within the parameters of Confederate experience, Lindsley's volume was an astonishingly incomplete record when compared with the *Official Record of the War of the Rebellion* (*OR*), which the U.S. government began publishing the following year. The *OR* detailed the evacuation of Nashville and the institution of military rule under Andrew Johnson; offered glimpses drawn from both Union and Confederate archives of the political divisions and shifting loyalties among Tennesseans; contained extensive reports on bushwhacking activity throughout Middle Tennessee; documented the dissolution of slavery, the emergence of contraband camps, and the organization of the United States Colored Troops around Nashville; and featured commentary from both sides on the collapse of the Confederate Army of Tennessee after the battle of Nashville in 1864. Instead of detailing and defining a *civil* war, the *Military Annals of Tennessee* presented triumphalist histories and memorial lists of Confederate regiments, sketched by the veterans themselves, stressing the self-sacrifice

of the white men involved in the military struggle while avoiding refer-
encing their objective: to defend the institution of slavery by seceding
from the United States.

Lindley's annals nonetheless held value for its contributors and subscribers, their contributions in effect providing an investment in their
community self-interest and self-idealization that has compounded over
the years. First, the *Military Annals of Tennessee* became a monument—a
memorial to the dead. As one local newspaper noted on receipt of Lindsley's book, "for the first time the patriot martyrs, who were buried without coffins, and in unmarked trenches, will have their names placed
in living letters before their families, friends, and comrades." The *Annals* provided a substitute for the well-tendered cemetery or monument,
a memorial-in-print to 9,108 named soldiers who had died during the
war with, the editor noted, "probably as many more . . . unrecorded."
The book in effect became Tennessee's first Confederate memorial, with
more than a hundred authors and many other contributors shaping a
community memory of the war and leaving a recorded legacy for future
generations. Testimonials of surviving veterans bore witness to their fallen
comrades, who were variously recorded as having died at the scene of a
specific battle, or "in battle" or "in hospital" or simply "some time during
service." Just as with the later monuments that would come to dominate
the private cemeteries and public squares of Tennessee, relatives and de-
scendants of those who had died could trace their names by finger and
feel an emotional attachment to the cause. One local editor observed
that the regimental sketches and roll call of the dead "cannot fail to make
it . . . dear to the surviving comrades and relatives and friends of those
chivalrous men who laid down their lives."[13]

Second, the *Annals* as an object itself instilled a sense of pride among
the defeated Confederates. Lindsley had the manuscript electrotyped at
the Southern Methodist Publishing House, ensuring that it was "hand-
somely gotten up" and illustrated with thirty-five steel plates of 116 like-
nesses from the burin of a New York engraver. Spanning 910 gilt-edged
pages bound in Turkish morocco, this expensive memento mori was just
as substantial as the family Bible. It was hailed locally on its publication in
1886 as "the book that we want to hand down to posterity." Whereas Sam
Watkins's *Co. Aytch*, priced at $1.50 in cloth, had contained the raw feel-
ings and sentiments of the "old web foot," Lindsley's volume, five times as
expensive, had given these ordinary private's recollections the discipline
and drill of a broader coordination. "The book is the greatest monument
yet erected to the Confederates," praised one subscriber. "It is, however,

but the foundation upon which to build." Writing from Beauvoir, Mississippi, the former Confederate president, Jefferson Davis, complimented Lindsley on his "beautiful" and "valuable volume." "I trust the example you have set will be followed by other states for the commemoration of Patriots," he added.[14]

Third, the annals was of both practical and material value to veterans and their families, particularly when state pensions were introduced for Confederate veterans (1891) and their widows (1905). Tennessee Confederate pensions, awarded to veterans of an honorable character, "unable to work due to war wound," were among the most generous, paying in 1901 up to $300 a year, which was twice what other southern states were paying and five times what Virginia paid. A card index, dating back to the late nineteenth century, in the Tennessee State Library and Archives of all veterans referenced in the *Annals* suggests that until the 1920s the book was the best available resource to verify service. When queried for the details of their service—"When did you enlist and in what command?" and "Gives the names of the regimental and company officers under whom you served"—both applicants and assessors would have referred to Lindsley's *Military Annals* as the most complete and authoritative source. When in the 1920s the Tennessee state archivist sent Tennessee's civil war veterans an extensive questionnaire, some Confederate veterans still referred to Lindsley's *Annals* as the reference point for details of their service.[15]

Fourth, the book became an investment in the future. As one supporter noted, "this will be a correct history . . . in which our children's children will be interested, and will be prized above all the books we have." Lindsley's *Annals*, while not a best seller, nonetheless entered the established historical record and became a reference point for later commentators, leaving, as one commentator remarked "a rich field for the future historian." Libraries and literary societies in the North, including the New York State Library, the New Hampshire State Library, the Chicago Public Library, Harvard University, and the Connecticut Historical Society, all added copies to their collections. An 1898 catalog of the most important books and pamphlets about the Civil War and slavery, published by a New York City bookseller, cited Lindsley's annals as the most significant of the regimental histories from Tennessee.[16]

"Shall this great military history of Confederate Tennessee be completed?," Lindsley asked rhetorically in his introduction to the *Military Annals*. "Shall the whole plan of a cyclopedia of Tennessee history be carried out?" Reviewing the book in the *Nation*, Jacob D. Cox, a former Union general and Republican governor of Ohio, acknowledged the stupendous effort involved and the "very great" value of the project to historians. But he thought Lindsley would struggle to find enough support for future volumes. "The monument can be justly considered out of proportion to the subject," he wrote. "In its present form, the book will hardly meet with any popular acceptance even in Tennessee." Cox had a point: priced at $7.50, the *Annals* sold modestly. Why was this? Perhaps the price point was wrong, with poor sales reflecting the economic realities of veterans' lives in the late 1880s. Perhaps the unevenness of the work created resentment among those families whose soldiers were not listed. In one estimation (by a twentieth-century state archivist), just 12 percent of total enlistments were recorded in Lindsley's volume. Why subscribe to a volume if the name you were looking for didn't appear? No further volumes were published in the subscriptions-only series; interest in Tennessee's history clearly wasn't as strong as Dr. Lindsley would have liked and perhaps also indicates that the strength of Confederate memorial communities in the mid-1880s wasn't yet as strong as it would become by 1900. Further, his incomplete history—partial toward one side and sketchy in detail—didn't live up to the original hype despite its luxurious production and the editor's efforts. Lindsley himself blamed the poor sales on consumer tendencies beyond his control, noting that if survivors contributed "the equivalent of what . . . they annually expend upon tobacco" the subscription base would have been greater. With an insufficient subscriber base to underwrite the costs of further volumes in the series, Lindsley shelved the broader project on Tennessee history to focus on editing thirteen volumes of the *State Board of Health Bulletin* from 1885 until his death in 1897. Yet his efforts in commemorating Confederates had served a purpose: assembling the *Military Annals of Tennessee* had been a therapeutic self-realization exercise for Tennessee's Confederate veterans stressing the virtue of the individual soldier almost in isolation from the cause for which they fought, enabling the connection to be made with the state's previous military volunteers.[17]

Sumner A. Cunningham was an *Annals* subscriber who later founded and edited the *Confederate Veteran*. Eulogizing Lindsley at his death in 1897, Cunningham hailed Lindsley's "Confederate Military Annals of Tennessee" as "the most valuable contribution to Confederate history ever published by an individual in any state." While conceding that Lindsley was "not a Confederate," Cunningham credited him with having "influenced the impulses" behind the development of the *Veteran* and having always encouraged him in pursuing his efforts to publish and rally the troops in retirement. Cunningham adopted the unsold copies of the *Annals*, and they were still being offered for sale (marked "scarce" and selling for five dollars) in the *Confederate Veteran* as late as 1922. To no small degree, the *Military Annals* was handmaiden to the *Veteran*, which by 1896 had become the official organ across the South of the United Confederate Veterans, with a circulation surpassing 160,000.[18]

When the Tennessee State Archives began to procure Civil War–era materials in the 1890s, Lindsley's work gathering the socialized memories of Confederate veterans, together with the official records he had procured from Washington, formed one of the cornerstones of the nascent collection. Almost eighty years elapsed before a full account of all Tennesseans in the Civil War was published, during the Civil War centennial. Today, Lindsley's *Annals* remains a central point of reference for genealogists and historians alike. In 2019, seven copies remained in the state library's collection, while an online database of Confederate regimental histories referenced Lindsley's book 144 times. Rare copies of the book circulate online with prices ranging from $950 to $1,375. The *Annals* remains a reference point for both scholars and lay historians, assuring Lindsley's Confederate contributors and subscribers a presence in the literature of the war more than 150 years after they laid down their arms. To posterity they had published their accounts of service to the Confederacy—it was all they had wished for, if not quite what the editor had originally hoped to achieve.

NOTES

1. *Pulaski (Tenn.) Citizen,* July 3, 1884; Daniel Wilson Holman, "Eleventh Tennessee Cavalry," in *The Military Annals of Tennessee: Confederate, First Series: Embracing a Review of Military Operations, with Regimental Histories and Memorial Rolls,* ed. John Berrien Lindsley (Nashville: J. M. Lindsley & Co., 1886), 690–720; Sam R. Watkins, *"Company Aytch"; or, A Side Show of the Big Show and Other Sketches,* ed. and intro. by M. Thomas Inge (1882; rpt., New York: Plume, 1999). For a study of Watkins's memoir, see Edward John Harcourt, "Would to God I Could Tear the Page from These Memoirs and from My Own Memory: *Co. Aytch* and the Confederate Sensibility of Loss," *Southern Cultures* (Winter 2017): 7–28.

2. On Lindsley's biography see John Edwin Windrow, *John Berrien Lindsley: Educator, Physician, Social Philosopher* (Chapel Hill: University of North Carolina Press, 1938), and Paul Keith Conkin, *Peabody College: From a Frontier Academy to the Frontiers of Teaching and Learning* (Nashville, Tenn.: Vanderbilt University Press, 2002), 74–77; Lindsley diary references, June 8, 1861, April 28, 1863, April 3

and 15, 1865, files 3 and 4, box 1, Lindsley Family Papers IV-D-4, Tennessee State Library and Archives (hereafter TSLA).

3. For Lindsley's 1878 outline of a full annals of Tennessee history, see Windrow, *John Berrien Lindsley*, 20–21n47, quoting undated diary entry from 1878; J. B. Henneman, "Historical Studies in the South since the War," *Sewanee Review* 3 (May 1893): 320–39; J. B. Lindsley to Edwin L. Drake, n.d., reprinted in Edwin L. Drake, ed. *The Annals of the Army of Tennessee and Early Western History, Including a Chronological Summary of Battles and Engagements in the Western Armies of the Confederacy* (Nashville, Tenn.: A. D. Haynes, 1878), 93–94.

4. Lindsley to Drake; Lindsley's reading is described in Windrow, *John Berrien Lindsley*, appendix F; Le Roy J. Halsey, *The Works of Philip Lindsley*, 3 vols. (Philadelphia: J. B. Lippincott, 1866). Michael Hackenberg, "Hawking Subscription Books in 1870: A Salesman's Prospectus from Western Pennsylvania," *The Papers of the Bibliographical Society of America* 78, no. 2 (Chicago: University of Chicago Press, 1984); Carl F. Kaestle, "Seeing the Sites: Readers, Publishers in Local Print Cultures in 1880," in *A History of the Book in America*, vol. 4, *Print in Motion: The Expansion of Publishing and Reading in the United States, 1880–1940*, ed. Carl F. Kaestle and Janice A. Radway (Chapel Hill: University of North Carolina Press, 2009); Robert J. Cook, *Civil War Memories: Contesting the Past in the United States since 1865* (Baltimore, Md.: Johns Hopkins University Press, 2017), 98–104 (including circulation figures).

5. S. R. Watkins to the editor, *Southern Bivouac*, September 10, 1883, quoted in M. Thomas Inge, ed., *Co. Aytch, or a Side Show of the Big Show and Other Sketches* (New York: Plume, 1999), x; Harcourt, "Would to God," 27n16.

6. The prospectus outlines the project's ambitious span: "the Creek War, the New Orleans Campaign, the First and Second Seminole Wars, the War of Texan Independence, the Mexican War, and the great War between the States." January 1883 prospectus, folder 5, Pamphlets Miscellaneous, Joseph H. Fussell Collection, TSLA.

7. For evidence of how Lindsley went about sourcing his material, see *McMinnville (Tenn.) Southern Standards*, June 21, 1884; *Clarksville (Tenn.) Weekly Chronicle*, January 27, 1883, March 22, June 28, and July 19, 1884; *Memphis Daily Appeal*, March 26, 1884; *Memphis Public Ledger*, May 26, 1883; "Military Annals of Tennessee from 1796–1882," *Milan (Tenn.) Exchange*, January 20, 1883; *Pulaski (Tenn.) Citizen*, July 3, 1884, August 27, 1885.

8. "Tennessee Federal Troops in the Sixties," *Confederate Veteran* 14 (May 1906): 207, original emphasis.

9. Lindsley's letter to the editor, *Bolivar (Tenn.) Bulletin*, February 7, 1884; Department of the Interior, *Compendium of the Eleventh Census: 1890*, part 3 (Washington, D.C.: Government Printing Office 1897); Alex W. Campbell, "Thirty-Fourth Tennessee Infantry," in Lindsley, *Military Annals*, 484–88; G. H. Baskette, "Eighteenth Tennessee Infantry," in Lindsley, *Military Annals*, 359–70; J. P. McGee, et al., "Twelfth Tennessee Infantry," in Lindsley, *Military Annals*, 306–10.

10. Joseph Love, "Forty-Eighth Tennessee Infantry (Voorhees's), in Lindsley, *Military Annals,* 546–49.

11. Alex. P. Stewart, "The Army of Tennessee: A Sketch," in Lindsley, *Military Annals,* 55–112; Jefferson Davis, *The Rise and Fall of the Confederate Government,* 2 vols. (1881; rpt., New York: Da Capo Press, 1990); Stewart, "Army of Tennessee," quote on 62–63.

12. *Fisk Herald,* March 1885.

13. *Clarksville (Tenn.) Weekly Chronicle,* June 28, 1884; *Memphis Daily Appeal,* December 9, 1884.

14. *Clarksville (Tenn.) Weekly Chronicle,* September 25, 1886; Jefferson Davis to J. Berrien Lindsley, March 11, 1887, reprinted in Windrow, *John Berrien Lindsley,* 198.

15. On Tennessee Confederate pensions, see Shari Eli and Laura Salisbury, "Patronage Politics and the Development of the Welfare State: Confederate Pensions in the American South," *Journal of Economic History* 76 (December 2016): 1083–84. On the state archivist questionnaire, see Gustavus W. Dyer et al., eds, *Tennessee Civil War Veterans Questionnaires: Confederate: Confederate Soldiers* (Easley, S.C.: Southern Historical Press, 1985), 1:1587.

16. "Dr. Lindsley's Confederate History," *Clarksville (Tenn.) Weekly Chronicle,* June 28, 1884; Lindsley obituary, *Southern Practitioner* 20 (January 1898): 39; *The American Civil War 1861–5 and Slavery,* catalog (New York: Francis P. Harper, February 1898), 58, 83.

17. Review of "Military Annals of Tennessee," *Nation,* March 10, 1887; the state archivist estimated that Lindsley's rosters contained only "about 12% of the total enlistments," see J. T. Moore Papers, box 15, ser. 3, RG 122, Tennessee State Librarian & Archivists Papers, TSLA; Lindsley to Drake.

18. Windrow, *John Berrien Lindsley,* 21; "Dr. John Berrien Lindsley," *Confederate Veteran* 5 (Dec. 1897): 605.

The wholesale grocer Brewster, Gordon and Co. of
Rochester, New York, marketed a complete line of canned
goods, spices, and cigars under the Veteran brand from
the 1860s until well into the twentieth century.

Attention Company
Marketing and Advertising

Brewster, Gordon and Co. was founded early in the 1860s, but its best-known line—named, plainly, "Veteran Brand" and featuring as a logo a distinguished but apparently generic veteran—did not appear until just after the war. At least two Brewsters and four Gordons served in the Civil War, and Charles H. Brewster, a cavalryman, was killed at Brandy Station, while Peter Gordon died in May 1864, so, although none of the founders was actually a veteran, they may have been inspired by brothers, cousins, or other relatives who had fought in the war.[1] In any event, their best-known brand, sold throughout the Northeast, no doubt attracted customers by connecting their merchandise to the steady, trustworthy, and even patriotic connotations projected by the image of the veteran that appeared on every can, tin, and pouch they sold.

Like these venerable Yankee grocers, for decades after the war advertisers eagerly offered Civil War images as representations of values that they believed were intrinsic to their products, no matter how far removed from the war they might be. Lion Coffee, marketed by Woolson Spice Company in Toledo, Ohio, ran numerous advertising campaigns during the decades after the war. One campaign, no doubt inspired by its founder's service in the Union army, emphasized soldiers' constant craving for coffee in camp, on the march, or whenever they had a moment to build a fire. "In war times," one ad went, "during the long and dreary marches, how the soldier relished his cup of Coffee! Today, a peaceful citizen, he enjoys it just the same." Another ad, calling Lion Coffee "the best beverage on earth," further linked its product to the war when it ordered, "ATTENTION COMPANY" and "HALT! STACK ARMS!" Civil War soldiers had never drunk a drop of Lion Coffee, which did not come on the market until the late 1860s, but the advertising campaign no doubt brought to the minds of consumers the stirring and patriotic nostalgia of the war years.[2]

In this section, four essays explore how wartime images—and the principles and ideals attached to them—appeared in ads for myriad products with, in many cases, even less of a relationship than Lion Coffee to the war or to the men who fought it. Anna Gibson Holloway and Jonathan W. White lead off by showing that the ironclads *Monitor* and *Merrimack* proved to be popular sources of advertising images almost as soon as they fought their iconic battle, coming to represent, among other things, U.S. industrial might and innovation. The next two essays highlight the ways in which Civil War images and ideas were used to market postwar products, often with a subtle—or not so subtle—promotion of reconciliation. Amanda Brickell Bellows reveals how advertisers "sold" reunion and ignored racial equality after the war, while Natalie Sweet examines the marketing power of educational and patriotic collectibles in the form of popular minibiographies of Confederate and Union generals that the Duke tobacco company used to promote its cigarettes. Crossing the Atlantic, David K. Thomson takes a different tack by looking at the way in which bonds sold by the Confederates to European investors—and the postwar debate over U.S. responsibilities to English buyers—represented competing ideas about commerce, debt, and loyalty long after the war.

NOTES

1. "E. F. Brewster, Jr., and Old Employees to Take Over Firm of Brewster, Gordon & Co.," *Simmons' Spice Mill* 42 (February 1919): 198; "Roster of Soldiers in the 'War of the Rebellion,'" Monroe County Library System, https://roccity library.org/genealogy-indexes/, accessed May 8, 2020.

2. *Ohio Soldier*, January 16, 1892, and July 4, 1891.

"American Originals"

The Monitor and Merrimack
as Marketing Machines

ANNA GIBSON HOLLOWAY AND JONATHAN W. WHITE

On April 20, 1861, Union forces abandoned the Gosport Navy Yard in Portsmouth, Virginia, setting fire to the vessels, dry dock, and buildings. Among several other vessels, the USS *Merrimack* burned and sank at her moorings. After taking control of the yard, Confederates raised the hull of the *Merrimack* from the Elizabeth River and began converting her into an ironclad ram—the CSS *Virginia*. They hoped this new weapon of war would be able to break the Union blockade at Hampton Roads. The Union's Department of the Navy countered by taking out advertisements in at least fifteen northern newspapers seeking proposals for ironclad steam vessels for the Union navy.[1] Swedish inventor John Ericsson, then living in New York City, submitted a radical design for a warship in which most of the ship's components were below the waterline and whose two cannons were housed in a revolving gun turret on the deck. How ironic that the *Monitor*—one of the most powerful marketing tools of the mid- to late nineteenth century—was born out of an advertisement in the newspapers.

Prior to the Battle of Hampton Roads (March 8–9, 1862), observers in the North and South had looked on the *Monitor* with skepticism, but soon this strange-looking vessel would capture the heart of the nation. She quickly appeared on patriotic tokens with the motto "Our Little *Monitor*," along with a likeness of the famous vessel.[2] These tokens served an important function in northern commerce, replacing pennies in shops and markets as the Union faced a shortage of hard currency during the war. But the *Monitor*'s image facilitated commercial transactions in other ways as well. In the wake of the Battle of Hampton Roads, the *Monitor* took a central place in marketing campaigns throughout the Union—a position she held for decades after the war. Initially she was presented to consumers as a symbol of Yankee strength and ingenuity—a victor over the evil Rebel ironclad. By the early twentieth century, however, advertisers paired her with the *Virginia* as a joint symbol of American greatness and honor. As a spirit of reconciliation gained traction among white Americans, the two warring ironclads became partners rather than adversaries in marketers' quest to sell products.

Wartime Marketing

The outbreak of the Civil War, in the words of historian Joanna Cohen, "sparked a dramatic fusion of patriotism with a broader commercial culture" through which the purchase of patriotic products gave northerners a strong emotional connection to the Union. The *Monitor* quickly became part of this process. Business owners sought to capitalize on the vessel's unique and powerful qualities in their marketing appeals, and Cohen notes that consumers could buy these goods "to express their patriotism."[3]

Within two days of the Battle of Hampton Roads, on March 11, Sleeper's of Philadelphia offered the first such advertisement:

> THE MONITOR'S A NOBLE CRAFT
>
> Of Excellent construction
> She forced the Merrimac to leave
> To save herself destruction
>
> The Monitor did fairly win
> The fame she has acquired
> And Sleeper for umbrellas has
> A fame to be desired.[4]

Not to be outdone, other Philadelphia companies entered the poetic fray. As in the antebellum period, advertisers continued to use puns and doggerel to sell products. Now they connected them to war news—something that northerners were eager to read about. Charles Stokes's One Price Clothing Store published some doggerel titled "An 'Ironic' Idyl," which made a clear connection between the strength of the *Monitor* and his product. Stokes's poem celebrated the *Monitor* for driving back the *Virginia*, reminding readers

> That *well-clad* ships, or men, will tell
> In daily strife.
> Thus STOKES' . . .
> *Clothes men with power* that will be felt, all
> Through their life.[5]

A well-clad man could be as powerful as a well-clad vessel of war.

These initial advertisements were followed on March 15 by ads from Philadelphia clothiers Towne Hall and Oak Hall. The first includes a poem titled "Latest Intelligence," extolling the virtues and strength of the Union's vessel:

> The *Monitor* punches
> The stout *Merrimac*
> Belaboring the monster
> With whack after whack.[6]

A few more lines later, the merchants urged readers to come to their shop to purchase from their spring line of clothing. The second poem, "The Monitor and Merrimac," recounted in silly rhymes how the Union ship had routed the *Virginia*. The poet-merchant concluded:

> The ships are best
> In iron dressed;
> But *men* who broadcloth wear
> Should make a call
> At TOWNE HALL
> To view the armor there.[7]

In the space of a few short hours, the *Monitor* was transformed from "Ericsson's Folly" to a celebrity endorsement for products and services. A Cleveland cobbler stated that the Confederates "can no more compete with the Yankees in the matter or iron ships than they can hope to rival the elegant boots and shoes manufactured by MCGUIRE." In Zanesville, Ohio, a local newspaper extolled the talents of a magician, saying that he was "the best man in his trade—a *Monitor* among the gunboats." Decks of playing cards featuring the two vessels appeared for sale on the streets of New York City by the summer of 1862. Sheet music for songs about ironclads flew off the shelves, as did gutta-percha photograph cases that featured the *Monitor* on the front cover. Newspapers in Washington, D.C., ran ads for "iron-clad Monitor Rotary Refrigerators" and "Monitor Cook

Stoves." In Wisconsin, the editors of the *Milwaukee Sentinel* advised readers to examine the "very attractive advertisement under the head of 'Little Monitor'" that appeared further on the page—an ad for an "important invention" for burning coal or kerosene oil called "Little Monitor." In the fall of 1862, when the *Monitor* entered the Washington Navy Yard for repairs, the town was consumed with *Monitor* madness. Even the local prostitutes celebrated her arrival by offering their services at brothels named the Monitor and the Iron-clad Battery.[8]

Shortly after Christmas the *Monitor* was ordered south to Beaufort, North Carolina. When she sank off Cape Hatteras in the early morning hours of December 31, 1862, sixteen men went down with the famous vessel, and news of the tragedy began to appear in major newspapers by January 4, 1863. The *Daily Milwaukee News* reported the sinking on page 4, while on page 3 of that same issue the persistent ad for "The Little Monitor" coal and kerosene stove ran as it had for days. In like manner, the *Providence (R.I.) Evening Press* carried word of the sinking on page 2, but the standard Monitor Cooking Stove advertisement still held pride of place on page 1. These ads were mute about the sinking, having been placed and typeset well before the event.[9]

A small ad in the January 9, 1863, edition of the *Hartford (Conn.) Daily Courant* was the first to use the tragedy to push products. Just four days after news of the sinking reached New England, the firm of Ford and Bartlett wrote in blazing letters, "THE MONITOR SUNK! But the Ship of State still floats down the river of time; and FORD & BARTLETT in a small boat, are coming, too with a few thousand dozen HOOP SKIRTS attached. Specimens to be seen at Weatherby & Co.'s. Sample dozens sent at the lowest cash wholesale prices, and all orders promptly filled, by FORD & BARTLETT, Vernon, Ct." A similar ad appeared on January 10, 1863, in the *Providence (R.I.) Daily Evening Press.* The Monitor stove ad moved from page 1 to page 3, and with its move, its message also changed: "STILL AFLOAT!" it declared, "OUR MONITOR HAS NOT SUNK." The advertisement went on to remind customers that "history has already made the name immortal, and the destruction of the original Monitor cannot destroy its prestige." One could display a stove with that same prestige in one's parlor. Frank Leslie's began running ads in the New York Herald on January 14, touting an upcoming issue that would feature "a beautiful engraving of THE LOSS OF THE MONITOR." Shortly after that the *Hartford (Conn.) Daily Courant* advertised a new product, the "Little Monitor Hand Lamp," which "will burn all night at the cost of ONE CENT."[10] Though she was gone, the little Monitor could still sell goods.

Prints and Parade Floats

Both during and after the war, printmakers and lithographers aimed to place images of the battle onto the walls of private homes and public spaces. With no photographs of the battle or of the ships to use as references, however, some of the early depictions were based on eyewitness accounts and others on wishful thinking. Although Hampton Roads was an amphitheater of sorts for twenty thousand battle observers, not all of them had a clear view of the wide-ranging, smoke-filled engagements, so even those present were not entirely sure of what they had seen. Not letting accuracy stand in the way of a sale, however, newspapers and printmakers provided the public with a vast number of images from which to choose. As historians Mark E. Neely Jr. and Harold Holzer write, "Unlike paintings, popular prints ordinarily originated with business firms attempting to maximize profits and not with patrons attempting to create image or prestige." And profit there was. Courier and Ives produced five images of the battle, four of which focused on the second day's fight between the two ironclads. Other firms followed suit. "Ugly or not," write Neely and Holzer, "the *Monitor,* and the *Virginia,* and many other Civil War ironclads churned across the walls of American parlors." Many featured the events of March 8 and 9 as occurring simultaneously so that the tragedy of the *Cumberland*'s sinking could be seen next to the ironclads engaged in battle.[11]

Commercial images of the battle—which first appeared within a month of the battle and continued to be produced well into the twentieth century—were printed almost exclusively by northern firms. These carried pro-Union messages, usually depicting the "little Monitor" in a David-versus-Goliath scene, with the righteous northern vessel defeating Confederate maritime monster. One Currier and Ives print titled *The First Fight between Iron Clad Ships of War* depicted the *Monitor* with only two guns to the *Virginia*'s ten, but the caption crowed that "the little 'Monitor' whipped the 'Merrimac' and the whole 'School' of Rebel Steamers." In November 1862, a Washington, D.C., paper reported that local bookstores were carrying "a spirited picture of the great naval engagement between the Monitor and Merrimac . . . which not only exhibits the two vessels with life-like accuracy, but gives at one view the Minnesota, the

Congress and the Cumberland, with the rebel steamers Jamestown and Yorktown." The two days of the battle conflated into a single image provided more action, which could translate into larger sales. "For sale at the bookstores in this city," concluded the report. "Everybody ought to have a copy."[12]

In the postwar period, companies continued to market images of the naval war to veterans. In 1896, one Richmond merchant advertised several lithographs in a local black newspaper, the *Richmond Planet*. Almost all of the images were of incidents in which the United States Colored Troops had played a heroic role—the assault of the Fifty-Fourth Massachusetts at Fort Wagner, the Battle of Olustee in Florida, Fort Pillow in Tennessee, and the Buffalo Soldiers fighting against Sitting Bull in the Dakotas. The final image in the advertisement seemed an unlikely one to include among the first four—a beautiful chromolithograph featuring the two-day Battle of Hampton Roads in one full-color image. Although the image itself likely included no African Americans, black men and women were in fact present at the battle. Many slaves and contrabands watched from the shorelines, and at least one black sailor—William H. Nichols of Brooklyn, New York—served belowdecks on the *Monitor* (the U.S. Navy had already been integrated for decades before the Civil War). This merchant in post-Reconstruction Virginia knew that black veterans there would be interested in this scene, along with the others that were more popularly connected with African Americans. It represented the strength of the Union as "the Monitor fir[es] into the Confederate ram, Merrimac" and the "stars and stripes and the stars and bars meet in deadly conflict." And it was a scene in which African Americans had participated.[13]

Farther north, Endicott and Co., a New York lithography firm, wrote to a Union naval veteran offering inducements for purchasing prints: "We send you a sample copy by to days mail and as your vessel occupies quite a prominent place in it we think the officers and crew would like to have some copies[.] If you will make out a list of those who want them and send the money to us with the addresses to which the copies are to be sent we will allow you an extra copy for every five names you obtain and will send them safely post paid by the following mail."[14] Lithography firms clearly recognized the role that veterans could play in promoting patriotic images of the conflict, and the pride they would feel in seeing their vessels depicted in historic (and victorious) scenes of battle.

The Battle of Hampton Roads inspired parade floats throughout the nation. Perhaps fittingly, some of the very men who had built the *Monitor* initiated the first parade. On March 29, 1862, four hundred workmen in Troy, New York, formed a torchlit procession to celebrate the success of the vessel they had helped build. Other communities similarly featured *Monitor* floats, including a forty-one-foot-long "monster model of the famous *Monitor*" in San Francisco on July 4, 1862, a "*miniature 'Monitor' on wheels*" in Columbus, Ohio, in October 1863, and a "fine working model of the Monitor" in Abraham Lincoln's second inaugural procession in March 1865. In the late nineteenth century, *Monitor* floats celebrated the Union warship's victory over the *Virginia*. One witness to an Independence Day parade in Evansville, Wisconsin, in 1884, reported that "the Monitor was loaded with soldiers and the Merrimac was covered with thick brown paper filled inside with rockets and when the Monitor drove up by the side of the Merrimac the rockets went off and lit the thing on fire." The crowd loved seeing the *Monitor* victorious. "You better bet there was hollering done," concluded the spectator.[15]

Farm and Household Products in Postwar America

The late nineteenth century saw the rise of mass production and distribution. As factory owners learned how to produce household items in large quantities, their business challenge became distribution. Marketers needed eye-catching advertisements to distinguish their products in the marketplace. The most colorful and intricate advertisements tended to be for commodities that were otherwise indistinguishable from their competitors, or items that catered to a specialized audience, such as farm implements or patent medicines.[16] The *Monitor* became an important part of the campaigns to peddle these products. The sheer quantity of *Monitor* products suggests that manufacturers, merchants, and marketers at least believed that the *Monitor* was a brand that would resonate with consumers. And they were almost certainly correct. The *Monitor* was something that the postwar public wanted to see and own. In short, her legacy became part of the art and story of the war in the service of capitalism.

The *Monitor* proved an enduring symbol in postwar America, and men and women alike celebrated her heroic qualities. She had been reliable, safe, durable, powerful, and scientifically designed. Many women saw in the *Monitor* something masculine to revere, and even love. An Iowan who visited "this masterpiece of science" in 1862 described the "awe" she felt when she stood in the turret and learned about "the mighty wonder of her power." The woman could not help herself as she kissed "the big guns . . . for their hard, big iron mouths are wonderously handsome in our eyes! Women love strength and defense, and many a fresh lip pressed the good guns of the *Monitor*." For years after the battle, Americans reflected on the significance of what had transpired at Hampton Roads. In 1869, a Massachusetts woman wrote to her parents, "I should like to witness such an engagement." In 1896, an older gentleman recollected witnessing the Battle of Hampton Roads. "This was 34 years ago," he wrote, "and though a mere boy, the grand scene of the explosion and the terrible noise of the cannonading is still fresh in my memory. It was grand and sublime; yet, horrible in its execution." In 1937, an ex-slave from Hampton recalled being held up by her mother so she could watch the battle. "Twas awful noise dem guns was makin' an' my mother said lots a men got kilt." Another ex-slave remembered the "flash of the guns" from that "strange fight." Veterans, of course, also often found eager listeners for their stories of life aboard those famous ships.[17] As a consequence of her special attributes—and her abiding place in northern popular culture—the *Monitor* served as a powerful branding tool to appeal to consumers. From fashion to farm equipment, food products to household appliances, scores—if not hundreds—of items came to be named after the *Monitor* or to bear her form or image in their own designs or advertising campaigns. Unlike the wartime advertisements, however, the postwar ads avoided use of humor. They instead appealed to peoples' memories of the *Monitor* as an effective war-making machine.

During and after the war articles of clothing were often named after the famous Union vessel. This rise in *Monitor* fashion was likely a response to the widely sold Merrimack textiles, which had been produced in Lowell, Massachusetts, along the Merrimack River, since 1823. In the antebellum era, manufacturers and marketers had named clothing after famous individuals in order to increase demand, such as the Jenny Lind cap. Now they would use the name of the country's most famous war-making machine. A gentleman could wear a Monitor checked shirt or a Monitor tie, while a lady could have a dress made from Monitor cloth that she could wear with her Monitor cloak and Monitor hat. Later in the century, she could add a pair of Monitor shoes to complete the ensemble, and she could purchase "little monitor infant shoes" and "little monitor school shoes" for her children. Wherever their clothes came from, they could be washed with a Monitor washboard and wrung out with a Monitor wringer, then dried by a Monitor stove. To remove wrinkles, a Monitor sad iron could be warmed up on a Monitor heater.

If a family could not afford to purchase these styles from the store, a woman could make her own on a Monitor sewing machine. G. L. Du

Advertisements for domestic wares utilized the *Monitor* as a symbol for dependability. Most of the trade cards used to sell Nellie Bly's Ironclad Enameled Iron Ware depicted scenes of domestic bliss juxtaposed with a small *Monitor* logo. This card, by contrast, features an inaccurate but rousing depiction of the famous vessel spewing pots and pans from opposite sides of the turret. In the actual vessel the guns had faced the same direction. (From the collection of Anna Gibson Holloway)

Laney and Co. of New York City produced an advertisement for sewing machines meant to appeal to female consumers—or perhaps to an aging veteran who might purchase one for his wife. In it, a woman sat hunched over her Little Monitor Sewing Machine while directly beneath her the Battle of Hampton Roads raged in a smoke-filled image. Quite a juxtaposition, but the message was clear. This sewing machine would be reliable—just like the *Monitor* at Hampton Roads.[18]

Scores of other Monitor brands and products were marketed to appeal to the wives, widows, and children of Civil War veterans. The prevalence of such items reveals the enduring significance of the war to U.S. women. As historian Kristin L. Hoganson writes, "In the late nineteenth and early twentieth centuries, middle-class Americans commonly regarded household interiors as expressions of the women who inhabited them." Kitchen staples and appliances abounded. Perhaps consumers believed they would be as indestructible as the vessel for which they were named; or perhaps they would be useful for protecting those in the home. Bread could be baked from Monitor flour and Monitor coffee drunk that had been ground in a Monitor grinder and brewed in a Mon-

This advertisement for the Little Monitor Sewing Machine juxtaposes depictions of a young woman seated at the machine with the "terrific combat between the 'Little Monitor' and 'Merrimac.'" Both "Little Monitors," according to the ad, were "invincible." (Trade Catalog Collection, Baker Library, Harvard Business School)

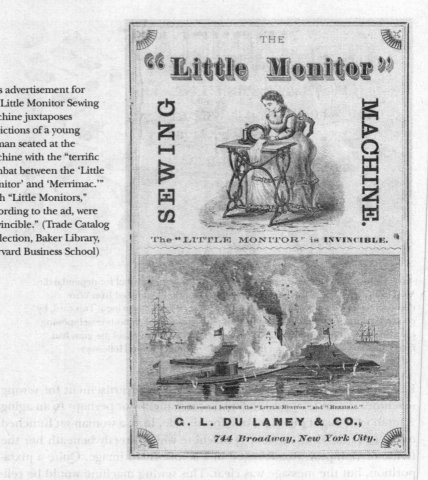

itor coffeepot. The Little Monitor Tea Company also offered a selection for those who didn't drink coffee. In the early to mid-twentieth century, perishable items could be stored in a General Electric Monitor-top refrigerator—a stylish appliance that featured a turret-like motor on top. One 1929 marketing booklet proclaimed that this "dependable," scientifically developed product "Makes it Safe to be Hungry." Another booklet promised consumers that "someday you will have a G-E refrigerator for protection to health." Every household, of course, also needed a set of durable cookware. In the late nineteenth and early twentieth centuries, the Ironclad Enameled Iron Ware Company produced a host of pots and pans that promised to be "absolutely free from mottles & rust spots." The company circulated a series of postcard advertisements that featured the *Monitor* and their products. In one, the *Monitor* fires dozens of pots, pans, kettles, colanders, buckets, and ladles from her inaccurately depicted guns. Others featured peaceful scenes of domestic life, but all of these included the company's trademark—the word "IRONCLAD" next to a vignette of the *Monitor*. One, featuring a woman in a kitchen, was captioned, "There is PEACE in the Kitchen For the MUSIC of the 'IRON CLAD' is heard in the Land." While Mother cooked, children could enjoy a game manufactured by Milton Bradley in 1866 that featured images of the battle that were illuminated by lantern light, or a double-turreted rolling toy *Monitor* that shot marbles out of its cannons, produced from 1883 to 1900 by the W. S. Bliss Toy Company.[19]

In the late nineteenth century the strength, ingenuity, and durability of the *Monitor* continued to appeal to men, whether Civil War veterans or their hardworking sons. On farms throughout the nation, Monitor rakes, Monitor seed drills, Monitor plows, Monitor incubators, Monitor windmills, and Monitor pumps were put to work. A turret-shaped Monitor Cupola could be added to ventilate barns. In one 1869 ad in Maine for "The Monitor Mower," consumers were promised that "the little Monitor . . . takes the grass down so easy, and don't hurt itself a bit doing it." Another ad for that same product claimed it to be "the most simple, practicable, lightest draft, and easiest managed machine in the world. The success of the Monitor is without parallel," concluding that it was "as much an improvement over the other Mowers as was the little Monitor over Iron clads, &c." In 1891, McCormick Harvesting Co. produced an advertisement featuring a large image of the battle (with the two days inaccurately combined into one image) with the tagline, "This fight settled the fate of the 'Wooden Walls' of the world and taught all nations that the War-Ship of the future must be—like the McCormick Harvester—a Machine of Steel."[20] Of course, the *Monitor* and *Virginia* were made of iron, not steel. But the point was clear. Moreover, unlike most advertisements of the era, McCormick's would have appealed to farmers who had fought for either side in the Civil War because the inclusion of both days' fights showed both vessels triumphing over their foes.

As Civil War veterans reached their golden years, the *Monitor* morphed into a tool to market products that might help them overcome the ailments of aging. Older men or women could purchase Wilbor's Monitor Hair Dye, a bottled chemical blend guaranteed to restore one's natural hair color. Meanwhile, in the 1890s, J. C. Childs and Co. advertised

Monitor Blend pure rye whiskey, which was an "Excellent Product of the Still" known for its "MEDICINAL and TONIC VIRTUES." If one doubted the medicinal qualities of whiskey, indulged in it too much, or suffered from other ailments associated with ill health or old age, Dr. Ray Vaughn Pierce's Pleasant Pellets were sure to be as effective as the *Monitor* in curing a whole host of ailments. In an advertisement that circulated in the 1890s and that featured the *Monitor* and the tagline, "Small But Effective," Dr. Pierce promised that his pills were "effective in conquering the enemy—disease." Whether a person was "grumpy, thick-headed and take a gloomy view of life," or suffered from "Sick Headache, Bilious Headache, Constipation, Indigestion, Bilious Attacks, and all derangements of the liver, stomach and bowels," Dr. Pierce's pellets would "clear up your system and start your liver into healthful action"—effective, just like that "little Monitor that met the Merrimac at Hampton Roads."[21]

Throughout the late nineteenth century, the CSS *Virginia* was never as commonly used in product names or advertisements. More often than not—as in the case of Dr. Pierce's Pleasant Pellets—the *Virginia* served as a foil to the victorious *Monitor*. Perhaps this was because of the confusion with her name. Was she the *Merrimac*? The *Merrimack*? Or the *Virginia*? This may also be because there was far less manufacturing and product development in the South. On occasion the *Virginia* was given her equal share in marketing campaigns—as in the McCormick Harvester poster, or a trade card produced by McLaughlin's Coffee of Chicago in 1889, which celebrated "peculiar war ships of the world." During the war years and into the postwar period, however, only one product consistently used both the *Monitor* and the *Virginia* together to sell products: tobacco. In 1864 the *Hartford (Conn.) Daily Courant* advertised imported cigars from Havana, including one brand called Monitor and Merrimac. In border regions in the immediate postwar period, advertisements for tobacco using both vessels appeared. For instance, in 1871, companies in West Virginia advertised several brands of "Kentucky Tobacco," including "Monitor" and "'Merrimac' Navy lbs." Between 1887 and 1911, at least three U.S. cigarette companies—and one from England—featured the two vessels on tobacco cards.[22] Of course, it made sense that these two vessels would be paired together in such marketing campaigns, as soldiers, sailors, and veterans from both sides were drawn to inexpensive smokes and chews. Indeed, tobacco ads featuring both the *Monitor* and the *Virginia* connected a product associated with masculinity with symbols that reflected bravery and manhood from the war. It was not until the 1920s that tobacco companies would begin pitching their products to young people.[23]

Reconciling the Enemy Vessels

Only in the early twentieth century were the *Monitor* and the *Virginia* finally and consistently paired together in marketing campaigns as equals. To be sure, some northern products—such as Memorial Day postcards—celebrated "The Monitor's Great Victory." But other advertising campaigns and events signaled a move toward reconciliation between the two historic ironclad vessels. The catalyst for this shift appears to have been the 1907 Jamestown Exposition. Spectators flocked to see the *Canonicus*, the last of the Civil War monitors, "on the actual scene of the Civil War conflict between the Monitor and the Merrimac." The exposition, which lasted from April 26 until December 1, also featured an enormous cycloramic depiction of the Battle of Hampton Roads "which was realistic in the extreme," as well as an electronic reproduction of the battle. Visitors to the exposition did not see a winner in this important duel. The decision to omit discussion of victory and defeat was purposeful so that "no exception can be taken by visitors from any section of the country." One Pennsylvania paper printed an account of the spectacle: "As the full red orb finally cast its brilliance over the waters of Hampton Roads, I saw coming from the direction of the sun the formidable enemy of the Merrimac—the Monitor, and then began the duel of the ironclads, a duel as terrific and awful as the annals of war record—a duel in which there appeared no supremacy, and there was no justly claimed victory." A southern woman left the exhibit with the same impression, writing, "Neither won but they compromised by the Merrimac going to Portsmouth and the Monitor to Fort Monroe."[24]

The intentional neutrality of the exhibition's producers had its desired effect. One journalist for a Utah newspaper noted that when the show ended, "a voice says, 'This way out, please,' and the show ends without arousing any controversial acrimony." Indeed, this reporter continued, "The management of the fair endeavors to minimize the arousal of feeling between blue and gray veterans." Over the ensuing years, the Battle of Hampton Roads exhibit made a national tour, stopping at a number of cities, including Seattle, Chicago, Pittsburgh, and Denver. Teachers and schoolchildren flocked to see it. "None," declared the superintendent of Pittsburgh public schools, "could afford to miss witnessing the greatest battle in the history of naval warfare fought over again in such a realistic way." This traveling exhibit taught a younger generation of Americans a reconciliationist account of the battle—that neither North nor South had won, and that both sides had fought valiantly. This message contrasted starkly to the voices of the veterans who still survived, many re-fighting the battle in newspapers, magazines, and commemorative book-lets as anniversaries of the battle passed, and participants passed away. Other recreations of the battle that celebrated both ships continued to appear throughout the nation in the early twentieth century.[25]

It is little wonder that in the twentieth century the two ironclad vessels appeared as partners more than as adversaries in promotional items and advertising campaigns. In some instances, the ships appeared in generic promotional materials that companies could personalize with their own store information, such as a 1937 "historical art calendar" that featured a number of scenes from U.S. history, including the "Battle of the Monitor and Merrimac." A 1908 medal from Greenpoint Bank in Brooklyn com-memorated "the first engagement between ironclads and revolutionized naval warfare," as well as that the *Monitor* had been assembled at Green-point. But unlike earlier depictions, this medal did not claim victory for the Union vessel (in fact, the reverse featured both U.S. and Confederate flags). Congress followed suit, authorizing a medal for "all naval veterans of the Civil War" that featured "the battle between the Monitor and the Merrimac" and was "supported by a blue and gray ribbon."[26]

In the early twentieth century, health product manufacturers used the *Monitor* and *Virginia* to appeal to aging veterans and their families. The makers of the medicine Athlophoros produced a postcard circa 1910 to appeal to men and women suffering from rheumatism. The front of the card featured two images from the Battle of Hampton Roads—one of the "Virginia sinking the Cumberland" from March 8, 1862, and the other of the "Monitor and Merrimac" on March 9. These two images were meant to appeal to consumers from both North and South, as ex-Confederates would look favorably on the first image, while Unionists would recall the *Monitor*'s fight with fondness. In a major ad campaign in 1912 and 1913, the Duffy Malt Whiskey Company of Rochester, New York, used a seven-ty-two-year-old Union nurse named Mrs. E. Kane of Brooklyn, New York, as its spokesperson. She claimed that twenty-three years ago her doctor had recommended drinking whiskey to improve her memory and health, and now "I can remember things that happened as far back as the battle off Hampton Roads, between the Monitor and the Merrimac, on March 8, 1862" (alas, her memory was off by a day). The Duffy advertisement in-cluded an image of the elderly woman and urged potential customers to "look at her photograph" and see "her brain alert, eyes bright and mem-ory clear." It then continued with language that would appeal to aging members of the Civil War generation: "If you are not aging gracefully, if you suffer from ills which you should not, if your faculties are becoming impaired, if the attention and interest of your friends are lessening, perhaps you can benefit from the experiences of Mrs. Kane." Duffy ran this ad in newspapers from Boston to New Orleans, and from Baltimore to San Francisco, and everywhere between.[27]

By the time of World War II, the two ironclad warships were unified in the public mind as one marketing machine. Perhaps most fittingly, a World War II–era ad for "Seagram's American Original—*Ancient Bottle* Gin" celebrated both vessels as American heroes, featuring an image of the second day of the Battle of Hampton Roads and declaring, "The first 'ironclad' warships, the MONITOR and the MERRIMAC, were both American Originals. They revolutionized the navies of the world."[28] The two original ironclad vessels of the Civil War would continue to inspire new generations of Americans—now as they went to face foreign enemies around the globe.

NOTES

The authors thank Christopher Newport University students Hannah Broughton, Danielle Forand, and Maggie Byers for assistance with research, and American studies professor Frank Garmon for his helpful comments.

1. *New York Times*, August 15, 1861; receipts for advertisements in RG 45 (Naval Records Collection of the Office of Naval Records and Library), entry 502 (subject File, 1775–1910), AC (Construction), box 22, National Archives, Washington, D.C.

2. David Schenkman, *Tokens and Medals: Commemorating the Battle between the Monitor and the Merrimac* (Hampton: Virginia Numismatic Association, 1979), [7–9].

3. Joanna Cohen, "'You Have No Flag Out Yet?': Commercial Connections and Patriotic Emotion in the Civil War North," *Journal of the Civil War Era* 9 (September 2019): 380, 401.

4. *Philadelphia Inquirer*, March 11, 1862.

5. *Philadelphia Inquirer*, March 14, 1862.

6. *Philadelphia Inquirer*, March 15, 1862.

7. Ibid.

8. Anna Gibson Holloway and Jonathan W. White, *"Our Little Monitor": The Greatest Invention of the Civil War* (Kent, Ohio: Kent State University Press, 2018), 91, 98–101, 106–7; *Washington (D.C.) Evening Star*, April 10, 17, 19, 1862, October 13–18, 1862, and January 7, 1863; "Antique Gutta Percha Union Case" (sold on eBay, September 25, 2018); *Milwaukee Sentinel*, November 3, 1862.

9. *Daily Milwaukee News*, January 4, 1863; *Providence (RI) Daily Evening Press*, January 5, 1863.

10. *Hartford (Conn.) Daily Courant*, January 8 and February 14, 1863; *Providence (R.I.) Daily Evening Press*, January 10, 1863; *New York Herald*, January 14 and 24, 1863.

11. Mark E. Neely Jr. and Harold Holzer, *The Union Image: Popular Prints of the Civil War North* (Chapel Hill: University of North Carolina Press, 2000), 115, 117.

12. *Portland (Me.) Daily Advertiser*, April 7, 1862; Currier and Ives, *The First Fight between Iron Clad Ships of War*, lithograph, 1862, Mariners' Museum, Newport News, Va. (hereafter TMM); *Washington (D.C.) Daily National Republican*, November 10, 1862.

13. *Richmond (Va.) Planet*, August 29, 1896; William H. Nichols File, Irwin M. Berent Papers (MS164), TMM.

14. Neely and Holzer, *Union Image*, 124.

15. Holloway and White, *Our Little Monitor*, 101–2; M. E. Furrow to Jasper M. Clark, July 6, 1884, collection of Jonathan W. White (hereafter JWW).

16. Susan Strasser, *Satisfaction Guaranteed: The Making of the American Mass Market* (New York: Pantheon, 1989); Alfred D. Chandler Jr., *The Visible Hand: The Managerial Revolution in American Business* (Cambridge, Mass.: Harvard University Press, 1977), 209–39.

17. "An Iowa Woman in Washington, D.C., 1861–1865," *Iowa Journal of History* 52 (January 1954): 71; Harriet Buss to parents, April 13, 1869, Harriet M. Buss Papers, Kislak Center for Special Collections, University of Pennsylvania; Lyons, *Rice County (Kans.) Eagle*, September 17, 1896; Charles L. Perdue Jr., Thomas E. Barden, and Robert K. Phillips, eds., *Weevils in the Wheat: Interviews with Virginia Ex-Slaves* (Charlottesville: University Press of Virginia, 1976), 69, 86; *Boston Globe*, May 30, 1886.

18. "'Up Pops the *Monitor*': The Battle of Hampton Roads in Popular Culture," exhibition curated by Anna Gibson Holloway, TMM, March 2011–August 2012; Anna Gibson Holloway and Jonathan W. White, "*Monitor* Pop!," *Civil War Times* 56 (February 2017): 26–33; *Charlotte News*, February 21, 1891; *State* (Columbia, S.C.), January 12 and 14, 1897, February 25, 1897; *Prescott (Ariz.) Evening Courier*, June 25, 1891.

19. Kristin L. Hoganson, *Consumers' Imperium: The Global Production of American Domesticity, 1865–1920* (Chapel Hill: University of North Carolina Press, 2007), 14; *Freeman* (Indianapolis), October 3, 10, 17, 24, and 31, 1891, November 7 and 14, 1891; Anna Holloway Image Collection on Ironclad Warships, (MS0438), TMM; Holloway and White, "*Monitor* Pop," 26–33.

20. *Maine Farmer*, June 6, 1867, and July 10, 1869; *Helena (Mont.) Independent Record*, May 15, 1884; McCormick Harvesting Co., "First Encounter of Ironclads" (1891), TMM.

21. *Boston Traveler*, June 5, 1866; Holloway and White, "*Monitor* Pop," 33.

22. *Hartford (Conn.) Daily Courant*, February 17, 1864; *Wheeling (W.V.) Daily Register*, April 14 and August 22, 1871; tobacco cards, JWW.

23. Richard W. Pollay, "Targeting Tactics in Selling Smoke: Youthful Aspects of 20th Century Cigarette Advertising," *Journal of Marketing Theory and Practice* 3 (Winter 1995): 1–22; Peter Morris, "'Personally, I Have Nothing against Smoking': The Lethal Alliance between Baseball and the Cigarette," *Nine: A Journal of Baseball History and Culture* 18 (Fall 2009): 38.

24. Cuyler Reynolds, *New York at the Jamestown Exposition* (Albany: J. B. Lyon, 1909), 123, 130, 178, 423; *Weekly Alert* (Jamestown, N.D.), May 23, 1907; *Allentown (Pa.) Morning Call*, August 9, 1907; *Charlotte (N.C.) News*, October 5, 1907.

25. *Salt Lake City Herald*, July 21, 1907; *Pittsburgh (Pa.) Post-Gazette*, September 25, 1910; *New-York Daily Tribune*, July 16, 1910; *Kansas City Star*, July 8, 1911; *Kalamazoo (Mich.) Gazette*, September 1, 1912. For veterans who protested that the exhibit got the story wrong, see *Camden (N.J.) Post-Telegram*, August 19, 1909; *Sioux City (Iowa) Journal*, May 25, 1910.

26. "1937 Wall Calendar" (sold on eBay, August 15, 2018); "USS Union Monitor Greenpoint Savings Bank Bronze Medal" (sold on eBay, September 25, 2018); *Norwich (Conn.) Morning Bulletin*, April 6, 1912.

27. Athlophoros advertisement, JWW; *New Orleans Times-Picayune*, October 13, 1910; *Boston Globe*, May 18, 1913.

28. Seagram's Gin advertisement, JWW.

"Let Us Have Peace"

Commercial Representations of Reunion and Reconciliation after the U.S. Civil War

AMANDA BRICKELL BELLOWS

Ulysses S. Grant, general-in-chief of the Union army during the Civil War, accepted his nomination as the Republican candidate during the presidential election of 1868 with conciliatory words. "Let us have peace," he declared, a statement that became both his campaign slogan and a key policy goal of his administration. As a Reconstruction-era president, Grant faced a divided people still recovering from the horrors of the U.S. Civil War. Outlining the challenges facing the country in his solemn inaugural address, Grant urged Americans to do their "share toward cementing a happy union." By Reconstruction's end, however, Grant's vision of a harmoniously reunited nation remained distant. African Americans had won legal status as U.S. citizens and black men obtained the franchise after the ratification of the Fourteenth and Fifteenth Amendments, but white supremacists intimidated and terrorized African Americans and those who supported their efforts to vote or run for office. During the subsequent Jim Crow era, when African Americans faced growing legal discrimination and racial violence, Americans pushed competing narratives about the meaning of the Civil War and Reconstruction.[1]

After Reconstruction, businesses produced advertisements that increasingly employed the language and imagery of reconciliation. These ads reflected late nineteenth-century public and private efforts to reunite the war-torn population, including the gathering of Civil War veterans' groups, the construction of monuments and memorials, and the publication of reconciliationist literature. As profit-driven entities, businesses that represented reunion sought to capitalize on these national trends to expand their consumer base. Rather than portraying peaceful and equitable race relations between white and black Americans, however, northern and southern companies primarily depicted the reconciliation of white supporters of the former Confederate and Union causes in illustrated advertisements.

Scholars of U.S. cultural history have written extensively about the role of advertisements and ephemera in shaping memories of the Civil War and emancipation. But historians have largely overlooked the subcategory of commercial depictions of reunion, advertisements that represented the postbellum reconciliation of white Americans. An examination of trade cards and pamphlets issued by northern and southern companies during the late nineteenth century reveals that businesses portrayed national reunion and reconciliation in a variety of ways. While some advertisements depicted friendly Union and Confederate soldiers putting aside their grievances to form new bonds of friendship by exchanging commodities or participating in shared commemorative events, others praised equally the deeds of Union and Confederate military commanders like Ulysses S. Grant and Robert E. Lee. Companies also deployed narratives and images that whitewashed the history of the Civil War by ignoring its central cause: slavery. Finally, some representations of post-emancipation reunion depicted white reconciliation that came at the expense of African Americans in ads that alluded to the federal government's unwillingness to protect their civil rights, portrayals that mirrored historical realities in Jim Crow America.[2]

The half-century that followed the Civil War was one of tremendous economic development, urbanization, and industrialization that transformed the chiefly agricultural nation into a productive powerhouse. Energized by the robust economy, U.S. businesses harnessed new printing and distribution technologies to create and disseminate advertisements for products that were increasingly affordable to a range of consumers. Many companies began selling individually packed products during the 1880s and used advertising to shape their brand names and help consumers recognize them. During the last two decades of the nineteenth century alone, the advertising volume in the United States grew from $200 million to $542 million.[3]

Trade cards were one of the most popular forms of advertising employed by manufacturers who competed to attract buyers. Created using new chromolithographic technology, these colorful printed advertisements featured an array of figures, scenes, and settings. Trade cards also often contained engaging text that described the characteristics of a company's product or history. At the turn of the century, companies were urged to use care when crafting messages to consumers through art and the printed word. For instance, the advertising agency J. Walter Thompson explained in its 1901 *Blue Book on Advertising* that an "advertisement must be virile, snappy, [and] magnetic" to attract buyers. The agency also believed that an ad required individual tailoring that would "give it color and flavor" to stand out among the competition.[4]

Businesses marketed particular goods to buyers based on consumption habits through gendered advertisements. For instance, during the late nineteenth century, social mores dictated that middle-class women belonged in the home, places that Kristen Hoganson argues were "loci not only of cultural production and reproduction but also of consumption." Businesses targeting female buyers responsible for purchasing household products created trade cards for soap, stove polish, and washing powder that depicted women completing domestic chores. By contrast, cards primarily advertised products like tobacco and beer to male consumers and more widely enjoyed foodstuffs like gelatin, gum drops, and peanuts to men, women, and children.[5]

Middle-class buyers, particularly women and children, collected trade cards and other forms of ephemera to display in personal scrapbooks. Some businesses sought to induce buyers to purchase more of their goods by encouraging them to collect a complete series of trade cards or by offering tickets for a chance to win expensive prizes in exchange for product wrappers. For instance, a late nineteenth-century trade card for David's Prize Soap presented a "list of presents" that included grand pianos, diamond bracelets, and sewing machines. If a consumer sent in twenty wrappers directly to the company "rolled like a newspaper, with a 3 cent stamp inside, and [her] address on the outside," David's Prize Soap Company would send her one ticket. Promotions like these encouraged brand loyalty among consumers who were otherwise willing to sample the merchandise of a company's competitors.[6]

Manufacturers placed trade cards in product packaging, distributed them to consumers via mail, or handed them out in stores. Millions of cards flooded the public sphere during the late nineteenth century, when the act of card collecting reached its peak in popularity. The engaging images that appeared on trade cards were not always designed with a particular product in mind. Lithographers like Louis Prang created stock cards that were intended to be used by multiple small businesses. Each manufacturer would order a version of the stock card with its company or product name stamped into the blank space provided on the front. Alternately, larger businesses contracted artists, maintained in-house advertising staff, or hired advertising agencies like J. Walter Thompson, Lord and Thomas, and N. W. Ayer and Son to create customized ads.[7]

An 1881 article in the *Scientific American* sheds light on the complex operations required to produce advertisements. At the Baltimore offices of Messrs. A. Vogeler and Co., a drug and chemical manufacturing company, employees engaged in extensive internal processes that generated an array of advertising materials. In the printing department, "thirteen steam presses [were] kept running day and night, printing . . . advertising work of every description . . . all of which is 'set up' by their own compositors." Nearby, the show card department churned out chromolithographic cards "in immense quantities" that were finished "plain, in gilt, or in colors" before being cut. Finally, the firm's advertising materials were delivered to the shipping department before their public release. Late nineteenth-century advertising procedures were more sophisticated and effective than ever before because companies invested heavily in the production of marketing materials for their wares.[8]

The themes of reunion and reconciliation regularly appeared in advertisements produced during the final decades of the nineteenth century. Reconciliation, however, was primarily a white phenomenon. White northerners and southerners reunited not by resolving their past differences but by cultivating a selective historical memory that ignored slavery as the root of the Civil War. Rather than defend African Americans' precarious liberty during the post-emancipation era, northern whites turned a blind eye to ex-Confederates' efforts to disfranchise, terrorize, and subjugate freedpeople. Consequently, historian John Neff contends, "black citizenship and political participation were sacrificed for the sake of white reconciliation."[9]

During the late nineteenth century, businesses used images of reconciliation to sell products primarily to white audiences. Their efforts were not without precedent; during the Civil War, Joanna Cohen found, businesses "commodified patriotism" to encourage consumption, blurring the lines between the political and the commercial. After the war, companies depicted white reconciliation and national reunion in trade cards and pamphlets in four distinct ways. First, they portrayed veterans from the Union and Confederate armies physically reuniting as they celebrated events like the nation's centennial or crossed enemy lines in the spirit of goodwill. In various sets of trade cards portraying famous historical heroes, businesses endorsed national reunion by lionizing Union and Confederate generals, Abraham Lincoln, and soldiers from both sides as heroes of the Civil War. A third technique for representing reconciliation was that of omission. In collectible trade cards that described the history of individual states or of the postwar South as a region, there is no mention of slavery, the cause of the Civil War. Finally, certain advertisements show the phenomena of reunion and reconciliation by portraying white political compromise at the expense of African Americans.[10]

Images of joyful, reunited Union and Confederate soldiers serve as significant examples of advertisements promoting reconciliation among former enemies. In 1876, the centennial of the signing of the Declaration of Independence proved to be an occasion for national self-reflection; Americans remembered not only the birth of their country but also the civil war that nearly destroyed it. A *Scribner's Monthly* editorial struck an optimistic note, expressing the hope that "this year is to do much to cast into forgetfulness the bitterness engendered by the civil war, and to make the nation as united and sympathetic in feeling as it is in the political fact." The author acknowledged the resentment still brewing among defeated rebels in 1876; however, he posited that the Centennial Exhibition in Philadelphia that year presented an opportunity for mutual understanding. "Of one thing we are certain," he promised, "if the South comes to the Centennial, it will receive such a welcome as will be accorded to no guests from any other part of the world." Without their presence, the author concluded, "there would be bitterness in our bread, sourness in our wine, and insignificance in our rejoicings."[11]

Philadelphia's Centennial Exposition offered the United States the opportunity to showcase its latest inventions, to express patriotism, and to promote the spirit of reunion among its people. Jennifer Black argues that "the nation's centennial celebration marked the beginning of the widespread commercial use of trade cards and a popular cultural fascination with them as reflected in the art of scrapbooking," due in part to lithographer Louis Prang's decision to introduce stock cards at the fair. Exhibitors showing off their wares to national and international fairgoers offered printed trade cards and ephemera to potential buyers as a way of marketing their products. According to Black, potential customers "moved through the Exposition collecting . . . portable lithographs along with holiday greeting cards, calling cards . . . and other printed materials."[12] They could exchange them with friends, take them home to show members of their family, or preserve them in their scrapbooks.

A trade card advertising the services of the Campbell Printing Building, standing on the exhibition grounds, presented to consumers the idealized vision of reconciliation so desired by the author of the *Scribner's*

"Campbell Press Building Trade Card." (AOB 3, box 2D, American Trade Card Collection, Robert B. Haas Family Arts Library, Yale University)

editorial. In it, a Confederate soldier, a Union soldier, and a British soldier hold hands while dancing joyfully around the Bunker Hill Monument, which commemorates the Revolutionary War–era Battle of Bunker Hill (1775) in Charlestown, Massachusetts. The flags of their respective armies adorn the monument and three intertwined rings bearing the dates of 1776, 1861, and 1876 float overhead. Two gravestones engraved with the name Hatchet suggest that the white veterans have effectively forgiven one another for their past disagreements; all three have "buried the hatchet." By alluding to the positive relations enjoyed in recent decades by former enemies, Great Britain and the United States, the advertisement assured consumers that, with the passage of time, reconciliation between former Unionists and Confederates was also possible.[13]

A second trade card produced by the Virginian tobacco company Myers Brothers and Co. and printed by a Michigan-based lithography firm advertised a product called Love Tobacco using a similar technique. Demand for tobacco products grew significantly during the late 1870s and early 1880s following changes to how tobacco was processed in Virginia and North Carolina. During the postbellum era, manufacturers began implementing a method called flue curing that resulted in tobacco that was easier to inhale and likely more addictive. Additional changes such as the mechanization of cigarette production and the growth of the advertising industry also contributed to the increasing popularity of to-

Myers Brothers and Co., Love
Tobacco, Richmond, Va., likely
early 1870s. (Box 22, Ephemera
Collection Trade Cards,
American Antiquarian Society)

bacco products. At the turn of the century, Myers Brothers and Co. sold
its Virginia-grown tobacco in Boston through an agent located at Central
Wharf. According to a publication that described businesses in Boston
in 1889, Myers Brothers and Co. was considered to be "one of the oldest
and largest tobacco manufactories in the United States, employing five
hundred to nine hundred hands, and producing a superior line of plug
and fine cut smoking and chewing tobaccos, which have a wide and permanent sale all over the country."[14]

Myers Brothers and Co.'s trade card for its Love Tobacco sought to attract northern and southern buyers alike through reconciliationist imagery that mirrored national efforts to reunite veterans during the same
period. The illustration shows a white Confederate soldier and a white
Union soldier exchanging precious goods across enemy lines during the
Civil War. "Haloo Johnny! Got any tobacco want to swap for coffee?" asks

the Union soldier. "All right, Yank!," the Confederate soldier replies. "Pass over the coffee; I've got the best tobacco made in the world." Here, Myers Brothers and Co. draws on readers' familiarity with the South as a famous tobacco-producing region; however, the advertisement avoids discussing the enslaved men and women whose labor supported the industry. Consumers were instead reminded of the transactions that sometimes occurred between Union and Confederate soldiers on picket duty. This representation of a harmonious exchange between Civil War soldiers had historical resonance for some veterans during the late nineteenth century. By purchasing Love Tobacco, buyers reenacted the practice of obtaining and using tobacco during the Civil War, a performance that was in itself a form of memorialization.[15]

Advertisers also strove to appeal to those who supported either the Union or Confederate causes through trade cards that honored military and political figures from both sides of the Civil War. For instance, W. F. McLaughlin and Co., a Chicago-based coffee producer, issued a series of trade cards celebrating historical individuals. Created by a northern lithography company, Major, Knapp, and Co., the cards depicted President Abraham Lincoln's inauguration as well as portraits of Union general Philip H. Sheridan, Union general Ulysses S. Grant, and Confederate general Robert E. Lee. Consumers were urged to collect all of the pictures from the series by mailing the company fifteen coffee wrappers and a letter stating the buyer's preference for a particular card. Furthermore, W. F. McLaughlin and Co. encouraged consumers not only to complete their series but also to publicly display the "beautifully colored" cards, which would be "an ornament to any parlor."[16]

Tobacco manufacturer W. Duke, Sons, and Company, based in Durham, North Carolina, and headed by a Confederate veteran, similarly published a *Heroes of the Civil War* album that contained the plates from its trade cards depicting famous Civil War generals (as Natalie Sweet discusses at length in her essay in this volume). The cards portrayed the stoic visages of Confederate generals and presented hagiographic biographies that praised their military accomplishments and personal virtues. The language sought to endear each general to both northern and southern audiences, an effort that likely stemmed from the tobacco company's interest in capturing more market share. W. Duke, Sons, and Company also pursued a democratic strategy of addressing supporters of both the Union and Confederate causes through its Battle Scenes series of trade cards. Not only famous generals, but also average Union and Confederate soldiers were portrayed, a decision that broadened the appeal of the cards by acknowledging the contributions of thousands of Americans. Trade cards like these endeavored to ameliorate enduring animosities among veterans and citizens by praising the actions of both Union and Confederate soldiers rather than focusing on the reasons they fought one another. By appealing to both northern and southern buyers, W. Duke, Sons sought to attract a wide consumer base.[17]

A third way in which businesses hoped to draw in northern and southern white buyers was by turning a blind eye to the role of slavery in prompting southern secession. In numerous trade cards, advertisers danced around the topics of slavery and postwar labor conditions for African Americans. For instance, W. Duke, Sons, and Company's Governors series (1888) explores the "interesting features" of the forty-eight U.S. states and territories. Each trade card features a prominent portrait of its current governor and illustrated representations of the state on the obverse, with a state map and text discussing its history, economy, and population on the reverse. Most descriptions avoid mentioning the Civil War, slavery, and emancipation. The cards focus instead on the states' Revolutionary War contributions, the dates of admission to the Union, and chief industries. The illustrations for the cards representing Louisiana, Alabama, Mississippi, and Tennessee depict African American laborers engaging in agricultural work, but the text on the reverse is silent about African Americans' historical or contemporary contributions to the states' economies. Mississippi, for example, is characterized as an "almost exclusively agricultural state; in the production of cotton it ranks first in the United States." The trade card describing Louisiana similarly calls it as "the largest sugar-producing State in our country" where "agriculture is the chief pursuit." Further, Alabama's commerce is "considerable, and its manufacturing interests are increasing rapidly; but its principal industry is agriculture, cotton and corn being the leading products." African American laborers are visually represented in miniature on the front of the cards, but they lack agency as historical actors. Only simple illustration titles like "Picking Cotton" and "Cutting Sugar Cane" directly describe the laborers' actions. Furthermore, the juxtaposition of the formal portrait of each state's white, male governor and the smaller figures of the African American workers on the obverse emphasizes the unequal power dynamics between whites and blacks in the Jim Crow South.[18]

An analogous advertisement depicting the late nineteenth-century U.S. South was produced by the New Home Sewing Machine Company. The trade card, published in 1882 and titled "The New Home in the Sunny South," portrays three white southern women outside of a grand house. At the center of an idyllic scene overlooking a river, the women converse while one uses her sewing machine. A white male figure on horseback approaches the women, accompanied by his dog. The source of the family's income, however, is mostly inferred. Tiny smudges of paint stand in for the laborers toiling in a nearby field. Once again, the work of African Americans is pushed into the background as the viewer is invited to rethink her existing conceptions of the American South. While the prewar South was corrupted by the existence of slavery, the postwar South now appears as a peaceful place, one without slave labor, in which modern technologies exist in a modified antebellum setting. Advertisements such as these ultimately sought to attract white northerners and southerners by shining a spotlight on the South that kept the subjects of unfree labor and black rights in the shadows.[19]

While most advertisements promoted goodwill between white northerners and southerners by ignoring African Americans, a handful of trade cards and ephemera deployed offensive representations of black men and women to sell products to white consumers during the postemancipation era. During Reconstruction, the states' ratification of the Reconstruction amendments granted African Americans citizenship and secured the franchise for black men. Between 1865 and 1877, thousands of African American men exercised their political rights by voting, running for office, and serving as elected officials. But after the Compromise of 1877, southern states attacked African Americans' hard-won rights by enacting discriminatory laws that curtailed their liberties and bolstered white supremacy. Southern Democrats used violence and terror to deprive freedpeople of their ability to vote and to gain a stronghold in statehouses across the South during the late nineteenth century. Northern Republicans lacked the political will and ability to deter Democrats, and life grew increasingly oppressive for black men and women in the Jim Crow South. Sectional reunion and white reconciliation were slowly achieved at the expense of African Americans.

While some companies used the war to market products, others employed disparaging images of African Americans that evoked negative ideas about Reconstruction. For instance, a late nineteenth-century advertisement for Van Stan's Stratena Cement, a glue product, mocked African American political leaders as corrupt and ineffectual. The Philadelphia-based company produced a trade card featuring an African American orator with cartoonish features touting the benefits of Stratena glue to a black audience. The fact that the image of the African American speaker was displayed on a stock card and could be tailored to a company's specific product suggests the universality of the representation; white audiences would be familiar with the scornful image of African Americans engaging in civic participation. In Van Stan's trade card, the orator speaks in dialect to his audience, assuring them that "one drop of dis yere Stratena on de conscience of a politician will make him stick to his principles." His statement seems to suggest that black politicians were inherently dishonest, a racist idea that gained traction during the post-emancipation era among white southerners who resisted African Americans' acquisition of political power and among turn-of-the-century Dunning School historians who promoted revisionist histories of black political participation during Reconstruction. Thus, the advertisement served to confirm white Americans' stereotypes of African American politicians as lacking morals and engaging in unethical practices.[20]

Finally, a late nineteenth-century pamphlet for the New York City–based company Hawley and Hoops's Breakfast Cocoa similarly rejected black political participation and civil rights. The trade card depicts two white politicians dining together while a black server, represented with exaggerated facial features, overhears their discussion. Discarded documents with titles like "Amendment to the Constitution," "Pensions," and "Congressional Report" cover the floor, signaling the lawmakers' lack of interest in tackling the thorny issues related to African Americans' civil liberties during Reconstruction. The caption reads,

> The senators who rant and plead
> About affairs of State,
> Upon this Cocoa have agreed
> Without the least debate.[21]

Thus, like the politicians who supported the Compromise of 1877, these fictional senators agree to ignore black rights for the sake of white political reunion.

The themes of national reunion and white reconciliation were even more explicitly referenced in two contemporaneous advertisements for consumer products. First, an illustration that subtly touted white reconciliation appeared in a Spicers and Peckham trade card promoting its Model Grand portable range stoves. The Rhode Island–based company produced an advertisement in which the figure of Uncle Sam impatiently awaits his meal. As an African American server prepares to present his dish, Uncle Sam expresses a message familiar to Americans who witnessed General Ulysses S. Grant's presidential campaign. "Let us have *piece!*," Uncle Sam says to the waiter, playing on Grant's campaign slogan that expressed his desire for national peace in 1868. It is plain that Uncle Sam will comfortably finish his meal, ignoring the needs of his African American server and those of the nation's freedpeople.[22]

In a comparable trade card selling Van Stan's Stratena Cement, the silhouettes of two figures appear to be stuck together as they attempt to walk in opposite directions. The caption for the illustration reads, "United We Stand, Divided We Fall," a phrase coined by Continental Congress delegate and songwriter John Dickinson in his melody, "The Liberty Song" (1768). The patriotic saying experienced a surge of popularity during the 1890s, when white reconciliation efforts multiplied as veterans' groups held reunions and constructed monuments commemorating the war and those who fought for Union and Confederate causes. Thus, the Stratena Cement advertisement's comical illustration of this phrase likely brought to consumers' minds the notions of national reunion and white reconciliation that circulated widely in the public sphere during the same period.[23]

In 1868, President Grant lamented that enduring disagreements still divided the nation. Thirty years later, however, white reconciliation seemed closer than ever. In an anecdote that reveals the changed national mood, writer Henry Wood describes an incident "simple in itself, but of great symbolic significance" that occurred during Republican president William McKinley's tour of the South in 1899. McKinley, a Union army veteran, donned what Wood called an "emblem of the 'Southern Confederacy'" in a "notable episode [that] caused great rejoicing and enthusiasm among the people with whom he was then an honored guest, and not much unfavorable comment was made in the North." McKinley's decision reflected the growing sympathy for the Confederate cause among the national population, particularly the youngest generation of Americans who had not directly experienced the Civil War. Wood concluded that McKinley's show of Confederate pride "thus virtually ended, morally and officially, nearly two score years of hatred, sectionalism, crimination and recrimination, which had continued after the formal close of the physical conflict."[24]

This episode serves as evidence that sectional reunion and white reconciliation were nearly complete at the turn of the twentieth century. The price of unity, however, was the sacrifice of African American interests. As historian David Blight argues, reunion was "achievable in the end only through new regimes of racial subjugation. . . . [T]he sections needed one another, almost as polar opposites that made the center hold and kept both an industrial economy humming and a New South on the course of revival."[25] An analysis of trade cards and ephemera reveals the extent to which American businesses participated in the process of post-war reconciliation. Seeking to maximize their profits, American businesses deployed images of reunion to sell products to white northerners and southerners alike. In the end, commercial images of heroic Civil War veterans, conciliatory politicians, and cartoonish or submissive African Americans serve as significant examples of visual culture that may ultimately have hastened the phenomenon of white reconciliation.

NOTES

1. Ulysses S. Grant, "Inaugural Address," March 4, 1869, American Presidency Project, https://www.presidency.ucsb.edu/node/203651, accessed July 31, 2020.

2. The advertisements studied in this chapter are housed in archival collections at Yale University, Duke University, and the American Antiquarian Society. For studies of advertisements and Civil War memory, see Kenneth Goings, *Mammy and Uncle Mose: Black Collectibles and American Stereotyping* (Bloomington: Indiana University Press, 1994); Karen Cox, *Dreaming of Dixie: How the South was Created in American Popular Culture* (Chapel Hill: University of North Carolina Press, 2011); Robert J. Cook, *Troubled Commemoration: The American Civil War Centennial, 1961–1965* (Baton Rouge: Louisiana State University Press, 2007); and Amanda Bellows, *American Slavery and Russian Serfdom in the Post-Emancipation Imagination* (Chapel Hill: University of North Carolina Press, 2020). In *Remembering the Civil War: Reunion and the Limits of Reconciliation* (Chapel Hill: University of North Carolina Press, 2013), Caroline E. Janney argues that race played a role in reconciliation, but was not the driving force of the phenomenon (199–200). By contrast, David Blight posits in *Race and Reunion: The Civil War in American Memory* (Cambridge, Mass.: Belknap Press of Harvard University, 2001) that reunion was made possible through racial oppression (139).

3. Juliann Sivulka, *Soap, Sex, and Cigarettes: A Cultural History of American Advertising* (Boston: Cengage Learning, 2011), 46.

4. *Blue Book on Advertising* (New York: J. Walter Thompson Company, 1901), 11, box DG4 c. 1, J. Walter Thompson Company, Domestic Advertisements Collection and Publications Collection, David M. Rubenstein Rare Book and Manuscript Library, Duke University.

5. Kristin Hoganson, *Consumers' Imperium: The Global Production of American Domesticity, 1865–1920* (Chapel Hill: University of North Carolina Press, 2007), 15; and "Cigarettes: Men," *Coffin Nails: The Tobacco Controversy of the Nineteenth Century,* published by *Harp Week,* https://tobacco.harpweek.com/hubpages/CommentaryPage.asp?Commentary=Men, accessed June 12, 2019.

6. David's Prize Soap Company, "David's Prize Soap," late nineteenth century, Ephemera Collection box 17, American Antiquarian Society; Jennifer M. Black,

"Corporate Calling Cards: Advertising Trade Cards and Logos in the United States, 1876–1890," *Journal of American Culture* 32, no. 4 (2009): 291–306.

7. Black, "Corporate Calling Cards," 292; Margaret Hale, "The Nineteenth-Century American Trade Card," *Business History Review* 74, no. 4 (2000): 683–88; Margaret Hale, "A New and Wonderful Invention: The Nineteenth-Century American Trade Card," September 5, 2000, Harvard Business School, https://hbswk.hbs.edu/archive/a-new-and-wonderful-invention-the-nineteenth-century-american-trade-card, accessed June 19, 2018; and T. J. Jackson Lears, *Fables of Abundance: A Cultural History of Advertising In America* (New York: Basic Books, 1995), 55.

8. "American Industries—No. 68, Proprietary Specialties," *Scientific American* 44, no. 13 (March 26, 1881): 194–95, quote on 194.

9. John Neff, *Honoring the Civil War Dead: Commemoration and the Problem of Reconciliation* (Lawrence: University of Kansas Press, 2005), 5.

10. Joanna Cohen, "'You Have No Flag Out Yet?': Commercial Connections and Patriotic Emotion in the Civil War North," *Journal of the Civil War Era* 9 (Sept. 2019): 378–409, quote on 378.

11. "The Centennial," *Scribner's Monthly* 11, no. 3 (1876): 433.

12. Black, "Corporate Calling Cards," 291–92.

13. The American colonists lost the Battle of Bunker Hill to the British in 1775, but they inflicted significant casualties on the British troops. The construction of the monument began fifty years later. "Campbell Press Building Trade Card," box AOB 3, box 2D, American Trade Card Collection, Robert B. Haas Family Arts Library, Yale University.

14. William Bennett, "The Cigarette Century," *Science* 80 (September–October 1980): 38–39; and *Illustrated Boston: The Metropolis of New England* (New York: American Publishing and Engraving Co., 1889), 194.

15. Civil War veterans engaged in reunions as early as the 1860s. Two blue-gray reunions occurred before 1883. "Reunions," Center for Civil War Research, University of Mississippi, http://www.civilwarcenter.olemiss.edu/reunions.html, accessed June 15, 2018. For additional detail on the Myers Bros. and Co. trade card, see Bellows, *American Slavery and Russian Serfdom*, 175. Myers Brothers and Co., "Love Tobacco," Richmond, Va., likely early 1870s, box 22, Ephemera Collection Trade Cards, American Antiquarian Society. See also Sue Eisenfeld, "Breaks in the Action," *New York Times*, February 7, 2014, accessed on at https://opinionator.blogs.nytimes.com/2014/02/07/breaks-in-the-action/ (dead), accessed June 8, 2020. For a discussion of the scarcity of resources during the Civil War, see Joan Cashin, *War Stuff: The Struggle for Human and Environmental Resources in the American Civil War* (Cambridge: Cambridge University Press, 2018).

16. McLaughlin's Coffee, "Inauguration of President Lincoln," late nineteenth century, Folio Trade Cards Late box 2, American Antiquarian Society.

17. Historian Edward Pollard's *The Lost Cause: A New Southern History of the War of the Confederates*, published in 1866, valorizes the Confederacy's objectives.

Proponents of the Lost Cause ideology during the late nineteenth century believed that the war was fought over states' rights, not slavery, and that the Confederate cause was not an immoral one. W. Duke, Sons, and Company, *Heroes of the Civil War*, 1889, W. Duke, Sons & Co. Advertising Materials 1880–1910, David M. Rubenstein Rare Book and Manuscript Library, https://repository.duke.edu/dc/wdukesons/dscsi05004, accessed June 20, 2018; and W. Duke, Sons, and Company, "Battle Scenes," 1887, W. Duke, Sons & Co. Advertising Materials.

18. Images of African American laborers on trade cards mirror the representations of enslaved African Americans on Confederate money that were intended to "validate [the] system that held its black laborers in perpetual slavery." Jules d'Hemecourt, "Beyond Face Value: Slavery Iconography in Confederate Currency," Louisiana State University Libraries Special Collections, http://exhibitions.blogs.lib.lsu.edu/?page_id=707, accessed June 8, 2020; W. Duke, Sons, and Company, "Governors, Coats of Arms and Interesting Features of the States and Territories of our Country," W. Duke, Sons & Co. Advertising Materials, https://repository.duke.edu/dc/wdukesons/dscsi05003, accessed June 21, 2018.

19. New Home Sewing Machine Company, "The New Home in the Sunny South," 1882, Box 1B, American Trade Card Collection.

20. Van Stan's Company, "Van Stan's Stratena," late nineteenth century, American Trade Card Collection.

21. Pamphlet for Hawley & Hoops' Breakfast Cocoa, late nineteenth century, Trade Cards Late Pamphlets Post 1876, American Antiquarian Society.

22. Spicers and Peckham, "The New 'Model Grand' Portable Range," folder "Ephemera Late Trade Cards not in ABE 17976," American Antiquarian Society. For additional analysis of this advertisement, see Bellows, *American Slavery and Russian Serfdom*, 175.

23. Van Stan Company, "Stratena Cement," box 4A, American Trade Card Collection; "United We Stand, Divided We Fall," Google Books Ngram Viewer, https://books.google.com/ngrams, accessed March 18, 2019; and "History of the Motto 'United We Stand,'" *Smithsonian Museum of American History*, https://amhistory.si.edu/1942/campaign/campaign24.html, accessed March 18, 2019.

24. Henry Wood, "Was the Civil War Necessary?," *Advocate of the Peace* 61, no. 3 (1899): 67–69.

25. Blight, *Race and Reunion*, 139.

Marketing the "Great Hero"

Duke Cigarette's Short Histories of Civil War Generals' Lives

NATALIE SWEET

In 1889, W. Duke, Sons and Company boasted that it had "made and sold during the last fiscal year 823 MILLION CIGARETTES . . . about 40 per cent. of all the American cigarettes used."[1] The company's rise coincided with the twilight years and deaths of former Civil War generals, which inspired a national wave of nostalgia. These two developments were related. Duke capitalized on Civil War nostalgia and the spirit of national reconciliation as a marketing tool by featuring portraits and histories of Civil War generals in cigarette package inserts. These capitalized on moralistic tales of wartime heroism that also took an ecumenical approach. Due to the company's desire to capture a nationwide audience, sectional balance became a must. The eventual popularity of the series led the company in 1889 to publish a special album, *Heroes of the Civil War*, a title that featured both Union and Confederate leaders. The specially curated set of Civil War tales helped shape a new generation's view of the conflict's leaders as conscientiously principled heroes.

W. Duke, Sons and Company's founder, Washington Duke, was a Confederate veteran. Like many farmers in the North Carolina Piedmont, however, his loyalty was divided in the years leading up to the war, and he chose to focus more on tobacco and cigarette production than on politics following the war. Throughout the 1870s, sales steadily grew. During the 1880s, Washington's son, James Buchanan "Buck" Duke, boosted sales even further through improved production and by including beautiful, suggestively clad women on inserts—small cardboard pieces that stiffened the packaging to protect the cigarettes. Although the inserts raised sales, some found the images distasteful and worried they would be a bad influence on youthful customers. Critics included Buck's father, Washington. As a result, only four years later, Duke's cigarette inserts added more edifying materials to the roster (images of attractive women were also still used), such as flags of the world's nations, coats of arms, and leaders of note. The decision critically carried consequences for public memory of the Civil War.

Increasing Addiction

Prior to the Civil War, both adults and children used tobacco. Although he was exaggerating, one Union soldier campaigning in the South claimed that "the little girls in these parts about seven or eight years old chew tobacco like veterans and babies smoke before they are weaned." Following the war, some Piedmont communities established boys clubs that featured tobacco cultivation as a part of their programs. As John C. Bunham explains, "tobacco provided a positive, relatively stable, and morally secure world for the people who furnished it to the public." Buck Duke grew up in this tobacco-soaked culture. His invention of cigarette inserts came in his midtwenties. He knew that images of actresses and trivia from around the world appealed to children as much as it did to young adults. They also appealed to consumers in urban New York and California as much as those in Durham or rural North Carolina. An addiction to card collecting would, with any luck, lead to a nationwide desire for Duke's cigarettes.[2]

The development of edifying content for the inserts was a public relations decision for the Duke Company. Nothing if not ambitious, Buck Duke believed in growing and maintaining a loyal customer base. However, the addictive nature of his tobacco could be found in every other cigarette company's product, too. Duke's cigarettes needed to meet another desire. To that end, Buck Duke looked to the female form. He invested heavily in advertising throughout the 1880s, and soon, the coquettish chromos within his cigarette packaging became a part of popular culture. "Charlotte [North Carolina] possess[es] the prettiest woman in the State. She is a blonde; and she weighs 133 pounds. Enclose $1 to this office for her picture and name," offered an 1889 ad in the *Progressive Farmer*. "Isn't your figure a little up?," quipped the Winston-based newspaper in its reprinting. "You forget that five cents will buy a package of Duke's cigarettes and a chromo." The *Progressive Farmer*'s audience could appreciate the joke.[3]

Yet, the eyebrow-raising inserts occasionally brought consternation. More problematically, they also brought lawsuits. In 1889, Duke defended against a libel suit brought by actress Gracie Wade. She asserted that the cigarette company had "'wrongfully and immodestly attach[ed] a picture of her head and face, reduced in size, to a ridiculous figure dressed in tights, exhibiting the lower limbs and tending to show that the plaintiff was a person of 'immoral character.'" Gracie Wade was just one of many famous actresses of the day to appear in a cigarette package—some, apparently, against their knowledge or assent.[4]

The development of the actress inserts connected cigarette smoking in the late nineteenth century to socially unacceptable behavior, which ran counter to earlier views of tobacco cultivation and consumption as a socially acceptable and manly activity. Even Buck Duke's devout Methodist father viewed the advertising scheme with disapproval. Washington Duke said that he had "always looked upon the distribution of this character of advertisement as wrong in its pernicious effects upon young men and womanhood." The patriarch knew the target audience for his son's scandalous inserts, as did the Methodist minister who approached the elder Duke with concern over the temptations Washington's son roused in the public. Indeed, beyond the elder Duke's written concern to his son, "there was some contemporary opinion that men discarded such material but that it was avidly sought by boys." Duke's advertising hinted that, with new products such as the cigarette holder, its products were targeted at boys who saw themselves as more grown up than their years. One advertisement enticed,

> "I am wiser and I'm Older,
>   And I've burned my upper lip
>   For I smoked without a holder."
>   (Duke could give this man a tip.)[5]

To those concerned about the moral effects of Buck Duke's inserts, it seemed clear that the chromos put young people, a targeted market, at risk.

There were, however, other options beyond seductively clad women that might appeal to potential customers. Late nineteenth-century economists such as the Wharton School's Simon Patten believed that "mass-produced abundance was an agent of the civilizing process"; why not include educational material in the mass-produced inserts? Following the introduction of the colorful chromos, the Duke Company ran a series with more instructional content—a collection of inserts that included world leaders, worldwide dress, presidential hopefuls, and flags of the world. In its Great American series, for example, the company chose fifty individuals it deemed worthy of emulation. Some were Civil War leaders, such as Abraham Lincoln, General Ulysses S. Grant, and Admiral David Farragut, while the American Revolution was represented by George Washington, Benjamin Franklin, Patrick Henry, and Alexander Hamilton. The series prized the country's inventors and artists, including Edgar Allen Poe, Noah Webster, Samuel Clemens, Samuel Morse, and Edwin Booth. Each card included a profile of the individual, a signature when available, and an image of the person posed in heroic action or alongside the invention or work of literature he or she created.[6]

If imitation is the sincerest form of flattery, it could also be viewed as a good indicator of the perceived popularity of Duke's insert strategy. For example, the Kinney Tobacco Company of New York began its own educational series of cards in 1888. On the back of an illuminated insert featuring the coat of arms of Michigan, the company proclaimed, "This is the most complete and correct collection of all military and naval uniforms throughout the world. Regiments forwarding COLORED sketches will be included as rapidly as possible." Kinney also promised to commission images of "military decorations, coats of arms, and flags of all nations."[7]

Duke's Great American series, along with its imitators, featured few words. The image was enough, and the back of the card simply included the list of other characters who could be collected. The same was even true of Duke's Presidential Possibilities series, which featured Abraham Lincoln's son, Robert Lincoln, among the twenty-five potential candidates for the 1888 election. In fact, the majority of the series created in 1888 relied solely on the artistic merit of the card. The exceptions were Duke's "History of . . ." series, which included "Histories of poor boys who have become rich, and other famous people" and "Civil War Generals." The cardboard inserts transformed into tiny, fifteen-page books that continued to serve a functional purpose while educating the smoker. In each of these series, characters possessed virtues that led to their success in life. Thomas Edison, for example, was "a man of herculean suggestiveness." John Jacob Astor's "judgment was extraordinarily sagacious, his habit industrious and methodical, and his memory exceedingly tenacious, retaining the slightest details."[8] The rare female figures were famed international actresses and singers, including Sarah Bernhardt, Etelka Gersker, and Helena Modjeska.

WORKING THE DUDE.

BROWN ELITE PHOTOGR

PHOTOGR

SEE A BOX OF CIGARETTES GIVEN AWAY WITH EVERY DOZEN PHOTOGRAPHS

As the cigarette-makers are giving away photographs as a bait for dudes, it wouldn't be a bad idea for the photographers to adopt something like the above, and work the dude for all he is worth.—*Chicago Ledger.*

The "Working the Dude" cartoon appeared in newspapers throughout the country. (*Frostburg Mining Journal,* September 7, 1889)

Despite the fact that moralists sometimes attacked the acting profession in the nineteenth century, the Duke histories carefully pointed out that the actresses carried themselves with nobility and dedicated themselves not only to beauty but also to studying such subjects as languages and history. While an actress might be admired for her physical form, the core of her character truly counted and was what separated her art from tawdriness. As would be key to its histories of Civil War generals, the inserts carefully highlighted the virtues of its subjects.

To its "lithographic work of the rarest merit," W. Duke, Sons and Company added the new concept of coupons; if a young man or woman purchased enough cigarettes, and then acquired one hundred coupons, he or she could submit those in return for a handsome album of the images. Only a year prior, the Coca-Cola company offered the first coupon for a free cola, but Duke used the coupon to entice customers to continue buying its product. The result was enriching content that could potentially uplift the masses and act as a much better moralizing force than chromos of lovely actresses. "'Who wouldn't be a boy again," asked the *United States Tobacco Journal* in 1888, "'so that he might know the delight of making a collection of cigarette pictures?'"[9]

Newspapers addressed the popularity of the appeal in an 1889 cartoon. The single-pane drawing, titled "Working the Dude," perfectly signaled the public's awareness of who collected chromos. A young man in fashionable striped pants and sporting a walking cane, a tall hat, and monocle, exits a photography store with a cigarette in his mouth. Late nineteenth-century commentators used the term "dude" to describe a young man who followed the latest trends. The cartoon's dude strolls past a sign that reads "A Box of Cigarettes Given Away With Every Dozen Photographs." "As the cigarette-makers are giving away photographs as a bait for dudes," the *Chicago Ledger* stated sarcastically, "it wouldn't be a bad idea for the photographers to adopt something like the above, and work the dude for all he is worth." Dudes, joined by impressionable children who sought the cards for trading and young women who admired the fashions and character studies on the cards, eagerly sought the photographs. It did not matter if the cards' subjects were attractive ladies, people of note, or Civil War generals; by encouraging collectability, Duke ensured that its target audience sought the cards. This audience, with its minimal firsthand experience of the Civil War, eagerly consumed Duke's history of Civil War generals.[10]

Timing Is Everything

In addition to his marketing genius, Duke's success also came from the fact that Buck concentrated on improving the mass production of cigarettes. Previously, factory workers had hand-rolled cigarettes, but Buck streamlined the manufacturing process and installed a Bonsack cigarette rolling machine in 1884. Steady improvements to the machine resulted in extraordinary results. At the same time, Buck also sought to eliminate competition from rival competitors by buying them out. If Duke's colorful inserts interested audiences in cigarettes, it was the rolling machine and declining competition that made the high number of sales possible in the mid 1880s. Historian Sarah Milov points out that cigarette sales only accounted for 2 percent of the tobacco market in the United States at the turn of the century, but this figure steadily changed as "demand for cigarettes surged amid unprecedented advertising expenditures." These facts, combined with the decision to run a series on Civil War heroes, came at a critical juncture in the development of Civil War memory. Key leaders from the war had died over the course of the 1880s. Under a heading "Only Three Left," the *Clarksville (Tenn.) Evening Chronicle* lamented in 1888, "If we except Maj. General Schofield . . . with

General Hood, only three of the leading heroes of our civil war now survive, viz: WT. [sic] Sherman, Jos. E. Johnston and G. T. Beauregard. All of the rest of the great leaders of either army have crossed the river." Within five years, those notable figures would also be dead. "They Go Quickly," observed a March 1891 headline from the Yorkville (S.C.) Enquirer, "The heroes of the civil war have disappeared much sooner after its close than did those of the Revolution. It was half a century after the Declaration of Independence before Adams and Jefferson died, and the year before . . . the White House had been vacated by a president who had joined the army in 1776. It is but thirty years now since the firing on Fort Sumter, and the great leaders of that period in both civil and military life are all gone."[11]

The 1888–89 run of Civil War cigarette inserts came at a time when the nation grappled with what it meant when a "great" generation aged and died. Some leaders, of course, had died during the conflict. Of course, the figurative river literally appeared by way of General Thomas "Stonewall" Jackson's own words, which appeared on his cigarette card: "'No, no, no; let us pass over the river, and rest under the shade of the trees.' Peace to his ashes! His remains rest under the trees.'" More traumatically, however, the assassination of President James Garfield had called to mind that of Abraham Lincoln. The author of his Civil War general card commemorated him by way of the words that Garfield had uttered on the sixteenth president's death. Garfield's "own sad end" in his short history concluded, "Fellow citizens, God reigns, and the Government in Washington lives.'" Even those generals who remained alive in 1888 (but whom the newspapers had either forgotten or had decided were of less importance) had their lives described as if they were on the edge of the immortal journey. With an air of finality, the insert author proclaimed of General Nathaniel Banks, "Although having passed the allotted time of three score and ten years, General Banks still retains all his active qualities of mind and brain. He is exceedingly popular among his neighbors, and enjoys the ease and comfort which are his after a life of hard-earned success." Banks died a few years later in 1894.[12]

Although the company took a unique approach to utilizing the Civil War in its advertisements, the Duke Company was not alone in commodifying the event. As historian David Blight has observed, the Durham-based company was but one of many that crafted the images of Civil War leaders into "salable memories in the name of good will and good business." Between the boom in cigarette production and distribution, the low cost of the cigarettes, and the appeal of collectability to young men

and women, Duke's inserts were able to sell a remarkable number of cigarettes even before the appearance of its Civil War advertisements. In
addition to appearing in newspapers across the Carolinas, ads for Duke
Cigarettes reached up to New York and down into Texas, appeared in
newspapers in Ohio, Illinois, and Idaho, and stretched all the way to
Utah, Washington, and even Hawaii. Dealers in urban areas and small
towns alike sought to draw in purchasers with advertisements proclaiming the Duke name. Measured against their own work and others crafting comparable edifying advertisements that would "prove advantageous
as an educator for the masses" and be "worthy of wide circulation among
the youth of the land," the *American Bookmaker* commended the Duke
Civil War cigarette album for being "a splendid specimen of a carefully directed effort in obtaining deserved success."[13]

Crafting the Hero

The cigarette inserts produced by W. Duke, Sons and Company are the
collective grandfather of all modern card collecting. New techniques
in color printing allowed eye-catching detail for each "hero's" portrait.
Stock battle scenes appeared on the back page of each insert. In some images, soldiers from both sides of the conflict loaded cannons and fired ri-
fles. Images of the most impressive naval technology to emerge from the
war, the ironclad, appeared on the back of more than one insert. Some
soldiers bore flags aloft or cradled dying comrades. Poignantly, more
than one young soldier bled out on the ground, the bright crimson of his
blood adding a stark splash of color to the tiny image.

The Duke company selected fifty generals and admirals to display. The
series divided the men evenly—twenty-five men representing the Union,
and twenty-five the Confederacy. Obvious choices included Generals Ulysses S. Grant, George B. McClellan, Robert E. Lee, and Thomas "Stonewall" Jackson. Political generals like General Benjamin Butler appeared,
too, as did Baden-born Franz Sigel. In his biography of Sigel, the series
writer explained that

> there is no more truly representative body of Americans than the commanders
> in our late war. Almost all of them were of humble birth, and exemplified in
> their own hard struggles against the adversity the life and spirit of the stur[d]y
> and progressive nation of which they so proudly claimed citizenship. They
> were distinctly Americans in birth, life, and character, and it is no matter for
> wonder, therefore, that the internal dissension and civil strife which threat-

ened to throw the government into chaos should have aroused in the minds of these brave men the intensest and most fervid feelings of patriotism.

Sigel may have been a "marked exception" in the series on account of his birthplace, but he shared the other patriotic characteristics that the writer saw necessary for inclusion.[14]

Best of all for the collector, the cards were highly portable—each insert measured a pocket-sized 1.5 by 3 inches. With no guarantee that any one of the more than fifty generals and admirals would appear in any given cigarette package, a serious collector found it essential to trade with friends and acquaintances and to buy multiple packages of cigarettes. However, another marketing innovation appeared in 1889: an individual could avoid the hard work of purchasing or trading by collecting coupons that were added to the inserts. After gathering a hundred coupons, the collector could receive a complete album of the images and biographies. This opportunity was an added bonus for older collectors, who sought a more formal and even prestigious way to preserve history. The title of the Civil War series on the individual inserts was "A Short History of [Name]," whereas the album was titled *Heroes of the Civil War*. The album title would have raised more eyebrows than the 1884 Duke series of actresses had it been produced twenty years prior, when many northerners still considered former Confederates to be traitors. Attitudes had changed by 1888, however. Time had also improved the reputations of some generals. Indeed, the title "hero" in the Duke Civil War album elevated to higher status leaders like General Braxton Bragg, who even the insert writer deemed "to have outlived [his] fame and usefulness" at end of life.[15]

The author or authors of the inserts remained anonymous. "Much care has been taken to have the sketches and histories accurate," readers of *Heroes of the Civil War* were assured, "and we offer this album to our patrons with full confidence, believing that all will enjoy it, and, while doing so, will have a kindly feeling for W. Duke, Sons & Co." The writing, however, obviously followed a set formula. A key feature of the inserts was the neat compartmentalization of each leader's life—it had to be, as the author only had fifteen paper-thin pages on which to document the subject's life. First came the general's rise, whether from humble origins or from privileged backgrounds. A description of the officer's valor during wartime formed the meat of each insert, followed by a conclusion reflecting on his postwar life. The fact that many of the subjects had recently died complemented the nineteenth-century notion that history was the story of great men—each insert read like a morality tale, with the path of

"A Short History of Gen. U. S. Grant" tobacco trading card produced by W. Duke, Sons & Co. (David M. Rubenstein Rare Book & Manuscript Library, Duke University)

honor and valor neatly charted for the reader to follow to the end of the subject's life.[16]

This is clear in the biographies of two of the Civil War's most popular figures: Generals Ulysses S. Grant and Robert E. Lee. Unsurprisingly, the biographies of these men are also the first that appeared, side by side, in the full-sized *Heroes of the Civil War* album. Collectors learned that Grant was born to "people of modest and humble circumstances." After "growing dissatisfied" following studies at West Point and a number of years in the army, he nonetheless "took a decided stand for the Union, raising a company of volunteers, whom he drilled thoroughly and accompanied to Springfield, Illinois." Showing "strategic skill that might well command the admiration of even his foes" during the Fort Donelson campaign, his star rose. After a string of successes, General Lee surrendered to Grant at Appomattox Court House, and the Union general was "feted and hailed throughout the Northern States as the hero of the Civil War." He then notably achieved the presidency of the country, and following that endeavor, committed himself to writing of his memoirs. When his end arrived, "the somber shadow of death fell across a name high on the honor roll of our national heroes."[17]

Robert E. Lee's biography read no less heroically than Grant's. An 1862 quote from Lord Wolsey declared that "Lee is stamped on my memory as a being apart and superior to all others in every way." The pronouncement appeared on the first page. The author traced Lee's family, noting that his father was a notable Revolutionary War soldier and his wife's lineage flowed from Martha Washington. He succeeded in every way as a youth and in school and served his country faithfully up until the time of the Civil War. It was then, the author noted, that "Lee resigned his commission in the United States Army, in obedience to his conscientious conviction that he was bound by the act of his state."[18]

Indeed, the anonymous author or authors of the Confederate inserts zeroed in on many of the subjects' "conscientious convictions." These men had not betrayed their country; rather, they had demonstrated extraordinary patriotism by refusing to abandon their states. For others, their economic and regional interests explained their choices. General Leonidas Polk, for example, "was a strong sympathizer with the doctrine of secession. His birth, education and associations were alike Southern; and his property, which was very considerable in land and slaves, aided to identify him with the project of establishing a Southern Confederacy." Regional affinities and economics explained decision making easily enough.[19]

Undeniably, the reasoning behind each general's entrance into battle mattered less as a character trait then the bravery and persistence he demonstrated. "Like Admiral Nelson," said the biography of General J. E. B. Stuart, "he seemed unaware of the meaning of the word fear." These were masculine role models any male reader could and should aspire to emulate. Despite losing an arm—and nearly his life—in battle, General Oliver O. Howard dutifully returned to fight at Antietam, earning him "the warm commendation and sympathy of his fellow officers." Bravery could also be defined by how one persistently pulled oneself up "by the bootstraps." "Two-fold glory should . . . attach itself to the name of Nathan Bedford Forrest," asserted the general's insert when remarking on his dogged pursuit of education, "for few of the many gallant men whose names grace the roll of honor of the Confederacy rose from such obscure birth to fortune and subsequently to renown." The author made no mention of Forrest's participation in the Fort Pillow Massacre or his postwar membership in the Ku Klux Klan; instead, the author reported that, after running the Selma, Marion and Memphis Railroad, Forrest had retired "and enjoyed the peace and quiet which his struggles had earned for him."[20]

Exuding masculinity and receiving one's just rewards in life, however, did not mean that the heroes showed no emotion. Indeed, the subject became more heroic when he demonstrated rare moments of tenderness, specifically when reflecting on those who died under his command. No hard-won peace was achieved without at least some heartache. Admiral Farragut's insert featured a quote describing the admiral's response the loss of 335 sailors at the 1864 Union victory at Mobile Bay. It was "the only time [he] ever saw the old gentleman cry; but tears came in his eyes like a little child" as Farragut watched the bodies of his men laid out on deck. The account of a leader's tears could even veer into the romantic if the subject faced a dire enough situation, as was the case of General George Pickett, whose voice was "tremulous with emotion" as he reported the disastrous events of his charge at Gettysburg to General Robert E. Lee. The author concluded by quoting Sir Walter Scott's Marmion and comparing Pickett's loss to "'Flodden's fatal field / Where shivered was fair Scotland's spear / And broken was her shield.'"[21]

It is easy to see how the inserts could have had a collective influence on their target audience's understanding of the war. The generals and admirals of Duke's inserts appeared just as young men were always told they should behave and in the manner that young ladies expected them to behave. The "heroes of the Civil War" were conscientious, brave, and showed enough tenderness so as not to appear heartless. According to these short histories, when the war was over, the generals from both sides (for the most part) returned home and contributed to their communities. These "short histories" of well-known commanders reflected the family narrative that Washington Duke's family wished to portray of its patriarch's life; he had loyally fought for the Confederacy but did not retain any sectional feelings after the war. When the war was lost, Washington had returned home to Durham to build a successful business and, eventually, becoming a Republican. His loyalty, acceptance of defeat, and hard work were the qualities worth understanding and celebrating.

Perhaps no better testament supports the inserts' appeal and longevity than their continuing collectability. Collectors eagerly pay $50 to $150 for individual inserts on public trading sites like eBay. In 1989 the inserts were combined into a single volume with an 1891 book *Generals and Battles of the Civil War*. Titled *Great Civil War Heroes and Their Battles*, the book still sells on Amazon. Various purchasers on the book's Amazon page hailed the book in reviews as "a very good introduction to the leaders of the Civil War" and one rated it "one of the best non-fiction books I've read in a long time."[22] The book's hagiographic approach continues to appeal to readers despite the widespread availability of robust, recent Civil War scholarship.

The Duke insert series has enjoyed a long shelf life. Designed to draw in a young audience bent on gathering full sets of collectable images, the company promoted its generals' conscientious convictions to an impressionable audience with little to no memory of that war. Copies numbered in the millions. The inserts' narratives portrayed the central players of both sides of the conflict in a heroic light and in a more affordable format than an expensive book. They lived in pockets, were eagerly traded hand to hand, and cost relatively little. Taking advantage of the late nineteenth-century interest in the Civil War, the Dukes created a profitable business plan by marketing cigarettes by promoting a heroic yet ecumenical version of the Civil War.

NOTES

1. "Read What the Manufacturers of Duke's Best Cigarettes Have to Say," *New York Evening World*, October 3, 1889.

2. Drew A. Swanson, "War Is Hell, So Have a Chew: The Persistence of Agroenvironmental Ideas in the Civil War Piedmont," in *The Blue, the Gray, and the Green: Toward and Environmental History of the Civil War*, ed. by Brian Allen Drake (Athens: University of Georgia Press, 2015), 163–90, quote on 168; John C. Bunham, *Bad Habits: Drinking, Smoking, Taking Drugs, Gambling, Sexual Misbehavior and Swearing in American History* (New York: New York University Press, 1993), 87.

3. "General News Items," *Progressive Farmer* (Winston, N.C.), July 9, 1889.

4. "A Suit about a Cigarette Picture," *Pittsburg Dispatch*, June 29, 1889.

5. Washington Duke to J. B. Duke, October 17, 1894, quoted in Robert F. Durden, *The Dukes of Durham, 1865–1929* (Durham, N.C.: Duke University Press, 1975), 60; Bunham, 88; *Tobacco*, November 19, 1886, quoted in Patrick G. Porter, "Advertising in the Early Cigarette Industry: W. Duke, Sons and Company of Durham," *North Carolina Historical Review* 48 (1971): 31–43, quote on 35.

6. Jackson Lears, *Fables of Abundance: A Cultural History of Advertising in America* (New York: Perseus Books Group, 1994), 115.

7. *State Arms of Michigan* (New York: Kinney Tobacco Company, 1888).

8. *History of Thos. Edison* (Park Place, N.Y.: Knapp & Company, 1888), 3; *A Life of John Jacob Astor* (Park Place, N.Y.: Knapp & Company, 1888) 3.

9. " Artistic Efforts," *Los Angeles Daily Herald*, May 3, 1888; letter in *United States Tobacco Journal* quoted in W. C. Roberts and Richard F. Knapp, "Paving the Way for the Tobacco Trust: From Hand Rolling to Mechanized Cigarette Production by W. Duke, Sons and Company," *North Carolina Historical Review* 69, no. 3 (July 1992): 257–81, quote on 264.

10. *Chicago Ledger*, quoted in "Working the Dude," *Democratic Northwest* (Napoleon, Ohio), August 8, 1889.

11. Sarah Milov, *The Cigarette: A Political History* (Cambridge, Mass.: Harvard University Press, 2019), 16–22; "Only Three Left," *Clarksville (Tenn.) Evening Chronicle*, November 12, 1888; "They Go Quickly," *Yorkville (S.C.) Enquirer*, March 4, 1891.

12. "A Short History of Gen. T. J. Jackson" (Park Place, N.Y.: Knapp & Company, 1888), 15; "A Short History of Gen. Garfield" (Park Place, N.Y.: Knapp & Company, 1888), 15; "A Short History of Gen. N. P. Banks" (Park Place, N.Y.: Knapp & Company, 1888), 15.

13. David W. Blight, *Race and Reunion: The Civil War in American Memory* (Cambridge, Mass.: Harvard University Press, 2001), 201; "Booklets and Brochures," in *American Bookmaker* (New York: Howard Lockwood and Company, 1890): 36.

14. "A Short History of Gen. F. Sigel" (Park Place, N.Y.: Knapp & Company, 1888), 3–4.

15. John Reeves, *The Lost Indictment of Robert E. Lee: The Forgotten Case Against an American Icon* (Lanham, Md.: Rowman & Littlefield, 2018), 1; "A Short History of Gen. Braxton Bragg" (Park Place, N.Y.: Knapp & Company, 1888), 15.

16. *The Heroes of the Civil War Album* (Durham, N.C.: W. Duke Sons and Company, 1888), 1.

17. "A Short History of Gen. U. S. Grant," (Park Place, N.Y.: Knapp & Company, 1888), 1–15.

18. "A Short History of Gen. Robert E. Lee" (Park Place, N.Y.: Knapp & Company, 1888), 1–15.

19. "A Short History of Gen. Leonidas Polk" (Park Place, N.Y.: Knapp & Company, 1888), 5.

20. "A Short History of Gen. O. O. Howard" (Park Place, N.Y.: Knapp & Company, 1888), 8–9; "A Short History of Gen. N. B. Forrest" (Park Place, N.Y.: Knapp & Company, 1888), 1, 15.

21. "A Short History of Adm'l Farragut" (Park Place, N.Y.: Knapp & Company, 1888), 13–14; "A Short History of Genl. G. E. Pickett" (Park Place, N.Y.: Knapp & Company, 1888), 15.

22. Steven J. Smallwood, "Very Good Introduction to Civil War Leaders," review of *Great Civil War Heroes and Their Battles*, ed. Walton Rawls; and Amor de

Soria, "Great Civil War Heroes and Their Battles a Wonderful and Interesting Read!," review of *Great Civil War Heroes and Their Battles*, ed. Walton Rawls, Amazon, October 19, 2011, https://www.amazon.com/Great-Civil-Heroes-Their-Battles/dp/0896595226/, accessed July 14, 2019.

Winning the Civil War

What Odds? ... Blessing and The Black ... May ... Bank ... purpose of Gen. ... Headquarters, Thayer ... ed. (Clinton State Univ ... 20). Online ... http ... Assassination on Great Inauguration of ... hthc ... (ore/9783 ... 0019 ... ee and Jun 1 2019.

"The National Debt May Be a National Blessing"

Debt as an Instrument of Character in the Civil War Era

DAVID K. THOMSON

In the summer of 1987, clerks of a prominent bank in London stumbled across an extraordinary find: seventy-five thousand Confederate bonds stashed in boxes. Despite the frequent flooding of the vaults by the nearby Thames River, the bonds remained in remarkably good condition. Even more noteworthy, the bonds survived the building's bombing in the 1940 Blitz. The bonds, with a face value of around $60 million, had been carefully bundled in wrappers labeled "1883." The bank had stored the bonds since the 1880s, although they had been moved to their present location—and apparently forgotten—in the 1920s, when "all hope" for redemption had been lost. The Associated Press news article detailing their discovery noted that the bonds would be auctioned by Sotheby's and were projected to fetch up to £220,000. According to Sotheby's, they had been asked to auction the bonds on behalf of the heirs of the trustees of the bonds, who hoped to reclaim at least part of the 125-year-old investment (and who unsurprisingly "asked not to be identified").[1]

Of the many burdens the Civil War placed on Americans, one of the least discussed is the financial obligations it created and the postwar debate about how to retire the nation's financial liability. Owing more than $2.6 billion by the summer of 1865, the U.S. government would face the challenge of not only paying a debt off, but also doing so with a southern population who had no qualms in repudiating such debt—just as they had done at the state level in the antebellum period. Financing the war required a degree of state-led financial innovation utterly at odds with American antebellum financial culture. The moral hazards of the anonymous marketplace from the antebellum era that criticized financiers as men of questionable character found itself replaced by a statist response that called on all of the citizenry to embrace an evolving financial world punctuated by wartime exigencies. Bondholding shifted from the domain of the economic elite to a wider swath of the population. As he had during the war, Philadelphia-based financier and U.S. "bond czar" Jay Cooke emerged with a central role in shaping U.S. financial policies in the postwar period. But Cooke and his allies on both sides of the Atlantic had to contend with a deeply divisive political issue surrounding debt.

In the aftermath of the Civil War, economic concerns weighed heavily on the minds of politicians in Washington and throughout the entire North. As Republicans waved the bloody shirt and Democrats decried class warfare, it appeared that debt as a politicized weapon would consume the Reconstruction period. Democratic propaganda suggested that the war had not been a "People's Contest," with people from all socioeconomic backgrounds purchasing the bonds. Although Civil War bond purchasers emanated from a wide swath of the population, stretching across gender, racial, sectional, and international lines, the latter part of Reconstruction witnessed a significant concentration of ownership of bonds in the hands of select financiers and financial institutions.

Bonds also served as a symbol of consumption by the time of the Civil War. Building off of antebellum growth in U.S. savings institutions by working-class Americans, the bond sales of the war and Reconstruction era reflected a new consumption of capital. As individuals began purchasing bonds directly rather than depositing their funds in saving institutions, these consumers served as logical extensions of the prewar development of nonelite participation in finance. This demographic widening of investors and consumers introduced a disruptive force in the relatively constant world of U.S. debt in the nineteenth century. While not a linear development, this increased interaction of a wider array of consumers (if only for a relatively brief moment) played a pivotal role in the evolution of the nation's understanding of financial consumption.[2]

The battles waged over the bonds became a fiercely partisan war. The postwar fiscal policy of the U.S. government centered above all else on the necessity of retiring the Civil War debt. But the process of retiring the debt raised questions about the possible ramifications of repudiation. For every Republican who called for the full repayment of debt, there was a Democrat (including former Confederates) who challenged the merits of full repayment. Union debt, in essence, became a highly divisive issue swirling around notions of American character, honor, and identity.

But what of Confederate debt? Confederate states and the government in Richmond had also issued tens of millions in bonds, many of which made their way across the Atlantic into the hands of European investors. The ratification of the Fourteenth Amendment to the Constitution, which dictated that Confederate debt would not be honored, initially settled the Confederate debt question. Yet Britons' insistence that the debt be repaid—and their threat to withhold future investment in the United States if it was not—ensured that the debate continued into the twentieth century. In many ways, the result of the war had transformed not only the worth of Confederate bonds—they were worth nothing, in fact—but also their meaning, which had also changed when they ceased to represent a burgeoning republic and became instead symbols of a failed rebellion—at least in American eyes.

British investors and their hostility to Confederate debt repudiation belied a changing dynamic over U.S. investment banking and the strength of the U.S. economy. In an odd way, the battle over Confederate debt served not to divide North and South but rather to unify the nation in response to British claims of aggrievement. In the Reconstruction period, U.S. banks opened branches overseas and bypassed traditional relationships with the long-established banks of London, while likewise latching on to other established as well as emerging markets. Such acts reveal a sophistication in the U.S. financial world and a greater integration with global financial markets. This shifted the financial balance in American capitalism moving forward. U.S. banks no longer served at the behest of London banks alone, but projected a newfound confidence and financial weight that contributed to the world's strongest economy by the turn of the century. In the end, these actions came to represent an important moment in the history of the fiscal state during a particular era of financial globalization.[3]

The end of the war brought relative stability to the treasury, but also great uncertainty as to the future of American debt. As a percentage of the gross domestic product, the public debt skyrocketed from 1.49 percent in 1860 to 27.1 percent by 1865. The U.S. government had no choice but to confront this issue directly. But as Franklin Noll and others have pointed out, an additional factor beyond the size of the debt proved to be the structure of the country's financial liabilities. In the summer of 1865, thirty-two financial instruments comprised American debt tied to widely varying interest rates (ranging from 4 to 7.3 percent). Perhaps most alarmingly, some 48 percent of the debt would come due in 1870. By the summer of 1865, the war may have concluded, but deep questions remained over how to pay for it.[4]

In the immediate aftermath of the war, Congress debated extensively on both Union and Confederate debt. Whether such debt was a "blessing" or a "burden" occupied many pages of newsprint in the United States for the remainder of 1865 and into 1866. The opinions on the matter, as one might expect, ranged widely. An article in the *Commercial and Financial Chronicle* equated war debt with capital improvements that in the long term would benefit the nation. "A national debt," the article stated, "may be so managed as to stimulate productive power and augment the force of inventive genius, to economise capital and open a beneficent reservoir for gathering together and rendering more productive ten thousand little fertilizing streams of national wealth." One of the most prominent pieces in support of the debt was (unsurprisingly) put forward by Jay Cooke's New York–based public relations machine. In *How Our National Debt May Be a National Blessing*, Samuel Wilkeson emphasized the power of a national debt to provide a "secure basis for national currency." Furthermore, Wilkeson contended, "We lay down the proposition that our national debt, made permanent and rightly managed, will be a national blessing."[5]

Despite many articles and pamphlets championing the national debt, there was some dissent, especially surrounding the notion of a national debt as a blessing. One author, when citing the "preposterous theory which considers a national debt as a 'national blessing,'" reiterated a popular refrain for the antidebt crowd when he noted that "it is capital to those only who hold it and a tax to everybody else." Secretary of the Treasury Hugh McCulloch differed sharply from his bond-selling partner Jay Cooke when he flatly stated that "there can be no reasonable doubt that a national debt is a national burden, for which there can be no substantial counterbalancing compensations." He added in a subsequent letter that "it would be foolish to call it a national blessing, it may be so managed as not to be a national calamity." A British economist at the time spoke to the fact that it was inherently a U.S. trait to pay off all debts. Americans, in the mind of this economist, had a "strong and controlling sense that debt was always and everywhere an evil; that it was a good thing to 'work off' the mortgage, even if it involved working very hard." Americans' aversion to debt had been exemplified by the complete payment of the national debt during the Jackson administration. It would stand to reason that the repayment of the U.S. debt in the postwar period served as a natural extension of this legacy of debt aversion.[6]

The extensive political discussions in the halls of Congress reinforced how paramount of an issue the debt question remained. Hardly a matter relegated to financial elites, the popular consumption of U.S. war bonds during the war and its immediate aftermath reflected an issue that impacted millions of Americans. In part, these bond purchasers signaled a changing dynamic of consumption that had emerged during the Jacksonian era. While not tied to material goods, the advertising campaign of the war conducted in newspapers and handbills attempted to drive a financial commodity into the hands of consumers—many of whom had never purchased a bond before. This served as a natural extension of what Wendy Woloson described as the work of "itinerant peddlers to transport goods into the hinterlands" and benefited from the antebellum "improvement of printing technologies to broadcast information and advertising on a national scale."[7] Jay Cooke's work as the federal agent for bond sales during the war laid bare these approaches to convince the American populace to consume the bonds.

While debates raged as to whether or not the debt was a blessing or a curse, others came to view the bonds and the funding of war debt more broadly as having larger and deeper meanings. The Union debt of several billions could not easily be paid off and thus would become a new reality of U.S. life and of government policy making. At the same time, the debt became more directly related to the outcome of the war. The debt, had, of course, paid at the most basic of levels for the everyday operations of the war: soldiers' pay, bullets, uniforms, food, and medicine. Bonds, therefore, served as more than just a financial IOU, but as an enduring symbol and practical reminder of the sacrifices made in the conflict. While perhaps not as poignant as an empty sleeve of a veteran, bonds nevertheless constituted a critical reminder of the costs of war and some of the long-lasting effects of such conflicts in the decades beyond the official end of hostilities. It is in this light, then, that one needs to examine U.S. debt—as a vital entity that challenged the character of an evolving financial marketplace in the postwar United States.

At the heart of the matter was the old debate between the creation of wealth through "active" capital and labor versus the creation of wealth through "inactive" means based in the financial sector. "Direct robbery by force could not have obtained this [oppression] so effectually as has been through the creation of a permanent national debt," claimed one critic. The same article railed against "moneyed institutions and heavy capitalists, who have immense sums to invest, and would like to have the nation guarantee the annual interest upon the same to themselves and their successors." Other commentators, such as President Andrew Johnson, even floated the idea of having interest payments count toward payment of bond principal to holders. In essence, there would no longer be a true interest payment, but just the beginning of the repayment of principal. Others pushed for the payment of interest in greenbacks rather than coin. Such disparate thoughts on the matter impacted any sort of financial policy decision making.[8]

The debate centered around the best way to tackle the debt. In the short term, taxation, along with custom duties, facilitated debt interest payments and the creation of a moderate budget surplus in the early postwar period. That said, taxation in and of itself could not solve the structure of the debt repayment nor remain viable for long, especially the income tax (with which the general populace was unaccustomed and to which they were generally opposed.) But something else needed to be done to address the debt issue. In buying government bonds, millions of northerners had purchased the right to be considered part of the Union war effort. For some, the patriotic duty of purchasing war debt mirrored their service on the front lines and their support network on the home front. The debt itself then served as a reminder of the great sacrifices made by so many throughout the North. However, according to historian Eric Foner, "most . . . viewed the sanctity of the national debt as a moral legacy of the war second only to emancipation itself."[9] Yet for others, the staggering wartime debt served, at a minimum, as a topic of great concern, and for still others as a threat to the nation's very existence.

The debt crisis quickly became a political game in Washington as Republicans and Democrats scurried to solidify or reaffirm their political relevance. One question that emerged in that summer of 1865 was whether or not the United States would assume the debts of the defeated Confederacy and of individual Confederate states, which totaled about $1.5 billion. While state debts had been assumed by the federal government following the Revolution, the massive state and federal debt incurred during the Civil War was altogether a different beast, and despite the fact that there were no constitutional barriers to assuming the debt, most assumed it was a nonissue. No one "outside of a lunatic asylum" thought the South would demand and succeed in payment of Confederate debt, claimed Democratic representative Benjamin Boyer of Pennsylvania. Similarly, the *New York Times* cited a Republican lawmaker who equated the assumption of such debt as akin to "fighting windmills" or waiting for "the sky to fall."[10]

When Congress reconvened in December 1865, it almost immediately passed a resolution declaring the national debt "sacred and inviolate." Yet that did little to quell the debate. The *Nation* reported concerns over the possibility of a combination of northern Democrats and former Confederates working to repudiate the debt. "It would hardly be a safe thing for the national credit to have such a body of men in Congress, reinforced as they would probably be, by a considerable number of Northern men ready to go for at least qualified repudiation." Massachusetts senator Henry Wilson took it a step further by expressing his fears over the possible repudiation of debt if left in the hands of former Confederates. For Wilson, the honoring of U.S. debt served a purpose "as sacred as the blood of our heroes poured out on the battlefields."[11]

The debt issue proved fundamental to electoral strategy for Republicans in the 1866 midterm elections. In particular, Republicans focused on the popular nature of investment. Targeting the wide swath of investors numbering in the millions at the war's end reflected a desire to emphasize the importance and power of debt as an American institution, while recognizing the democratization of investment and the importance of honoring that debt. Former Union general Benjamin Butler spoke to those themes when he warned a crowd in Massachusetts that if Democrats were elected "what would your 7:30s be worth?" But perhaps the *New York Herald* stated it best: "Herein lies the secret of the astounding popular strength of [the Fourteenth Amendment]. . . . No man who has a fifty dollar government bond salted down would trust its redemption to the chances of the casting vote in Congress of a Southerner who has lost his thousands in Confederate script."[12] Such quotes reinforced a changing dynamic by the end of the war. Government bonds—long relegated to financial elites—had made their way into larger swaths of the populace. As a result, honoring the debt at full value became a topic of great concern to a larger proportion of the population than ever before. Investing in bonds had been marketed during the war as a way to prove one's loyalty to the Union, a concept that remained integral to Republicans' postwar fusing of patriotism and self-interest in defense of the debt. The product purchased by investors and the meanings they attached to it were politically sacrosanct.

Such beliefs marked a deviation from the initial beliefs in Congress following the end of the war. Justin Morrill, a senator from Vermont and a bondholder himself, exclaimed in 1866 that "a permanent national debt is not an American institution, as our history has already twice proven, and though it may take a number of years to wholly extinguish the present debt, the policy of gradual extinction can and should be steadily pursued." Other members of Congress reiterated the sentiments of James

Garfield and John Sherman, who emphasized that the national honor required repaying the loans in specie. Theodore Pomeroy (N.Y.) stated, "I am ashamed to have a proposition made at the close of the Thirty-Ninth Congress to pay off the debt of the United States or any portion of it otherwise than by bonds payable, principal and interest, in gold, or else by gold itself." Henry Corbett (Oreg.) quipped, "public credit should be 'like Caesar's wife, above suspicion.'"[13]

Many Democrats seized on the "Ohio Idea" prominently championed by George Hunt Pendleton (George McClellan's vice presidential running mate in 1864). Slamming Republicans for ineptitude and corruption when it came to the public debt, he (and an increasing percentage of Democrats) called for the repayment of principle whenever possible in depreciated greenbacks. Additionally, many Democrats also questioned the motives of the current bondholders. Many of the "patriotic purchasers" of the war itself had sold their bonds, and many Democrats found the motivations of those purchasers more suspect. While such resale of bonds proved true by the early 1870s, it remained less prominent at the time of the 1868 elections.

Republicans and their allies in the press attacked any such schemes as akin to repudiation of the debt. The Republican Party in 1868 made a plank on its platform denouncing repudiation in any form. Even after Ulysses Grant's election in the fall of 1868, Republicans still had to contend with the actions of lame duck president Andrew Johnson. During Johnson's annual message in December 1868, he broke with his party to call for a repudiation of the debt. In an ironic twist, Johnson equated the continued servicing of the debt as a new form of slavery: "The borrowers would become the servants to the lenders—the lenders the masters of the people." Congress responded with a House resolution the following week declaring "that all forms and degrees of repudiation of national indebtedness are odious to the American people." Congress then passed a bill in early March 1869, promising the government's repayment of all bonds in coin. Although the bill never became law because of a pocket veto by Johnson, Grant's term began soon thereafter, and one of the first pieces of legislation passed during his administration was the Public Credit Act. Passed into law on March 18, 1869, the law pledged that all U.S. obligations would be paid out "in coin or its equivalent." The crisis over how bonds would be repaid was resolved, and it was no coincidence that a drastic increase in European investment in U.S. sovereign debt coincided with the Public Credit Act.[14]

It took another year after the passage of the Public Credit Act for Congress to take up the issue of refinancing the debt. Initially proposed by new Treasury Secretary George Boutwell in December 1869, the act passed on July 14, 1870. The act authorized the Secretary of the Treasury to issue $500 million in ten-year bonds at 5 percent, $300 million in fifteen-year bonds at 4.5. percent, and $1 billion in thirty-year bonds at 4 percent. Discussion continued on some of the details, but the initial political battle was over. Nevertheless, partisan and geographic differences still remained, and U.S. debt in the postwar period acted as a legacy of the war—but could still be interpreted widely depending on your political allegiances.

But the Union had not been alone in the sales of debt instruments during the Civil War. The Confederacy had floated a series of bond issues during the war—many of which were subscribed to by members of the Confederacy not through payment in currency or specie, but in goods, most notably cotton. Additionally, the Confederacy could claim the distinction of being the only side in the Civil War to engineer a foreign loan through a financial institution. The £3 million ($15 million) Erlanger Loan, named after the Parisian banking house that floated the loan, found a ready class of investors, particularly in Britain. The cotton-hungry island had long associations with the U.S. South and many wealthier Britons had financial stakes in the success of the Confederacy—even before the issuance of bonds. British capitalists allegedly purchased the bonds in droves in the war while optimism reigned that the Confederacy would emerge victorious. The defeat of the Confederacy in 1865 left the fate of Confederate debt in limbo (at least in the minds of many Europeans). The United States had defaulted at the state level in the early 1840s with disastrous consequences—would they do so once more with debt on the part of a failed rebellion? Once more, British financiers and advocates for assumption of the debt merely had to point to the actions undertaken by Secretary of the Treasury Alexander Hamilton to absorb state debt following the Revolutionary War as an example of past precedent.

In December 1862, Thomas Haines Dudley, the U.S. consul in Liverpool, wrote to Secretary of State William Seward regarding the early vestiges of Confederate loans in Britain. "Referring to previous dispatch and the raising of money for the Rebels on Confederate bonds in England I have now to report that there is no doubt about the matter," Dudley solemnly reported. He added further, "from what I learn seven hundred thousand pounds sterling have been raised." "Perhaps," Dudley concluded ominously, "the worst feature about it [the bond issue] is that ev-

A $500 8 percent Confederate bond issued February 20, 1863. Per the bond issue, the holder of said bond would receive $500 principal and outstanding interest on July 1, 1868. (Image courtesy of Tennessee State Library and Archives, Nashville)

ery man who holds a bond has an interest in the success of the Confederacy. It is just that much stock invested in the concern, if it succeeds the bonds are good, if it fails they are worthless, that is the war, they will regard it and will use all their means and efforts to secure its success." By December 1862, Dudley was able to confirm that a £3 million bond issue (separate from the Erlanger Loan) had been successful in raising funds for the Confederacy. Nevertheless, Dudley worked tirelessly with a group of informants (many of them police officers) as well as U.S. ambassador to Brussels Henry Sanford to undercut Confederate financial efforts in England. Dudley brought this information to the British government in an effort to quash the construction of ships for the Confederate cause. Thus, while Union bonds did not flourish in Liverpool, the market remained vital to understanding British markets writ large.[15]

Even before the war ended, the northern press bemoaned how easily the British had gotten off. One *New York Times* article from late April 1865 revealed just one element of the disdain shared by many in the North for the financial support (perceived or otherwise) the Confederacy had received from Great Britain during the war. Such beliefs were amplified in December 1865, when a list of British subscribers to the Confederate cotton loan became public. It fell under the verbose and provocative title, "THE REBEL LOAN.; A More Complete List of British Subscribers. Who Got Their Interest and Who Did Not. Probable Misuse of Respectable Names. The Subterfuge of the Proprietors of the London Times. Some Account of Some of the Subscribers. Newspaper Writers and Their Situations in the Loan." Warning that the names could not be entirely verified, the list nevertheless identified individuals who contributed some £800,000 worth of capital toward the Confederate cause, although the article noted that interest had not been paid since November 1864, and even then to only a portion of the subscribers. Notable names on the list included "J. V. Craford" [*sic*], the British consul to Cuba; "J. Rutter," the British consul to Uruguay; Lieutenant Colonel Arthur Freemantle (a British military observer subsequently made famous by the movie *Gettysburg*, 1993); William Gladstone (British Chancellor of the Exchequer at the time); and several members of the British Parliament. While some individuals denied the claims in the *Times*, it nevertheless reinforced a perception of and animosity toward the British in the war's aftermath.[16]

But it was not until the Gilded Age that British financiers began to advocate in earnest for honoring the Confederate debt. In the early 1880s, a slew of articles emerged regarding British interest in the repayment of Confederate war debt. In May 1881, a committee organized in London and consisting of Confederate bondholders discussed among other items how the bonds should be honored and paid out by the federal government. "G. Lindo," the secretary of the committee, denied on numerous occasions that the committee was making any kind of threats. Such claims, however, seemed disingenuous because in the very next paragraph Lindo made such bold declarations as, "the time has come when the restriction imposed by the 14th Amendment should be removed, so far as it prohibits the Southern States . . . from effecting a just and equitable settlement of the debts legally contracted by them." Lindo further added, "the committee are sanguine that the day will come when America will listen to the voice of justice and will recognize, or at least will permit the recognition of, obligations entered into in good faith on both sides, and still undischarged." Numerous editorials appeared in British newspapers stressing the importance to America of honoring this debt. A letter to the editor of the *Manchester (U.K.) Guardian* proclaimed, "whatever may be the present effect upon the mind of the American nation of the various statements issued affecting the value of the Confederate Debt, the Committee are sanguine that the day will come when America will listen to the voice of justice, and will recognize, or at least will permit the recognition of, obligations entered into in good faith on both sides, and still undischarged."[17]

Yet for all the bravado regarding moral and legal obligations on the part of the federal government, others viewed such actions as greed and manipulation on the part of European bankers. The 1883 article "The Confederate Bonds Game in Europe" offered a more subversive set of intentions on the part of these European bankers. In the article, an American gentleman "well acquainted with the views of London, German, Dutch and Paris bankers" laid out the nineteenth-century equivalent of "pump and dump schemes" to inflate Confederate debt. The bankers (according to this American gentleman) formed "committees" in an attempt to raise awareness of the debt and artificially inflate the prices by some speculators and wishful thinkers. These bankers would eliminate their personal investments in the Confederacy only when it became apparent that it would never be honored and its value began to slip. This approach of buying low, inflating the price, and selling high netted a tidy profit.[18]

Nevertheless, the Confederate debt debate of the 1880s reached a fever pitch in 1886, when members of Congress entrusted a former New York Supreme Court justice, William Fullerton, to submit to the House Committee on War Claims a ruling as to whether or not the Confederate debt should be honored. Fullerton denounced the act of secession and war, but he indicated that the United States had no legal authority to nullify these Confederate debts—being a third party to the agreement itself. Therefore, the U.S. government was under no obligation to repay the debts; instead, the former Confederate states had that burden. Such a public statement (the judge acknowledged he was "advocating an unpopular measure") further stoked the fire of British calls for repayment.

The fact remained that Britain still represented one of the world's largest economies by the latter part of the nineteenth century. The threat of British banks withholding capital investment until the debt had been honored still remained a valid threat and real fear—especially for certain cash strapped southern states. While the United States was gaining greater strength on the world stage and would soon call itself the world's creditor, those developments remained on the horizon.[19]

Despite Fullerton's opinion, there remained a great reluctance to pay the debt off among those in the North and South alike. Increasingly, newspapers published items that not only chastised the actions of the British but noted the unified opposition of both northerners and southerners. As one article in the *San Francisco Chronicle* noted,

> There is an impression among the English holders of Confederate bonds that these bonds will be paid at least in part. That such an impression prevails may seem to Americans even more ridiculous than it did twenty five years ago. . . . Many times since the war has ended the North laughed over these bonds and their English owners. Of late years may be, the South has laughed over these same bonds. . . . North and South laughed, after a manner of the two sections, over this transaction and much was said in private and public of the ignorance among Englishmen of American institutions, and of their utter idiocy in supposing that the Confederate bonds were valuable except as waste paper.[20]

Even as late as 1900, a newspaper in Alabama was marveling over the ill-conceived beliefs of British bankers when it came to honoring southern debt: "It is surprising that there are still in England many persons who still cherish the delusion that the bonds of the Southern Confederacy will be paid. These exceedingly credulous mortals are not all cranks." Yet calls for honoring the debt continued into the twentieth century. They ranged from Canadian journalists to members of the British House of Commons. The British only amplified the rhetoric of redemption as calls emerged following World War I and the question of debts owed the United States that were associated with that war. Questions ranged over the repayment of war debts to the United States. More than one British member of Parliament called for the outstanding Confederate debt to be subtracted from the balance of the British debt to U.S. creditors. In 1926, Chancellor of the Exchequer and future British prime minister Winston Churchill echoed the sentiments of earlier members of Parliament, who called on Britain to withhold certain debt repayments tied to World War I from American creditors until they had begun repayment on debt tied to the Confederacy and even delinquent state debts from the 1830s. Yet the United States (buoyed by its new position as the world's creditor) held firm and refused to honor this Confederate debt. The Confederate bonds made their way into the vaults of London banks and attics of homes in the U.S. South and can now be found for sale online today for a fraction of their face value.[21]

The debt incurred by the sale of Civil War bonds represented the hundreds of thousands of simple transactions that funded the Union war effort. The billions of dollars in debt accumulated by both North and South proved an issue of great consequence in the postwar period. Civil War debt served as a new class of consumption for a nation of burgeoning consumers. Building on the tactics of the Jacksonian era with traveling salesmen, elaborate use of the press, and a patriotic flair (with a dash of self-interest), bond salesmen crisscrossed the nation. Jay Cooke's nation of agents sold the Union to the people writ large, and in the Reconstruction era this class of consumers drove the debt debate in Congress. While northern debt became one of the most contested political battles during the early days of Reconstruction, Confederate debt proved the opposite. The repudiation of Confederate debt reflected a newfound confidence on the part of the U.S. financial sector and previewed a creditor nation that would soon eclipse the powerful British, portending a new era of financial capitalism.

NOTES

1. Graham Heathcote, "Confederate Bonds Found in London," *Palm Beach (Fla.) Post*, November 19, 1987, 13D; see also Graham Heathcote, "U.S. Civil War Bonds Found in London Vault," Associated Press, October 31, 1987, https://apnews.com/3c5450f9f7df619bba1722be2dc3acee, accessed August 2, 2020.

2. Nicholas Osborne, "Little Capitalists: The Social Economy of Saving in the United States, 1816–1914" (PhD diss., Columbia University, 2014), 11.

3. Such a concept was also posited by Jay Sexton; see his "International Finance in the Civil War Era," in *The Transnational Significance of the American Civil War*, ed. Jörg Nagler, Don H. Doyle, and Marcus Gräser (London: Palgrave Mc-Millian, 2016), 91–106.

4. *Annual Report of the Secretary of the Treasury on the State of the Finances, Statistical Appendix, 1980* (Washington, D.C.: Government Printing Office, 1980), 61; *Annual Report of the Secretary of the Treasury on the State of the Finances, 1867* (Washington, D.C.: Government Printing Office, 1868), iii–iv; *Annual Report of the Secretary of the Treasury on the State of the Finances, 1865* (Washington, D.C.: Government Printing Office, 1865), 50–55. Franklin Noll, "Repudiation! The Crisis of United States Civil War Debt, 1865–1870," unpublished paper for the Graduate

Institute of International and Development Studies, Geneva, Switzerland, conference entitled "Government Debt Crises: Politics, Economics, and History," 2–3. I am deeply indebted to Franklin Noll for sharing this paper with me.

5. Samuel Wilkeson, *How Our National Debt May Be a National Blessing: The Debt Is Public Wealth, Political Union, Protection of Industry, Secure Basis for National Currency, the Orphans' and Widows' Savings Fund* (Philadelphia: McLaughlin Brothers, 1865), 1.

6. *Commercial and Financial Chronicle*, August 19, 1865, 226; Wilkeson, *How Our National Debt May Be a National Blessing*, 5–6.

7. Wendy A. Woloson, "The Rise of Consumer Culture in the Age of Jackson," in *A Companion to the Era of Andrew Jackson*, ed. Sean Patrick Adams (Chichester, U.K.: Wiley-Blackwell, 2013), 489–508, quote on 490.

8. "Conversion of the National Debt into Capital," *Lippincott's Monthly Magazine* 1 (June 1868): 641, 639, quoted in Robert Patterson, *Federal Debt-Management Policies: 1865–1879* (Durham, N.C.: Duke University Press, 1954), 57.

9. Eric Foner, *Reconstruction: America's Unfinished Revolution 1863–1877* (New York: HarperCollins, 2002), 311.

10. Joseph B. James, *The Framing of the Fourteenth Amendment* (Urbana: University of Illinois Press, 1965), 24, quoted in Noll, "Repudiation!," 11.

11. Howard K. Beale, *The Critical Year: A Study of Andrew Johnson and Reconstruction* (New York: Harcourt, Brace, 1930), 333; *Cong. Globe*, 39th Cong., 1st Sess. (1865), 701, quoted in Noll, "Repudiation!,, 13–14.

12. James, *Framing of the Fourteenth Amendment*, quoted in Noll, "Repudiation!," 15. The "7:30" bond issue was the single largest of the war—a 7.3 percent treasury note. This particular issue numbered $800 million.

13. Nicolas Barreyre, *Gold and Freedom: The Political Economy of Reconstruction*, transl. Arthur Goldhammer (Charlottesville: University of Virginia Press, 2015), 54n42. Ultimately, the national debt would never be eliminated again as it had during the presidency of Andrew Jackson and would never drop below $900 million. Barreyre, *Gold and Freedom*, 55.

14. Edward McPherson, *The Political History of the United States of America during the Period of Reconstruction*, 2nd ed. (Washington, D.C.: Solomons & Chapman, 1875), 386–88; Noll, "Repudiation!," 18–20.

15. Thomas Haines Dudley to William Seward, December 5, 1862, Thomas Haines Dudley Papers, Huntington Library, San Marino, California; Dudley to W. Seward, December 8, 1862, Dudley Papers. Examples of Dudley's work with informants to flood the British government with information regarding the Confederate outfitting of ships can be seen in Dudley to W. Seward, July 25, December 2, December 5, and December 8, 1862, Dudley Papers. Concerns also arose in Europe regarding the prospect of counterfeiting of bonds, bills, and treasury notes that would take shape and make its way across the ocean to the United States. Dudley to Seward, October 4, 1862, Dudley Papers; John Bigelow to

Salmon Chase, February 17, 1862, Salmon P. Chase Papers, Historical Society of Pennsylvania, Philadelphia.

16. "THE REBEL LOAN; A More Complete List of British Subscribers. Who Got Their Interest and Who Did Not. Probable Misuse of Respectable Names. The Subterfuge of the Proprietors of the London Times. Some Account of Some of the Subscribers. Newspaper Writers and Their Situations in the Loan," *New York Times*, December 9, 1865, 1.

17. "The Confederate Debt," *Bristol (U.K.) Mercury and Daily Post, Western Countries and South Wales Advertiser*, December 1, 1881, 2; "The Confederate Debt," *Manchester (U.K.) Guardian*, November 30, 1881, 7.

18. "The Confederate Bonds Game in Europe," *Vermont Phoenix and Record and Farmer* (Brattleboro), August 10, 1883.

19. "Confederate Debt: Judge Fullerton Says the United States Should Acknowledge the Liability," *Boston Globe*, June 26, 1886, 8.

20. James Gordon Bennett, "Confederate Bonds: Will the British Get Their Payment? A Clever Scheme of Rich Bankers. No Coin for American Projects Till an Installment Is Paid on the Bonds," *San Francisco Chronicle*, October 4, 1889.

21. "Confederate Bonds," *Citizens Journal* (Troy, Ala.), September 15, 1900.

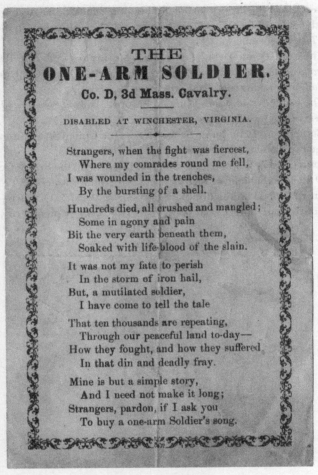

THE
ONE-ARM SOLDIER.

Co. D, 3d Mass. Cavalry.

DISABLED AT WINCHESTER, VIRGINIA.

Strangers, when the fight was fiercest,
  Where my comrades round me fell,
I was wounded in the trenches,
  By the bursting of a shell.

Hundreds died, all crushed and mangled;
  Some in agony and pain
Bit the very earth beneath them,
  Soaked with life-blood of the slain.

It was not my fate to perish
  In the storm of iron hail,
But, a mutilated soldier,
  I have come to tell the tale

That ten thousands are repeating,
  Through our peaceful land to-day—
How they fought, and how they suffered,
  In that din and deadly fray.

Mine is but a simple story,
  And I need not make it long;
Strangers, pardon, if I ask you
  To buy a one-arm Soldier's song.

"The One-Arm Soldier" describes the maiming of a Massachusetts cavalryman at Winchester, and his struggle to not only make ends meet after the war but also to tell his "simple story" so others could understand the costs of war. The last line implored readers "to buy a one-arm Soldier's song." ("The One-Arm Soldier, Co. D, 3d Mass. Cavalry, Disabled at Winchester, Virginia" [Massachusetts?, ca. 1865], American Broadsides and Ephemera, series 1, no. 1456, Harvard Medical Library, Cambridge, Massachusetts)

SECTION THREE

Coming to Tell the Tale
Imagining the War

Soldiers were among the first entrepreneurs to try to make money from the war. "The One-Arm Soldier" was one such effort; the unnamed Massachusetts trooper clearly hoped that friends, neighbors, and family members would help him adapt to his life as a disabled veteran by buying copies of the poem. The same poem was published in at least four other, slightly different versions that changed the battles and the men's wounds, altered a few words, or in one case added a stanza: "The One Armed Boy, Wounded at Petersburg, Va.," "The One-Armed Soldier, William Harrington, . . . Wounded at Ken[n]esaw Mountain, Georgia," "The One Arm and one Leg Soldier, Wounded at the Battle of Shiloh," and "Disabled at Petersburg, the One-Legged Soldier."

Although not without controversy—many Americans were uncomfortable with former soldiers using their wounds to elicit sympathy and charity—the poem acknowledged that no one who had not served could imagine the violence of war. Nor could they imagine the demands war made on soldiers' honor, patriotism, and perseverance. The war tore bodies apart, inflicted psychological wounds, and challenged precious moral assumptions. As Caroline Janney points out in the essay that closes this section, the grievously wounded lecturer and pamphleteer John Chase used his own body as a living text to help others "imagine" the horrors of war.[1]

The essays in this section examine ways in which images of war entered forms of entertainment popular among middle-class Americans. Barbara A. Gannon shows how the stereoviews of graphic war images were marketed during and just after the war, fell out of favor, and returned as two-dimensional images in the mammoth *Photographic History of the Civil War*. Children and youth were also targeted by toy makers and publishers. Margaret Fairgrieve Milanick tells the story of the Myriopticon, a miniature version of the popular panoramas that had shown war "news" throughout the Union and Confederacy during the war. Transforming these familiar images into a parlor game, the Myriopticon sold a particular vision of the war to northern families. Oliver Optic, the pro-

lific writer and editor of juvenile novels and magazines, is at the center of
Paul Ringel's essay, which shows the ebb and flow of the popular trilogies
that he wrote about teenagers fighting in the war. James Marten's essay
turns to Civil War speakers on the Gilded Age lecture circuit, demonstrat-
ing how this familiar form of entertainment not only imparted knowledge, but also offered comforting images and memories for audiences a
generation after the war ended. Finally, cycloramas—the massive, circular paintings of key battles—were, according to Caroline E. Janney, staged
as money-making efforts that nevertheless inspired different meanings
among the audiences who paid to see them.

NOTES

1. J. F. Chase, *John F. Chase, member of the 5th Main Battery and 3d Regiment* . . .
(Augusta, Maine: J. F. Chase, ca. 1886).

Marketing the Dead

The Civil War in 3-D and 2-D

BARBARA A. GANNON

Oliver Wendell Holmes Sr. traveled to Antietam right after the battle, looking for his wounded son. There he witnessed the horrific aftermath of the bloodiest one-day battle in U.S. history. Not long after, he examined Alexander Gardner's photographs of the battle's aftermath. "The photographs bear witness to the accuracy of some of our own sketches," he wrote in a July 1863 article for the *Atlantic Monthly*. "The 'ditch' is . . . still encumbered with the dead, and strewed, as we saw it and the neighboring fields with fragments and tatters. The 'colonel's [dead] gray horse' is given in another picture just as we saw him lying." Holmes understood the value of these photographs. "It was so nearly like visiting the battlefield to look over these views that all emotions excited by the actual sight the stained and sordid scene, strewed with rags and wrecks, came back to us, and we buried them in the recesses of our cabinet as we would have buried the mutilated remains of the dead they too vividly represented." Holmes emphasized that these views gave "some conception of what a repulsive brutal sickening hideous thing it is this dashing together of two frantic mobs to which we give the name of armies." For the first time, Americans far from the battlefield were exposed to the war's horrors.[1]

Civil War–era photography made it possible for civilians to witness the horrors of war. Union photographers often recorded the aftermaths of battles on stereographs, known more commonly as stereoviews, a format featuring two pictures on one card that presented a three-dimensional (3-D) image when placed in a stereoscope, better known as a stereo viewer. Ironically, Oliver Wendell Holmes Sr. created the inexpensive stereo viewer that allowed civilians to see the battlefield and its casualties.

Indeed, most contemporaries who saw the photos viewed them in this way. Yet today, most Americans remember these gruesome photographs as two-dimensional (2-D) photographs.[2]

Because stereoviews represented one of the most popular types of photography in the nineteenth and early twentieth centuries, it is surprising that the 3-D version of the Antietam dead and other scenes capturing America's bloodiest battle seem forgotten now. According to art historian Emily Godbey, the 3-D camera was "the primary battlefield tool, not the bulkier plate camera" that produced 2-D photographs. As a result, most of Gardner's photographs, including those of the dead, were 3-D. Gardner took sixty-three photographs of the battle's immediate aftermath; eight were 2-D photographs, while the rest were 3-D stereoviews. The images of dead soldiers were all stereoviews. Godbey explains that the 3-D Civil War photographs were converted to 2-D pictures in the twentieth century. As a result, Americans forgot "a critical element of Civil War photography as it was practiced at Antietam and Gettysburg, as contemporary audiences experienced it: the predominance of stereographic images." Indeed, stereoviews dominated photographic entertainment throughout the era. One historian has estimated that between 1858 and 1920, American photographers created up to 5 million different views. While the numbers of copies sold from these negatives remains unknown, it is likely in the hundreds of millions. Despite Americans' embrace of 3-D stereoviews as their preferred form of consuming visual imagery, photographs originally in 3-D were reproduced as 2-D. This essay addresses questions related to the consumption and marketing of these historic images to identify why the 3-D Civil War images transitioned to 2-D despite stereoviews' enormous popularity.[3]

Ironically, it was the success of the stereoviews and viewers—the first mass-marketed home-entertainment system—that explains the Civil War's transformation into a 2-D war. From 1890 until about 1920, large-scale commercial entities produced stereoviews for the home. Stereoview purveyors marketed exotic overseas photographs and unique domestic scenes as a refined and educational pastime for the middle class. Stereoviews also provided less-refined entertainment for the home parlor, including domestic comedies of love and marriage. Civil War photographs neither uplifted, educated, nor entertained, and as a result they remained outside the mainstream stereoview market. Instead, groups of Union veterans and their families and friends viewed war images in theaters or churches to raise funds for their organizations. Moreover, Civil War stereoviews chronicled the Federal war and not the Confederate effort, which narrowed their potential market. By the time of the war's fiftieth anniversary, the reuniting of the nation created a market for a photographic record that included Confederate images. As a result, *The Photographic History of the Civil War in Ten Volumes*, first published in 1911, reconciled the war's legacy by converting the 3-D Union war into a 2-D homage to both sides that became the authoritative visual record of the war.

Scholars have examined the 3-D Civil War before it was compressed into a 2-D history. Emily Godbey contends that Civil War stereoviews' "horrific subject matter . . . at once commanded attention and repulsed viewers"; however, "the novelty of the three-dimensional image created something akin to mediation, which provided a sort of buffer against the true horror of the images presented in this manner." Other scholars examined stereoviews as part of a gendered analysis of nineteenth-century U.S. life. In *Women's Views: The Narrative Stereograph in Nineteenth-Century America*, Melody Davis emphasizes the gendered components of 3-D stereographic photographs by focusing on the fictional comic narratives of family and domestic life so popular in this era. Davis contends that a "woman at home was the primary customer." As a result, "publishers issued titles that would appeal to her tastes, so that feminine culture and sensibility governed the market for narrative views." Consumption related to domesticity also had an international dimension. In *Consumers' Imperium: The Global Production of American Domesticity 1865–1920*, Kristin L. Hoganson identified elite white women's consumption of imported goods to assert their cosmopolitanism. Middle-class women may have settled for a less-expensive library of stereoviews showcasing exotic overseas locations to suggest that they shared this sophisticated world view.[4]

The photographic revolution that led to stereoviews, of actual as well as fictional scenes, began in the decades before the Civil War. In 1859, Oliver Wendell Holmes Sr. described in an enormously influential essay the technical transformation that allowed men and women to capture and hold visual impressions. After examining the development of photography, he described the importance of the newer 3-D medium—assuming that stereoviews would eventually be universally available. "The time will come when a man who wishes to see any object, natural or artificial, will go to the Imperial, National, or City Stereographic Library and call for [it] . . . as he would for a book at any common library." Critical to the story of Civil War prints, libraries never became the main distribution point for stereoviews. Instead, 3-D photographs became an entirely new line of profitable pop-culture products. Holmes facilitated this for-profit market by designing an inexpensive stereoscopic viewer. He eschewed profit himself by refusing to patent this apparatus. When almost every middle-class home had a viewer, each family could own a personal library of stereoviews. As a result, producing and selling stereoviews became a profitable commercial enterprise.[5]

After Fort Sumter, photographers leveraged this new technology to capture images of the first widely photographed war. Mathew Brady, a photographer based in Washington, D.C., at the time, gets much of the credit for this visual record, although his most important contributions were to finance and organize other professional photographers' work. Initially, these men captured routine military scenes, including camp life. When war came to battlefields in Maryland and Pennsylvania, locations much more accessible to Brady's photographers than those farther south, Alexander Gardner responded with his 3-D camera. He was the first photographer to capture dead American soldiers on film and the last to have their efforts distributed with no restrictions. The public shock at such grim visages of dead American soldiers made both the government and the media reluctant to publicize war's gruesome reality, making such wartime images rare until at least the 1960s. Since Gardner took these pictures for Brady's studio, it was Brady who shared them with the public. In the decades after the war, people reproduced these images from Brady's negatives.[6]

Initially, Americans did not see the dead in either 2-D or 3-D photographs. Because technology had not advanced enough to print photographs in newspapers, *Harper's Weekly* reproduced woodcuts of Gardner's work in October 1862. But in that same month, photographs of the wages of war became available when Brady exhibited Antietam stereoviews in his New York gallery. The public responded enthusiastically: "Crowds of people are constantly going up the stairs; follow them, and you find them bending over photographic views of that fearful battlefield, taken immediately after the action," reported a *New York Times* reviewer. "You will see hushed, reveren[t] groups standing around these weird copies of carnage, bending down to look in the pale faces of the dead, chained by the strange spell that dwells in dead men's eyes." Exhibit visitors were stooped over because they viewed these 3-D images in a special box stereo viewer. The images provided little mediation of the war's horror. "It seems somewhat singular that the same sun that looked down on the faces of the slain, blistering them, blotting out from the bodies all semblance to humanity, and hastening corruption, should have thus caught their features upon canvas, and given them perpetuity for-

The "Sunken Road" at Antietam, 1862, stereograph by Alexander Gardner. (Library of Congress Prints and Photographs Division Civil War Photograph Collection)

ever." The effect of the 3-D Civil War was clear. "Mr. Brady has done something to bring home to us the terrible reality and earnestness of the war. If he has not brought bodies and laid them in our door-yards and along streets, he has done something very like it."[7]

During the war, Americans flocked to similar exhibits. In New York, someone placed an ad for a display of "MAGNIFICENT STEREOVIEWS including thrilling war tableaus" to raise money for a "National Home for Invalid Soldiers." The war was not the sole attraction. The exhibit also included "beautiful scenes in Architecture, Statuary, and Landscape." The Oddfellows, a fraternal organization, raised money by charging twenty-five cents for adults and fifteen cents for children to see the "GREAT STEREOSCOPIC EXHIBITION of the AMERICAN CIVIL WAR." They also advertised views of statuary, buildings, and portraits, among other things, suggesting that they viewed the Civil War scenes as part of a broader market for stereoviews. The Oddfellows and the patrons of the National Home may have answered the classified ad that offered "stereoscopic views of the war, suitable for a hall, tent, or open exhibitions."[8]

Northerners who could not attend these displays wanted to see the battle's aftermath. In response, Brady established a partnership with E. and H. T. Anthony Company (A&A), the first large-scale producer of stereographic views in the United States. Gardner, who broke with Brady and began his own business in late 1862, also collaborated with this company,

which had been in business for about three years. In 1859, the same year
that Holmes published his *Atlantic Monthly* essay, A&A had sold its first
series of stereographic views capturing New York scenes. In addition to
domestic scenes, it also sold photographs of exotic overseas locations.
These prints became the staple of the stereoview market and provided
a type of virtual tourism for consumers. Once war came, A&A advertised
"War Scenes" and other types of photographs, including "foreign cities
and landscapes" in newspapers across the loyal states. Based on the ads'
wording and format, the company considered war scenes one type of stereoview marketed alongside their other views.[9]

After the Civil War, A&A reproduced the Brady negatives and promoted a series of over 1,200 stereographic views titled the "War for the
Union." Once again, the company advertised Civil War views alongside its
other products. Between 1865 and 1868, it promoted these views in newspapers across the states that had remained loyal to the Union, including
Ohio, Wisconsin, Pennsylvania, Vermont, Iowa, Minnesota, Indiana, and
Kansas. But A&A even placed ads in South Carolina. Yet by 1869, the
company no longer marketed and sold the "War for the Union" series.[10]

The war's twenty-fifth anniversary prompted a renewed interest in wartime stereographic views. By this time, Taylor and Huntington of Hartford, Connecticut, had obtained the Brady negatives and wanted to take
advantage of middle-aged veterans' nostalgia for their short military
careers. John C. Taylor, a member of the Grand Army of the Republic
(GAR)—the Union army's largest veterans' organization—bought seven
thousand war-related stereoviews from A&A and sold them under his
company's name. According to its catalog, the "War for the Union" consisted of "*ORIGINAL PHOTOGRAPHS* taken during the War of the Rebellion." The catalog copy explained the importance of this series: "A quar-
ter of a century has passed away since the sun painted these real scenes
of that great war. . . . Of course no more 'negatives' can be made as the
scenes represented by this series of war views have passed away forever."
The company targeted Civil War veterans and highlighted Taylor's status
as a veteran himself: "These views vividly renew the memories of our war
days. The camp, the march, the battlefields, the forts and trenches, the
wounded, the prisoners, the dead, [and] the hurriedly made grave."[11]

Although rare, a few images portrayed African Americans. The catalog
offered an image of "A Slave Pen, Alexandria, Virginia." The image suggested that time might have erased the memory of slavery: "People of this
generation can hardly make it seem possible that such an 'institution' was
ever tolerated under the stars and stripes, in this 'land of the free.'" Yet

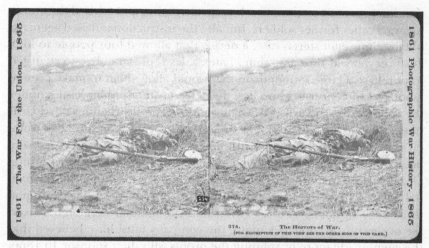

"The Horrors of War," stereograph by Alexander Gardner, Gettysburg 1863. (Library of Congress Prints and Photographs Division, Civil War Photograph Collection)

the images on offer did not present African Americans with respect or in a particularly positive light. Another picture was of "a Group of Contrabands . . . happy and thankful to remain under the protection of 'Massa Linkums soldiers.'" The collection even included a photograph of an African American soldier's body hanging from a scaffold after having been accused of rape.[12]

The Taylor and Huntington series also featured Gardner's photographs of other Union soldiers whose lives ended during the war. Sometimes only their bones remained. In one picture, "the boot still hang[s] on the fleshless bones." In another, the caption identified "the skulls and skeleton remains of our unknown heroes." Some of the more grisly images captured the enemy dead. "A dead confederate [is shown] just as he fell. . . . His head is partly shot away and his brains are scattered about in the mud." The series also recorded the fates of some of the Union dead. In a stereoview titled the "Horrors of War," a Union soldier "killed by a shell at Gettysburg . . . can be seen with his arm torn off" and "completely disemboweled." After describing this individual's wretched death, the description asked the viewer to imagine this single body as part of "a battlefield covering nearly twenty-five square miles, and covered with thousands of dead, many of them mangled even worse than this one and you can have a faint idea of Gettysburg."[13]

Selling the dead in 3-D presented a marketing challenge; Taylor's solution was to recruit veterans as sales representatives and advised these men to target other former soldiers. Initially, the instructions advised agents to obtain a museum stereo case, a device that allowed four people to look at stereoviews at the same time. Later, sales representatives were urged to purchase a large stereopticon that would allow them to make presentations to audiences in churches, theaters, or other public venues under the sponsorship of Civil War organizations. The instructions cited GAR posts, their sons and daughter's organizations, and their affiliated women's auxiliary as their primary customers. Taylor provided sales representatives with specific guidance on cost and profit sharing for fund-raising. Organizations might prefer a fixed fee for the service; however, the manual advised that "the best and most satisfactory terms . . . are an equal division of the net receipts." Given that the manual suggested a fixed fee of seventy-five dollars a night, the company must have believed that the agent made more by splitting the profits with their sponsor. In 1890, seventy-five dollars represented a not inconsiderable profit for a charity benefit. While a valuable contribution to veterans' charitable efforts, the company's partnership with the GAR and its affiliates indicated that the men and women of the northern Civil War generation represented the target market for Civil War stereoviews. The real war remained a specialized business that did not survive this cohort.[14]

Just as the stereoview became a specialized market that targeted veterans, large companies mass-produced and marketed a wide variety of stereoviews to the public. Consumers could order directly out of catalogs, but door-to-door sales representatives made unsolicited calls at private households. By 1901, Underwood and Underwood dominated the market, producing twenty-five thousand stereoviews a day and three hundred thousand stereo viewers in a year. A well-trained sales force made their company successful. Underwood significantly modified Ebenezer Hannaford's *Success in Canvasing: A Manual of Practical Hints and Instructions, Specially Adapted for the Use of Book Canvassers of the Better Class* (1875) and published this tailored version for its sales force.[15]

Underwood's adaptation provided each sales representative with detailed instructions. Interestingly, the writer's first admonition was to read Holmes's *Atlantic Monthly* essay. The manual provided a dialogue, or "sample remarks," as part of a sales pitch. "As Dr. Holmes says, this is no *toy*, but rather a divine gift, which can thus bring us into the very presence of the most important people and the most interesting places the world over." Once the aspiring sale representative read Holmes, they should familiarize themselves with their products; the manual recommended that they study the "Tour of the Holy Land" series first. Most views depicted exotic locations like Japan, the Vatican, Sweden, Hawaii, and Russia; the only scene tangentially related to the Civil War was a cotton plantation in Georgia. But Underwood did not eschew conflict in general; it sold contemporary war views. The manual reported that the company had stereograph photographers "*at the front* with Lord Roberts in Bloemfontein, South Africa" in the Boer War and others documenting the insurgency in the Philippines.[16]

The manual emphasized both the quality of the goods and the people who bought them. As in newspaper advertisements, typographic and graphic elements were liberally deployed to highlight points of emphasis for prospective sellers. Salesmen were to "USE PROMINENT NAMES to influence" clients, with a sample dialogue showing them how. "'Dr. So and So liked that very much, He thought it was about the finest. . . . Or 'Mr. So and So was greatly pleased with these views.'" Such "*Local Personal* INFLUENCE of this kind is *impossible* for anyone to resist entirely." If a woman hesitated to make a purchase without her husband's permission, the manual advised the sales representative to use the names of neighbors who had already purchased sets to close the sale. "The ladies all around you, Mrs. Seaton, Mrs. McManus, Mrs. Jarvis, Mrs. Plain, and the lady right across the street here, Mrs. Calhoun, and a large number of others, are [buying] them WITHOUT consulting their husbands, and I am sure *your* husband will appreciate these very much and be pleased with your purchase." Clearly, failure to buy these views would cause one to fall behind neighbors who had purchased them. It is unlikely that pictures of the Civil War dead had the same appeal.[17]

In addition, Underwood sales representatives also sold domestic scenes, another popular topic. "Love Courtship and Marriage," also known as "Is Marriage a Failure," included "18 inimitable views . . . enjoyed heartily by the general public and may be relied upon to sell whenever it is shown." The peddler was advised to sell a larger set such as the "Trip Around the World" that included seventy-two stereoviews, because "these [domestic scenes] always succeed when all other sets fail to sell." Clearly, Civil War scenes might not have fit the typical clientele for the domestic and exotic scenes that dominated the market.[18]

Despite the efforts of door-to-door sales representatives, companies still sold stereoviews in the early twentieth century through newspapers. However, the advertisements in the *National Tribune*—the GAR's national paper—demonstrated that even the aging Civil War generation failed to see these images as suitable for home libraries. It was not that stereoviews were unpopular. Readers often wrote to the paper about how they appreciated the photographs. One GAR comrade wrote from Ohio that he was "well pleased" with his order, which included a stereo viewer and five sets of images, including the "Life of Christ." In fact, the *National Tribune* used stereo viewers and views to sell subscriptions. According to a frequently published ad, "the *National Tribune* has made arrangements with a large manufacturer of [stereo viewers] for such a very large supply [so] that we are enabled to sell them at the very lowest price." Indeed, "The price is so low" that the *Tribune* could offer its readers "a very handsome and serviceable" stereo viewer together with a year's subscription to the *National Tribune* for only $1.25. Although the *National Tribune*'s audience was predominantly male, the ad showed a woman using the stereoscope, suggesting that Davis correctly identified the gendered nature of this market. If someone owned a stereoscope and wanted new views, the Tribune offered a one-year subscription and one series of views for one dollar.[19]

Instead of offering Civil War views, *Tribune* officials advertised every other kind of stereoscopic view for sale or with a subscription. One could order the photographs of the "Wonders of the Old World." The comrade from Ohio who enjoyed "The Life of Christ" had received "25 Stereoscopic views of the life of Christ, the most realistic set of stereoscopic views ever produced" Including a "painting of Christ's last moment on Calvary." In addition to the usual tourist and religious offerings, customers could order entertainment views including the "Home Pet" that included "25 groups of children and pets." Those would did not like animals could sample "A New Series of Comics" featuring "25 new and mirth provoking comic scenes from life." Clearly, stereoviews foreshadowed the content of the modern-day Internet by offering animals, kids, and even humorous memes. Another ad offered a stereoscope and views for anyone who generated three new subscriptions to the *National Tribune*. The newspaper offered fifty "views from every civilized land." In this case, most photographs featured American and European cities and sites. If the GAR national newspaper, which reminded its readers of the Union war on every page, did not believe that Civil War views sold subscriptions, then we might surmise that no other businesses thought that there was a market for these photographs.[20]

As Civil War soldiers passed into history, the Civil War memory market changed. In 1911, at the beginning of the semicentennial, *The Photographic History of the Civil War in Ten Volumes* portrayed the war in almost 3,400 photographs with accompanying text. Still acknowledged by many as the standard photographic history of the war, it was reprinted

just before the centennial in 1958 and again in 1987. Unlike the ste-
reoview sets of an earlier generation, this was not simply a record of the
Union War; the compilers dedicated the series to "the men in Blue and
Gray whose valor and devotion have become the priceless heritage of a
united nation." In contrast, a half-century earlier, when Alexander Gardner described the Gettysburg dead in his *Photographic Sketchbook of the
War* (1866), he rejected any notion of equality between the combatants.
Confederates died in "frantic efforts to break the steady line of patriots,
whose heroism only excelled theirs in motive, [Confederates] paid with
life the price of their treason."[21]

The acknowledgments of *The Photographic History* explain the 1911
collection's dedication to the Blue and the Gray. The editor thanks former Confederate officers, the United Daughters of the Confederacy
(UDC), and other "owners of indispensable pictures who have so gen-
erously contributed them for this purpose." The editor's introduction
might have been written by the UDC—guardians of Confederate memory and its Lost Cause. The war demonstrated "how a devoted people
whose fathers had stood shoulder to shoulder for liberty in the American Revolution . . . parted at the dividing line of a great economic problem and stood arrayed against each other in the greatest fratricidal tragedy that the world has ever witnessed." Rather than an account of what
stereoviews presented as a "War for the Union," *The Photographic History*
provided an "undying record of valor of those who fought for independence from it—each according to his own interpretation of the Constitution that bound them into a great republic of states." If race mattered in
this retelling, it was the white or Anglo-Saxon race: "no Grecian phalanx
or Roman legion ever knew truer manhood than in those days on the
American continent when the Anglo-Saxon met the Anglo-Saxon." The
editor appealed to a universal brotherhood among the "Civilized world"
that did not include the uncivilized races. Ironically, less than four years
after the publication of *The Photographic History*, the "civilized" people of
the world began a war so horrific that Civil War photographs would come
to seem like quaint relics of a simpler time.[22]

A search of all ten volumes of *The Photographic History* identified only a
handful of references to slaves or slavery. Under a picture of "Contraban
[*sic*]," the writer explains that slaves who reached Union lines had been
treated as contraband of war. His explanation of their wartime usefulness
reflects the racial views of the day. While the writer knew "of no single instance on record in which false or misleading information was knowingly
given by the colored man" to Union authorities, "in a large number of

cases [it was] by no means trustworthy. The darkey had no capacity for accuracy of observation or for precision of statement." The author lists African American ineptitude under a picture of sloppily dressed former slaves. Only one picture of black soldiers is included in the main body of the work, but these "Colored convalescent troops" were neither fighting nor drilling. The editors found a place for fighting and drilling black soldiers in a final section titled "The Light Side." Five pictures of black soldiers illustrated the poem "Sambos Right to be Kilt," a satirical wartime poem by a white soldier applauding the enlistment of African American soldiers. The "faithful slave" receives equal billing. A photograph captures a number of well-dressed slaves. The text reassures the reader that these men and women "remained quietly at work on large plantations."[23]

Despite the decline in popularity of Civil War views, people did buy images of the Spanish-American, Philippine-American, and the Russo-Japanese wars. Yet none of these photographs captured the same gruesome images of the U.S. war dead. In twentieth-century wars, American soldiers' horrific sacrifices remained unseen because federal officials censored the media. No media outlet challenged this type of censorship. No independent photographers selected scenes to photograph, nor did they exhibit or mass-market images of dead U.S. soldiers. The evolution of the pictorial presentation of Civil War scenes may reflect more than the triumph of the lost cause or national reunion. A more urgent issue for a nation beginning a century when each generation fought its own war was to forget the gruesome reality of war. It is no coincidence that no one questioned the nation's seemingly endless wars until television brought the Vietnam War home live and in 2-D color to living rooms across the nation.[24]

NOTES

1. Oliver Wendell Holmes [Sr.], "My Hunt after the Captain," *Atlantic Monthly*, December 1862, https://www.theatlantic.com/magazine/archive/1862/12/my-hunt-after-the-captain/308750/, accessed July 26, 2019; "Doings of the Sunbeam," *Atlantic Monthly*, July 1863, 11–12, https://www.unz.com/print/AtlanticMonthly-1863jul-00001/, accessed August 21, 2020.

2. Bob Zeller, *The Blue and the Gray in Black and White: A History of Civil War Photography* (Westport, Conn.: Praeger, 2005), 23.

3. Emily Godbey, "'Terrible Fascination': Civil War Stereographs of the Dead," *History of Photography* 36, no. 3 (2012): 267; William A. Frassanito, *Antietam: The Photographic Legacy of America's Bloodiest Day* (New York: Charles Scribner's Sons, 1978), 53. Frassanito's study uses photographs and not stereoviews

to document Antietam images. In his description of each photograph, he lists the types of negatives Gardner produced for each image, either "stereo" for 3-D views or plate for 2-D photographs. Robert Wilson, *Mathew Brady: Portrait of a Nation* (New York: Bloomsbury, 2013), 134; William Culp Darrah, *Stereoviews: A History of Stereographs in America and Their Collection* (Gettysburg, Pa.: Time and News, 1964), 12.

4. Godbey, "'Terrible Fascination," 267, 268; Melody Davis, *Women's Views: The Narrative Stereograph in Nineteenth-Century America* (Durham: University of New Hampshire Press, 2015), 4; Kristin L. Hoganson, *Consumers' Imperium: The Global Production of American Domesticity, 1865–1920* (Chapel Hill: University of North Carolina Press, 2007).

5. Oliver Wendell Holmes [Sr.], "The Stereoscope and the Stereograph," *Atlantic*, June 1859, https://www.theatlantic.com/magazine/archive/1859/06 /the-stereoscope-and-the-stereograph/303361/, accessed July 2, 2019; "Gregory P. Garvey, "Exploring Perception, Cognition, and Neural Pathways of Stereo Vision and the Split-Brain Human-Computer Interface," in *Knowledge Visualization and Visual Literacy in Science Education*, ed. Anna Ursyn (Hershey, Pa.: IGI Global, 2016), 41–43.

6. Zeller, *Blue and the Gray*, 65–81.

7. Ibid., 80; "Scenes on the Battlefield of Antietam," *Harper's Weekly*, October 18, 1862, 664; "Brady's Photographs: Pictures of the Dead at Antietam," *New York Times*, October 30, 1862, https://www.nytimes.com/1862/10/20 /archives/bradys-photographs-pictures-of-the-dead-at-antietam.html, accessed March 10, 2019.

8. "St. Nicholas Hall," *New York Herald*, January 15, 1864, 7; "Odd Fellows Hall," *Washington D.C. Evening Star*, May 30, 1863; "For Sale-Stereoscopic Views," *Chicago Daily Tribune*, August 9, 1864.

9. T. K. Treadwell, *The Stereoscopic Views Issued by the Anthony Company* (np. : Institute of Photographic Research, 2002) https://stereoworld.org/wp-content/ uploads/2016/03/anthonybook-1.pdf, accessed August 22, 2020; "E. & H. T. Anthony Company," *Eaton (Ohio) Democratic Press*, November 17, 1864. One reason Gardner split with Brady was the latter's unwillingness to credit the photographers. When Gardner published his own collection of photographs, he credited the photographers. Alexander Gardner, *Gardner's Photographic Sketchbook of the War*, 2 vols. (Washington, D.C.: Philp & Solomons, 1866), https://www.loc .gov/pictures/item/01021785/, accessed June 7, 2020.

10. For the assessment of A&A after the war, I searched the Library of Congress's Chronicling America database, a collection of historical newspapers 1865–68 and 1869–73. In the latter period, there were no advertisements for wartime stereoviews. Between 1865 and 1868, I found extensive advertising. See Library of Congress, "Chronicling America: Historic American Newspapers," https://chroniclingamerica.loc.gov/, accessed July 26, 2019. For examples, see *Urbana (Ohio) Union*, December 26, 1866; *Mineral Point (Wisc.) Weekly Tribune*,

July 12, 1865; *Cambria Freeman* (Ebensburg, Pa.), July 18, 1867; *Lamoille News-dealer* (Hyde Park, Vt.), February 6, 1867; *Weekly New Oregon (Iowa) Plain Dealer*, March 1, 1867; *The St. Cloud (Minn.) Journal*, September 5, 1867; *Jasper (Ind.) Weekly Courier*, February 16, 1867; *Oskaloosa (Kans.) Independent*, July 22, 1865; *Newberry (S.C.) Herald*, November 7, 1866, 1.

11. *War Memories: Catalogue of Officials War Views*, War Photographic and Exhibition Company, Hartford, Conn., 1891, 1.

12. Ibid., 2, 3.

13. Ibid., 3, 4.

14. Ibid., 18–20, 24.

15. Robert Taft, *Photography and the American Scene* (New York: Dover, 1938), 502. Walter A. Friedman, *Birth of a Salesman: The Transformation of Selling in America* (Cambridge, Mass.: Harvard University Press, 2004), 34–55; *Manual of Instruction: To Be Studied and Followed by Our Agents* (New York: Underwood and Underwood, 1900), 1, 2; Ebenezer Hanaford, *Success in Canvasing: A Manual of Practical Hints and Instructions, Specially Adapted for the Use of Book Canvassers of the Better Class* (N.p.: Ebenezer Hannaford, 1875).

16. *Manual of Instruction*: 2, 3, 4, 5, 11–19, 39, original emphasis.

17. Ibid., 19, 21.

18. Ibid., 42.

19. "Scattering," *National Tribune* (Washington, D.C.), December 19, 1907, 8; "Stereoscope and View Offer," *National Tribune*, March 28, 1907, 8. See Library of Congress, "Chronicling America: Historic American Newspapers," https://chroniclingamerica.loc.gov/, accessed July 26, 2019. The same ad ran in the *Tribune* a number of times in 1907 and 1908.

20. "Stereoscope and View Offer," *National Tribune*, December 5, 1907, 6; "Seeing the World," *National Tribune*, October 4, 1906, 8.

21. Francis Trevelyan Miller, ed., *The Photographic History of the Civil War in Ten Volumes* (New York: Review of Reviews Co., 1911), vol. 1, dedication page; Allan Nevins, James I. Robertson Jr., and Bell I Wiley, eds., *Civil War Books: A Critical Bibliography* (Baton Rouge: Louisiana State University Press, 1969), 2:22; Gardner, *Gardner's Photographic Sketchbook of the War*, http://www.loc.gov/pictures/phpdata/pageturner.php?type=&agg=ppmsca&item=12834&turnType=byImage&seq=79, assessed June 7, 2020.

22. Miller, *Photographic History*, 1:14, 1:16, 1:18, 1:16, 1:18. Karen Cox, *Dixie's Daughters: The United Daughters of the Confederacy and the Preservation of Confederate Culture* (Gainesville: University Press of Florida, 2003).

23. Miller, *Photographic History*, , 9:180, 7:113, 9:173–80, 9:183; Zeller, *Blue and the Gray*, 191–92, 194. Although the poem "Sambo's Right to Be Kil't" is sometimes cited as a racist call for black troops, it was actually a satirical piece written by an officer who supported arming African Americans. See Barbara A. Gannon, *The Won Cause: Black and White Comradeship in the Grand Army of the Republic* (Chapel Hill: University of North Carolina), 117–118.

24. John Waldsmith, *Stereo Views: An Illustrated History and Price Guide* (Iola, Wisc.: Krause, 2002), 180; Alan Axelrod, *Selling the Great War: The Making of American Propaganda* (New York: St. Martin's Press, 2009); Michael Mandelbaum, "Vietnam: The Television War," *Daedalus* 111, no. 4 (1982): 157–69, http://www.jstor.org/stable/20024822, accessed August 15, 2019.

43. John Welshons, *Awakening from Grief: Finding the Road Back to Joy* (Little Falls, NJ: Open Heart, 2000); Alan D. Wolfelt, *Healing the Grief: The Martha's Vineyard Bereavement Companion* (New York: St. Martin's Press, 2009); Michael Bamberger, *Wandering Home* (New York: Penguin, 2011); and Thomas G. Long, "Gone from My Sight, 2009, 242.

Big Ideas in a Little Box

Nation Building in Milton Bradley's Myriopticon

MARGARET FAIRGRIEVE MILANICK

Milton Bradley and Company, a Massachusetts-based purveyor of family parlor games and portable games for soldiers, manufactured a miniature moving panorama titled *Myriopticon: A Historical Panorama of the Rebellion* in 1866. The Myriopticon consisted of a paper scroll of twenty-four chromolithographed scenes, all but one copied from illustrations on the pages of *Harper's Weekly,* and all housed in a decorated pasteboard box about five inches tall and eight inches wide. The product presumed an operator who turned a hand crank to advance each scene into position behind a proscenium cutout as a lecturer recited descriptions of the images and their significance. The scroll and the stage were accompanied by several accessories: a seven-page script, a sheet of admission tickets, and an advertising poster. The Myriopticon performances took place in the family parlor; the "Directions to the Proprietor of the Myriopticon" recommend drawing the parlor draperies to "increase the effect" of the show.

Milton Bradley and Company's Myriopticon recalled the Great Rebellion in wartime images and interpretations familiar to Union audiences. It repurposed those familiar historical scenes in order to curate a particular narrative that replaced the idea of sectionalism, which characterized the nation in the years leading up to and during the Civil War, with the idea of a unified nation resting firmly on the foundations of the North's economic power. Further, its domestic performance replicated the gendered division of labor and values of middle-class respectability and deportment required for the maintenance of that economic system. For one, the narrative rendered women invisible; only two scenes included women, placed in the margins in supporting roles. Men, on the other

hand, took active part in all the scenes. The Myriopticon worked alongside other middle-class media to define what the Union believed a unified U.S. society should be and how its young performers and viewers
could appropriately participate in it. It did so, moreover, in a clear sequence that established causality and indicated the preservation of the
union was ordained because of the righteousness of the Union cause and
the North's ability to fight a modern war. Ultimately, the ideological message produced by the game focused on the triumph of the North's economic power in industrial might, in resource wealth, and in institutional
organization. In addition, the images showed boys how they might play
multiple specialized roles in order to participate in the inevitable march
of progress as they came of age.

Milton Bradley and Company situated the Myriopticon within middle-
class social expectations and standards of deportment represented by
the "museum theater," the respectable, family-oriented theater first created in the 1840s and 1850s by P. T. Barnum in New York City and Mo-
ses Kimball in Boston to resemble the middle-class parlor, the epicenter
of respectable domesticity and cosmopolitanism.[1] The "Directions to the
Proprietor of the Myriopticon" that came with every game included instructions suggesting how to create a "museum theater" in your parlor.
The advertising poster provided tongue-in-cheek guidance for proper
behavior in this respectable theater: audience members were "to remain
seated till the close of the first scene," while "Gentlemen with bricks in
their hats will please deposit them at the Ticket Office for safe keeping." The proscenium cutout, complete with chromolithographed drapery decoration, provided a proper frame for every scene. The Myriopticon's success was highlighted in a letter sent by a satisfied customer,
B. R. Davis.[2] Davis described how every evening his family (he, his wife,
their five children, and his brother) gathered in the parlor to participate
in the Myriopticon performance. The family appointed him, as the authority figure of the typical American family of the period, as both hand-
crank operator and narrator. They created a theater in their parlor by
arranging the drapery and the lighting to focus attention on the proscenium and on him as the performer, and they invited the neighbors over
to watch the performance, too.

Placing the performance of a story about the Great Rebellion within
the family parlor during Reconstruction connected the Myriopticon with
an educational mission. Public opinion between the North and South
was very divided given that the cultural, political, and economic systems
of the South had been defined by slavery. Public opinion, however, was

also divided in the North. Milton Bradley and Company produced the Myriopticon in a northern political climate in which Republicans dominated both national and state politics, including significant majorities in both houses of Congress and in governor's mansions.[3] Still, in 1864 Lincoln won 91 percent of the electoral college but only 55 percent of the popular vote, highlighting strong Democratic opposition. These divisions led public figures to make public education a cornerstone of congressional Reconstruction.[4] Reconstruction would not be about rebuilding but would instead propagate the message that the southern states should adopt the industrial, capitalist American culture practiced in the North.

The Myriopticon fit well with the reeducation efforts of Reconstruction. The twenty-four scenes do not romanticize the story of the Great Rebellion with one victorious battle after another. The Myriopticon, for example, features several notable Union defeats, including Bull Run, the 1862 Peninsula Campaign, and the disastrous Battle of Fredericksburg. A majority of the images represent the equipment of war and the institutional organization necessary to prosecute a modern war. The Myriopticon curated a memory of the Great Rebellion that made visible the struggle involved and the resiliency required to put down the rebellion.

The Myriopticon's twenty-four moving scenes and script recorded what reasonably informed Union families already knew to be important subjects concerning the war. Americans had witnessed the war primarily through illustrated news magazines, and *Harper's Weekly*, produced by Harper and Brothers publishing house in New York City, was the premier illustrated news magazine in the country during the war. Given the wartime pressure from the U.S. public for current news, large, successful news outlets such as Harper and Brothers could afford to hire and embed their own artists in the military services to report and illustrate the war. All but the last image in the Myriopticon first appeared in *Harper's Weekly*.

The images in the Myriopticon were already familiar to middle-class families not only because they had already seen them in *Harper's Weekly*, but also because *Harper's Weekly* editorials interpreted the images. That periodical's illustrations, news, and editorials became central to shaping public opinion. The *North American Review*, in its April 1865 issue, called *Harper's Weekly* "the most powerful of the organs of public opinion." Citing its "vast circulation, deservedly secured and maintained by the excellence and variety of its illustrations of the scenes and events of the war," the literary journal concluded *Harper's Weekly* "has done its full part in the furtherance of the great cause of Union, of Freedom, and of Law."[5]

In addition to employing the powerful interaction of images and text, the Myriopticon relied on the prevailing wisdom of mid-nineteenth-century historical writing through its chronological organization of the scenes. Emma Willard introduced her soon-popular textbook, *History of the United States, or Republic of America: With a Chronological Table and a Series of Progressive Maps* (1864), by asserting that chronological order was the only way to ground "the mass of knowledge" in "objective" reality.[6] Facts and dates were considered to be of utmost importance. Indeed, the "Directions to the Proprietor of the Myriopticon" included with every Myriopticon game informed the performer that the script's "historical statements and dates are intended to be absolutely accurate." The battle scenes included in the game were placed in chronological order, and the seven-page script included dates and facts about the war. The scene sequence deviated from chronological order only at the end of the story, which was purposefully altered for dramatic effect to suggest that the demise of the Confederacy was ordained.

Although Milton Bradley and Company repurposed *Harper's Weekly* images, the Myriopticon show did not just recycle those images but also emphasized the same subject matter as very early histories of the war written by authors sympathetic to the Union. More than one-third of the images and all the events described in the Myriopticon later appeared in *Harper's Pictorial History of the Great Rebellion*, an illustrated narrative of the war published in two volumes by Harper and Brothers, the first volume in 1866 and the second volume in 1868. Well-known historian Benson J. Lossing stressed these same events in his *Pictorial History of the Civil War in the United States of America*, published in 1866. The attendant circumstances of war so prominent in the Myriopticon, such as the technology for communications, special forces and their specialized weapons, new naval ships and weaponry and newly developed institutions for the care of the wounded, are also illuminated in Lossing's history.

The blended visual and text format of the Myriopticon was familiar to families from the stereoscope cards that permeated the domestic setting of their parlors. Both Mathew Brady's and Alexander Gardner's studios produced photographs of the war that were displayed in galleries and widely distributed in popular stereograph card sets. Although today many Americans visualize the Civil War through surviving photographs, photography was not the primary source for the scenes in the Myriopticon. Of the twenty-four scenes, "Contrabands Coming into Camp" is the only event to have appeared also as a photograph (by David B. Woodbury and composed slightly differently).[7] The image in the Myriopticon, however, is a copy of the *Harper's Weekly* version of this event sketched by Al-

fred R. Waud, a full-time paid staff artist for *Harper's Weekly* embedded
with the Army of the Potomac. The image appeared in the January 31,
1863, issue.[8]

Whereas the Myriopticon's visual and text format, parlor viewing, and
some of the subject matter including the equipment of war was similar
to stereography, the style of the scenes employed in the game differed
dramatically. Photographs of the era could only capture static subjects
such as portraits, dead bodies, and the equipment of war after fighting.
Sketches, however, could capture movement. The scenes utilized in the
Myriopticon were active, placing the viewer in the "smoky sway of battle,"
as *Harper's Weekly* stated in its "Our Artists during the War" article.[9] The
Myriopticon scenes reproduced the action and movement of the sketches
made by artists in the many theaters of war. The Myriopticon advertising
poster that came with the game proclaimed that "this Panorama is copied
from the sketches of our most celebrated artists, taken from nature, on
the spot, as soon after the events therein depicted transpired as was con-
sistent with their personal safety."

What also set the Myriopticon apart was that the illustrations not only
depicted motion, they were set in motion by the operator of the hand
crank. In this way, Milton Bradley and Company connected the Myriopticon to the full-scale moving panoramas that first became popular in
the United States in the 1840s and 1850s (as discussed in Janney's essay). The company's *1871–72 Work and Play Annual of Home Amusements
and Social Sports* included an advertisement for the Myriopticon designed
to stir parents' memories of the very popular Mississippi River panoramas of their childhoods. The Myriopticon, by association, became the
perfect domestic version of fond childhood memories. The broadside
included with the game was designed to recall one of the most famous,
Banvard's Mammoth Panorama of the Mississippi River. Like the Myriopticon, Banvard's panorama combined news and commentary to orient the
viewer while a presenter editorialized the facts through a script to make
the images comprehensible and meaningful for the viewer. Viewers were
also familiar with the many full-scale moving panoramas about the battles
of the Civil War, such as George W. Williams's *Great Painting of the WAR!
of 1861* produced in 1862 and Goodwin and Woodward's *Polyrama of the
War* from 1863.[10]

In imitation of full-scale moving panoramas, the Myriopticon's twenty-
four scenes were placed one after the other in the scroll. This linear format, chronologically configured and set in motion, gave rise to a narrative of time with a beginning, middle, and end that asserted causal-

ity, making the Union's win inevitable because of its superior economic power and resources, allowing it to lead a modern war effort.[11] As the political scientist and historian Benedict Anderson writes, history is created in "uptime" from the past to the present, and in retrospect with the understanding that a particular endpoint has already been determined.[12]

The story arc of the Myriopticon opened by showing how, in the beginning, the South aggressively started the war by rebelling against its own nation, and in doing so, brought total disaster on itself. The heart of the narrative made visible the Union's struggle but eventual triumph because of the righteousness of its cause and because of what its economic system enabled it to do. The ideological messages inherent in the Myriopticon narrative established war as a masculine arena; there was no place for women except to watch and serve from the sidelines. The game likewise emphasized the equipment of war in action and the role of the western theater in Union victory. Moreover, by including two scenes concerning the effects of war on African Americans, the Myriopticon highlighted the important role they played in the war and grappled with defining a nation that included black men.

In the first four opening scenes, the texts and images together juxtapose the Revolutionary Era with the rebellion to highlight the Confederacy's actions as treasonous. This is in no way a new interpretation; in fact, wartime Union newspapers promoted this as a dominant theme. In the first scene, the Myriopticon represents the heroism of Major Robert Anderson and his men in the face of South Carolinian treason. The Myriopticon script reminds viewers the ancestors of those very South Carolinians fought valiantly against the British during the Revolutionary War to form the United States of America, but now their treachery has made that nation vulnerable. Just how vulnerable was both shown in this scene and related in the script, as Major Anderson and his men were forced to flee Fort Moultrie to occupy Fort Sumter under cover of darkness on December 26, 1860. Viewers would have known that Anderson was "the hero of the hour" since contemporary newspaper accounts referred to him that way and gauged how successful his move was by reporting a rise in the stock market, a key indicator for the economic system of the North.[13]

The second scene establishes the Confederates as the aggressors in the Great Rebellion. It spans two proscenium widths in the Myriopticon, just as the original image from which it was copied in *Harper's Weekly* spans two pages in that magazine.[14] The scene visually echoes Lincoln's first inaugural address, on March 4, 1861, when he told the South: "In your hands,

Scene 2. The bombardment of Fort Sumter by rebels, April 12–13, 1861, Milton Bradley's Myriopticon. (Beinecke Rare Book and Manuscript Library, Yale University)

my dissatisfied fellow countrymen, and not in mine, is the momentous issue of civil war. The government will not assail you. You can have no conflict, without being yourselves the aggressors." The Myriopticon image presents the second day of the bombardment of Fort Sumter, April 13, 1861, which the script reminds viewers ignited not only the fort but also the war. Civil War histories of the time describe Fort Sumter as the Rock of Gibraltar, a metaphor for the monumental strength of the U.S. government.[15] The viewer is placed in the rebel batteries to clearly show southerners as the aggressor, firing on their own countrymen. Placed on either side of the firing cannon are two rebels in red shirts. Their placement directs the viewer's attention along the barrel of the big gun to the cannon ball beginning its trajectory. Streaks of red lead the viewers' eyes to its target, "Fort Sumter on fire!" This image became iconic and was reproduced in many popular media forms, such as on period envelopes printed with the rallying cry "Remember Fort Sumter!"[16]

In the next two scenes, the Myriopticon sets up the Union's vision of the essential differences between Union and Confederate citizens and foreshadows the outcome of the story: disciplined, unified order wins over emotionalism, disobedience, and rebellion. In scene 3, the Union soldiers in blue uniforms on the left present a cohesive, disciplined group aiming their muskets on command and are referred to in the Myriopti-

"Bombardment of Fort Sumter by the Batteries of the Confederate States, April 13, 1861." (*Harper's Weekly*, April 27, 1861)

con script as "the 6th Massachusetts regiment" and as "among the first that rallied to the defence of their country." On the right, a hodgepodge of legs, heads, arms, and hands holding a variety of weapons is described by the Myriopticon script as "a mob in the streets of Baltimore." Scene 4 underscores this distinction by memorializing the murder of Colonel Elmer Ellsworth at the hands of a man referred to in the script only as "Jackson." Readers of *Harper's Weekly* knew well the exploits of this young, dashing officer and his Zouave regiment recruited from the ranks of the New York City Fire Department. The charismatic, self-reliant, and industrious Fire Zouave Union commander was contrasted against James Jackson, identified in the Myriopticon script as "a hotel-keeper in Alexandria, Va.," but known to readers of *Harper's Weekly* as a notorious secessionist leader and "a man of violent habit . . . and like too many Southerners, was prompt with knife and pistol."[17]

The Myriopticon establishes the righteousness of the Union's cause by connecting the beginning scenes to the origin story of the nation and making the Union the legitimate heir to American revolutionary ideals. For example, the Myriopticon script for scene 3 editorializes: "This was the first blood shed in the great rebellion and it singularly occurred on the same day of the same month with the first blood of the American

Revolution shed at Lexington, Massachusetts, in 1775." In other words, the Sixth Massachusetts fought for freedom from the tyranny of "aggressive slavers" just as the American patriots, among them the ancestors of the southerners in the Baltimore scene, fought for freedom from British tyranny in the American Revolutionary War. The viewer of scene 4 would have understood that Colonel Ellsworth was the first Union officer killed in the war and would have connected that death to the founding of the nation, as news stories and editorials of the period pointed this out. The Lounger, a weekly column on *Harper's Weekly's* editorial page, dated June 8, 1861, connected Ellsworth's death to the death of General Joseph Warren eighty-six years earlier, the first officer killed when British troops stormed the redoubt of Breed's Hill in the Battle of Bunker Hill. The editorial explains that, "as Warren died in the beginning of the struggle to obtain Constitutional liberty, so dies Ellsworth at the opening of the war to maintain and perpetuate it."[18]

Having established the Confederacy's treachery and the Union's allegiance to Revolutionary ideals, the Myriopticon's next seventeen scenes illustrate five reasons for the Union's eventual victory: industrial development, new communication technologies, medical advances on the battlefield, new labor resources, and a new model of leadership for a modern war. The scenes construct traits for the individual to emulate, among them self-discipline and virtuousness, which supported the powerful economic system of the North that made the nation's reunification possible and allowed viewers to envision their own participation. Satisfied customer Davis made this clear in his letter to Milton Bradley and Company when he writes about his brother: "In the part about the first Battle of Bull Run where he was at and fought, he always speaks up in a loud voice to say he was one of those who holt up at Centerville [*sic*] and not among the cowards who run on to Washington."[19]

The Myriopticon establishes the importance of an industrial base and the institutional organization needed to effectively implement it in order to design, manufacture, and operate new war equipment. In scene 16, for example, a sharpshooter concealed in a tree fills the frame, allowing the Myriopticon narrative to highlight the importance of the rifle and the training needed to use it effectively. This self-disciplined individual wears a red shirt so the viewer can readily see him, although in battle he would wear camouflage green or gray. He offers a study in concentration as he aims a breech-loading rifle at a target not visible to the audience. In the words of the Myriopticon script, he "fires whenever he sees the head of an enemy." But *Harper's Weekly* readers would have understood that these special-forces members were used as skirmishers at the front to pick off enemy officers and gunners and would have even known something about the sharpshooter's training and rifle. With concealment of utmost importance, a breech-loading rifle allowed the sharpshooter to load the gun from many different positions, even clinging to the branches up in a tree.

The Myriopticon likewise introduces the importance of communications to modern warfare. In the foreground of scene 14, running men in blue uniforms unravel a wire on a reel. The Myriopticon script informs the audience that members of the U.S. Telegraph Corps are "erecting telegraph wires on the battlefield under fire." A smoky battlefield with massed armies serves as the background. In the middle ground, a two wheeled horse-drawn cart that houses transmitting and receiving equipment waits as the two men string telegraph wire from pole to pole in the foreground. The Myriopticon script informs the audience that "in an engagement a telegraph wire is frequently followed up as fast as ground is gained, and thereby a commander at his headquarters is constantly informed of operations in the several parts of the field." This battle scene reminds viewers that the Union's ability to wage modern warfare by creating a network of communication with the telegraph led to its successful war effort.

The Myriopticon also portrays the Union's timely care of the wounded soldier. The script orients the viewer of scene 15 by announcing that they are looking at the "celebrated" stone bridge made famous in "a terrible fight by the forces under Burnside" to ensure the audience identifies this as the Battle of Antietam. The public was made aware of the human costs of saving the Union at Antietam, the bloodiest single day of the war, from static images of dead soldiers by Mathew Brady, Alexander Gardner, and other photographers published widely on stereoscope cards used in the parlor setting.[20] But the Myriopticon, instead presents a scene of organized action, which the script informs the viewer "represents the wounded being cared for." Instead of a celebration of the first Union victory in the eastern theater, the image depicted surgeons, wounded soldiers, ambulances, and stretcher bearers. The color red draws the viewer's attention to splotches of blood on a draped table and on a soldier transported on a stretcher. The viewer traces the efficient coordination of care from operating table to stretcher transport to waiting ambulance to the arrival of another ambulance on Burnside's Bridge. *Harper's Weekly* had kept families well-informed during the war years of the efforts of the U.S. Sanitary Commission, charged with development and oversight of best practices for the care of Union soldiers.[21]

Perhaps most surprisingly, the Myriopticon also highlights emancipated slaves and free men of color as necessary to a successful Union war effort. In scene 18, the script identifies a mutigenerational black family group as "contrabands coming into camp, and having just arrived are now sitting for their pictures." They are posed in front of their dilapidated mule cart. The black men were neutralized in this scene by their domestic situation, poverty, and static poses. *Harper's Weekly* kept readers informed week after week about the efforts extended by the government to employ runaway and then emancipated slaves. Scene 18 is placed chronologically at January 1, 1863: the date the Emancipation Proclamation took effect. The audience of the Myriopticon performance likely would have read many editorials and news articles on the topic of what to do about the four million slaves held in the South. A *Harper's Weekly* editorial titled "To Our Southern Readers," published a month after the war began, states that "actual war between Slave and Free States ultimately involves abolition." Another, dated January 10, 1863, states that "our recent reverses supply additional motives for securing the active aide of 4,000,000 slaves, if it can be done. . . . Necessity will compel us to use them as soldiers."[22]

In scene 23, a regiment of black soldiers marches in formation led by their commanding officer, the charred ruins of buildings forming a backdrop. The Myriopticon script notes that the audience was looking at "the colored troops of the United States" entering "Charleston, S.C., where originated the whole plot of the rebellion." The Myriopticon performance, therefore, brings this conflict full circle, from the firing on Fort Sumter that began the war in Charleston Harbor to the fall of Charleston at the close of the war, signifying the end of the slave system and the launch of a new labor resource. The Myriopticon scene pictures former slaves cheering on the triumphal march of the Fifty-Fifth Regiment of the United States Colored Troops. Viewers of the Myriopticon performance would recall the *Harper's Weekly* illustration "Marching On!," and the commentary provided in which this event was pronounced a revolution in relations between "the negro and his master."[23] African Americans now had a new master—the industrial capitalist economic system.

Finally, the Myriopticon introduced a new model of leadership for a modern industrial war. Scene 9 outlines the first Union victory that occurred at the Battle of Fort Donelson by introducing the leader who

Scene 23. The Fifty-Fifth Massachusetts Colored Regiment entering
Charleston, South Carolina February 21, 1865, Milton Bradley's Myriopticon.
(Beinecke Rare Book and Manuscript Library, Yale University)

"'Marching On!' The Fifty-fifth Massachusetts Colored Regiment Singing John Brown's
March in the Streets of Charleston, February 21, 1865." (*Harper's Weekly*, March 18, 1865)

eventually brought the war to a conclusion that saved the nation, Ulysses S. Grant. The scene focuses on three boats in the middle of a river belching black smoke with Fort Donelson in the background, marked by a flying flag. The boats represented formidable weapons of the U.S. Navy. The script observes that the successful surrender of this fort also took serious fighting by the U.S. Army under the command of General Grant. The visual and the script worked together to inform the viewer that the successful outcome of the battle sprang from Grant's leadership in the use of war strategies and modern weapons made possible by the industrial capitalist age.

The Myriopticon emphasizes the role of the western theater in Union victory. The performance includes six scenes of battle victories from this theater and highlights the fact that the western theater witnessed an almost unbroken string of Union successes. The Myriopticon suggests that the war's turning point happened not at Gettysburg but during the Vicksburg Campaign, secured through the modern leadership of Major General Ulysses S. Grant. In scene 19, Grant rides in on a white horse to save the nation. Victory at Vicksburg, July 4, 1863, solidified Grant's reputation as a fighting general who commanded from the field rather than from behind a desk. Pictured with his sword drawn, leading the Union to victory, a direct connection is made to George Washington, the military leader of the American Revolution and the father of the nation, always also shown as a leader who commanded from the field of battle. Victory at Vicksburg opened up the route to Atlanta. In scene 20, Union soldiers literally and figuratively washed up after taking the heart of the Confederacy in September 1864.

The last three scenes in the Myriopticon describe the apocalyptic end of the ill-fated rebellion. Positioned as a metaphor for that end, scene 22 describes the sinking of the CSS *Alabama*. This is the only event out of chronological order, having occurred in June 1864, and contrary to all other events narrated in the script, this event is undated, even though the "Directions to the Proprietor of the Myriopticon" impress on the presenter their importance. Placed in the center of the scene, a large ship lists at the stern, its masts and rigging in disarray. Viewers had been kept so well-informed by news media sources of the *Alabama*'s treasonous exploits against Union commerce on the high seas over the two previous years that the script needed only to inform the viewer they are witnessing "the sinking of the *Alabama* by *Kearsarge* off Cherbourg, France" for the viewer to grasp the critical blow the United States had dealt to the Confederacy. *Harper's Weekly* ended its story announcing the *Alabama*'s destruction by quoting from John Milton's "Lycidas," about shipwreck and the fates: "'Built I' the eclipse and rigged with the curses dark' she has gone down to her own place. May the Rebellion of which she was a fitting instrument, soon follow her!"[24] This sinking ship of the Confederacy, therefore, became a metaphor for the inevitability of Union victory. Scene 23 illuminates the end of the Confederacy's slave system against the backdrop of the ruins of Charleston. The final scene depicts the defeated Confederate army in retreat, silhouetted against towering flames, as Richmond, the head of the Confederacy, is destroyed.

This final scene of apocalypse brings the story arc to a conclusion that deliberately spells out defeat for the Confederacy. Although every other scene in the moving panorama show was copied from the pages of *Harper's Weekly*, this scene of Richmond in flames was not. Whereas the magazine ran an illustration of the Union Army marching in triumph into Richmond, the Myriopticon presents Richmond burning to the ground. The story arc required that, according to fate, the Confederacy "go down to her own place" in flames.

At the very beginning of the war, *Harper's Weekly* wrote in an editorial titled "A Political Catechism for Children" that this ending was ordained. The last lines of this editorial read "But if you have read your Bible right, and have the true instincts of a free-born American Boy in you, you can not doubt how the contest will end."[25] The Myriopticon narrative shows why this end was inevitable.

Satisfied customer of the Myriopticon B. R. Davis ended his letter to Milton Bradley and Company by writing: "I thank you for making it and hope many buy so as to make it less crowded in our parlor these evenings."[26] Assigned as purchasers by Victorian gender codes, women reinforced the message of the Myriopticon in the parlor by purchasing Currier and Ives prints of the war, stereoscope card sets, *Harper's Weekly* news magazines, history books of the Civil War, and sheet music with songs of the Civil War for the parlor organ to entertain guests and family. Even though women were relegated in the Myriopticon narrative to watching and supporting, their role as educators of the virtuous citizen ensured that boys, male citizens in training, would understand the message and the roles they could play in the industrial capitalist economic system that won the war.

What message would a boy see and hear in the narrative of the war portrayed in the Myriopticon? First, he saw the divine righteousness of the cause of Union. From the second scene, where he was placed behind the canons being fired by the rebels, he saw Confederates in rebellion firing illegally on his nation, and therefore he knew the war must be fought. He understood who the hero of the Union cause was and why, because Grant understood how industries moved people and products. He learned that only men waged war and played an active part as citizens of the nation. He learned the importance of and respect for organizing the war effort by institutions. He understood that men needed to specialize and become experts, necessary attributes in the new postwar world he would come of age in. The Myriopticon visualized ample examples of this specialization: special forces like sharpshooters, trained ambulance drivers and stretcher bearers, telegraph and signal corpsmen, engineers, inventors, artillerymen, surgeons. The Myriopticon allowed any boy to dream of what he wanted to be when he grew up. It is not surprising, therefore, that the letter sent to Milton Bradley and Company was written by a father; after all, the company made the nuclear family the center for instruction in the traits to emulate in this newly reunified nation.

NOTES

1. Katherine C. Grier, *Culture and Comfort: Parlor Making and Middle-Class Identity, 1850–1930* (Washington, D.C.: Smithsonian Institution Press, 1998), 10.

2. James J. Shea, as told to Charles Mercer, *It's All in the Game* (New York: G. P. Putnam's Sons, [1960]), 81.

3. John White, *Reconstruction after the American Civil War* (London: Longman Group, 1977), 23.

4. Ibid., 30.

5. "Harper's Weekly, Journal of Civilization, 1857–1864," review by *North American Review* 100, no. 207 (April 1865): 623, 624.

6. Emma Willard, *History of the United States, or Republic of America: With a Chronological Table* (New York: A. S. Barnes and Burr, 1864), iii.

7. "Arrival of Negro Family in the Lines," Library of Congress, https://www.loc.gov/photos/?q=LC-B811-657, accessed March 17, 2019.

8. "Contrabands Coming into Camp in Consequence of the Proclamation," *Harper's Weekly* 7, no. 318 (January 31, 1863): 68.

9. "Our Artists during the War," *Harper's Weekly* 9, no. 440 (June 3, 1865): 339.

10. Erkki Huhtamo, *Illusions in Motion* (Cambridge, Mass.: MIT Press, 2013), 264–65. Neither of these full-scale moving panoramas have survived to the present day. However, broadsides advertising both are in Huhtamo's collection, and reveal some of the same events included in the Myriopticon such as "Fort Sumter on Fire!" "The Riot in Baltimore," "The Death of Ellsworth!," and "Grand Naval Battle in Hampton Roads!" The illustration for the battle between the *Mer-*

rimac and the *Monitor* is included on the broadside for *Polyrama of the War!* and is the same one that appeared in *Harper's Weekly* and the Myriopticon.

11. Patricia M. Burnham and Lucretia Hoover Giese, eds., *Redefining American History Painting* (New York: Cambridge University Press, 1995), 11.

12. Benedict Anderson, *Imagined Communities: Reflections on the Origin and Spread of Nationalism* (New York: Verso, 2006), 205.

13. Alfred H. Guernsey and Henry M. Alden, *Harper's Pictorial History of the Great Rebellion in the United States* (New York: Harper and Brothers, 1866), 29.

14. "Bombardment of Fort Sumter by the Batteries of the Confederate States, April 13, 1861," *Harper's Weekly* 5, no. 226 (April 27, 1861): 264–65.

15. Guernsey and Alden, *Harper's Pictorial History*, 61.

16. Civil War envelope (1861), Library of Congress, https://www.loc.gov /item/2011648573/, accessed March 17, 2019.

17. "The Murder of Ellsworth," *Harper's Weekly* 5, no. 233 (June 15, 1861): 369.

18. Ibid.; "The Irrepressible Conflict Again," *Harper's Weekly* 7, no. 321 (February 21, 1863): 114; "Ellsworth," *Harper's Weekly* 5, no. 232 (June 8, 1861): 354

19. Shea and Mercer, *It's All in the Game*, 82.

20. Emily Godbey, "'Terrible Fascination:' Civil War Stereographs of the Dead," *History of Photography* 36, no. 3 (July 9, 2012): 265–74, quote on 268.

21. Just a sampling of issues includes "The Health of the Volunteer," *Harper's Weekly* 5, no. 236 (July 6, 1861): 418; almost the entire issue of *Harper's Weekly* 8, no. 382 (April 23, 1864); "Mississippi Valley Sanitary Fair," *Harper's Weekly* 8, no. 385 (May 14, 1864): 306.

22. "To Our Southern Readers," *Harper's Weekly* 5, no. 230 (May 25, 1861): 322. "Negro Emancipation," *Harper's Weekly* 7, no. 315 (January 10, 1863): 18.

23. "Marching On!," *Harper's Weekly* 9, no. 429 (March 18, 1865): 165, 172.

24. "The 'Alabama,'" *Harper's Weekly* 8, no. 394 (July 16, 1864): 450.

25. "A Political Catechism for Children," *Harper's Weekly* 5, no. 245 (September 7, 1861): 562.

26. Shea and Mercer, *It's All in the Game*, 82.

"A Victorious Union"

Oliver Optic Sells the Civil War to
Northern Youths, 1863–1898

PAUL RINGEL

Christy Passford and Dexter (Deck) Lyon, the sixteen-year-old heroes of Oliver Optic's Blue and Gray novels (a series that ran from 1888 through 1898), are indomitable products of successful, white, northern families. Christy, whose father is a wealthy New York merchant, first learns about the outbreak of the Civil War when he returns from an international cruise aboard the family yacht. Deck, the son of a New Hampshire farmer, initially encounters the conflict when his family moves to Kentucky to take over his deceased uncle's plantation. Over the course of twelve books, these model northern boys experience an unrelenting series of triumphs. Christy helps to retrieve his sister Florry from his uncle's Alabama plantation, outmaneuvers a series of Confederate spies and naval officers, and ends the war as the twenty-one-year-old commander of a warship. Deck joins a Union regiment his father organized, proves a master military strategist and a daring (bordering on reckless) fighter, and rises to the rank of colonel in the Union army. The Lyons even solve the nation's slavery dilemma. They inherit more than one hundred slaves and agree to free them after five years; in the meantime, they treat their slaves uncommonly well, refusing to sell them and even arming them to defend the family property.

These postwar northern success fantasies are quite different from Optic's best-selling wartime Army and Navy series, which ran from 1863 through 1866 and offered a harrowing (if still validating) portrayal of young men's experiences in the Union military. The contrast reflects the fluid relationship that the author, whose real name was William Taylor Adams, developed with the Civil War and its memory over this period.

Part of this relationship was driven by the usual market factors; as did the children's publishing industry as a whole, Adams grappled with the immediate call for stories that interpreted the war for young people as it happened, and then mostly ignored the conflict for the next two decades as war fatigue settled in. His return to the subject at the end of the 1880s aligned with a national resurgence of interest in war-related products, and his justification for this second series of books reflected the reconciliatory impulse that fueled this demand.

Adams, though, pursued this strategy much longer and with more pro-northern vigor than his mostly younger colleagues, and with less commercial success than he achieved during the 1860s. His unrestrained glorification of Union boys in his Blue and Gray books exemplified another trend in the children's book industry: the idealization of northern white middle-class ideals of nation building and child rearing. This practice began in the 1850s as both a market strategy and moral economic strategy, and as postwar retailers shifted toward a message of national unity that honored southern as well as northern values, children's books and magazines did not follow. Instead, they continued to sell U.S. families a historical memory of the war that was firmly and confidently northern.

This choice was partly commercial; the large majority of the American children's literature industry's audience came from states that had remained loyal to the Union. It was also the product of a publishing tradition that had generated commercially successful children's books in this manner for nearly half a century. Most of these books embraced the rapidly urbanizing northeastern cultures that made the U.S. children's literature industry both viable (by creating concentrated audiences that made profits possible with limited regional distribution) and necessary (by removing families from largely self-contained rural communities and exposing children to a range of commercial entertainments).

The writers, editors, and publishers of these books and magazines were also overwhelmingly northerners who believed that their white, Protestant, middle-class homes in expanding commercial regions served as ideal incubators for producing physically, morally, and intellectually strong young Americans. Children's publishing had begun in the United States primarily as a moral endeavor, and the industry's late nineteenth-century leaders retained a belief in the social importance of their custodianship over their audience's reading materials. They further perceived that by upholding that responsibility, they helped to destigmatize their commercial efforts to expand children's role as consumers.[1] The Oliver

Optic Civil War stories of the 1860s and the 1880s–90s reinforce these intertwined agendas by presenting the Union victory as an affirmation of the superiority of northern child-rearing culture.

Adams was one of the few authors who participated in both waves of Civil War stories, and his forty-year career at the ideological and commercial epicenter of the children's publishing industry illuminates how those waves fit into the industry's development. A longtime teacher and principal at schools in and around Boston, during the late antebellum period he invigorated the children's market by breaking down divisions between didactic and sensational literature that were vexing mid-nineteenth-century U.S. publishers.[2] A growing urban print culture of penny press, story papers, and crime magazines made the evangelical instructional reading that had dominated the previous generation of children's literature less appealing for older boys with access to sources outside the home. Sellers pursuing this audience had to address its consumer demands directly, and still satisfy the instructional demands of adults who remained the primary purchasers of these items.[3]

In his first book for young readers, *The Boat Club, or, The Bunkers of Rippleton* (1854), Adams began to develop that balance by presenting the adventures of northern boys growing up in a child-rearing culture based on mentored independence. *The Boat Club* and its sequels established a pattern of strong but gradually diminishing paternal oversight for Adams's predominantly boy characters. Protagonist Frank Sedley and his friends enjoy excursions and competitions on a New England lake, initially under the careful supervision of his father Captain Sedley and Uncle Ben, "an old seaman, who had sailed a great many years in the employ" of the captain.[4] Uncle Ben taught the boys to row, and Frank's father formulated the idea for the club and showed them how to run their organization. Having received this guidance, and with the dictates of Protestant morality clearly instilled within their leader (Frank chooses to donate his spending money to a poor widow rather than buying fireworks for the Fourth of July), these boys received the exciting—and in children's literature of the time, rare—opportunity to entertain themselves in an environment beyond direct adult control.

The best-selling Boat Club novels (the original book ran through more than sixty printings) launched Adams's publishing career, during which he wrote over one hundred novels and nearly one thousand stories, and helped to establish the series format that became critical to the marketing of U.S. children's literature.[5] For Adams, they also introduced a pattern of paternal guidance as essential to young men's development that persisted even as boys in his books roamed progressively farther away from home on more extreme adventures. In the Blue and Grey series, which debuted more than thirty years after the Boat Club books, Christy's father, Horatio Passford, is also his son's employer, counselor, and confidante, and Deck's father, Noah Lyon, doubles as his commanding officer.

By 1860, Adams's approach of appealing to both adult and juvenile customers by celebrating the merits of a gradually liberating system of northern child-rearing had proven a reliable method of selling children's literature, but the war threw this strategy into disarray. Initially, with northern families separating due to the war effort, some publishers abandoned their cautious approach to young readers and embraced the ardent patriotism that was sweeping the region. They produced stories about drummer boys on the battlefield and homebound children dreaming of joining their brothers and fathers in the Union army. Other sources, such as the soon-to-be national best-selling *Youth's Companion* magazine, sought to temper young Unionists' martial enthusiasm. *Companion* editor Daniel Sharp Ford published no stories on the war until eight months after it began, and then told his young readers they could prove "a better patriot by staying at home." In a story about a boy attempting to enlist in the army, his father tells him, "This is not your place. You are too young for that."[6]

Adams did not engage in this debate; neither his novels nor his magazine, *Student and Schoolmate*, addressed the war during its opening stages. By 1863, as the war's impact on families reached previously unfathomable levels and both the hyperpatriotic and the tightly restricted method of explaining the conflict to U.S. children proved unsustainable, *Student* joined other publications in cautiously teaching children about the conflict through nonfiction articles "that presented in a rather matter-of-fact way the nuts and bolts of life in the army." Adams decried the "cheap patriotism" of earlier stories and published letters from soldiers as well as a series called "Campaigning," which described the organization of armies and how they were deployed in battle.[7]

The first Civil War novels for children appeared later that year, and in this format Adams returned to and expanded on his initial formula. *The Soldier Boy*, his first war novel, presents the experiences of sixteen-year-old Tom Somers, a typically upstanding Oliver Optic protagonist, during his initial months in the Union army. Adams's publisher Lee and Shepard "vigorously" advertised the book, and its commercial success spawned the Army and Navy series.[8] Over the next four years, Adams wrote five additional books about Tom and his twin brother Jack, who joined the navy. The adventures in these wartime books are considerably more dramatic than in Adams's earlier novels, but he retained his sense of moral responsibility to his young readers and his faith in the character foundation provided by their northern home environments.

One of the fundamental privations that Adams highlights when the Somers boys join the Union forces is separation from their families. When Tom says good-bye to his mother as his company departed for war early in *The Soldier Boy*, "he could no longer restrain the tears." Though a friend makes fun of him for it, this emotional connection to his family was regenerating rather than debilitating for his performance as a soldier. At Manassas, his first battle, "his heart rose up in his throat" as the fighting reached him, but, "determined not to disgrace the name he bore," he performs admirably (even as his friend ran away).[9]

Jack Somers, Tom's twin and the hero of *The Sailor Boy*, also sheds tears at the thought of leaving his mother and home when he departs for the military. This devotion to maternal love was typical of mid-nineteenth-century children's literature, but such scenes are unusual among Optic books because there is no mention of the boys' father. Captain Somers is a mostly absent figure throughout the Army and Navy series. He travels to Virginia just after the firing on Fort Sumter and goes missing behind enemy lines; though he reemerges and returns home safely later in the series, he does not assume the advisory role typical of Adams's fictional fathers.

In addition to this wartime hazard of lost parental supervision (and particularly the anomalous—for Adams's books—loss of paternal guidance), the Optic Civil War novels emphasize the physical dangers of the conflict. Beyond the obvious threat of death and disability, Adams repeatedly describes how military work dangerously sapped the strength of still-developing boys. After a year in the Union army, the cumulative effect of the war becomes too much for Tom Somers's body. Springing forward to lead a charge at Antietam, he falls to the ground with a flesh wound. The narrator comments that "his constitution had not yet fully developed; his muscles were not hardened, and the fatigues of battle and march had a more serious effect on him than the ounce of lead that struck him on the forehead." Doctors give Tom medical leave, and though he works to strengthen his body over the course of several sequels, the young soldier remains susceptible to illness throughout the remainder of the war, even as he continues to rise through the ranks. Jack did not suffer from the same persistent ailments as his brother, but when he tells his mentor and veteran sailor, Tom Longworth, that he had been chosen for the boarding party of an enemy ship, Tom calls it "murder to send little boys like that . . . you're a good boy enough, my lad; but you aren't no more fit for such work than the Evil Sperit is for a missionary."[10]

Despite the social and physical toll that the Civil War imposed on its young men, Adams expresses confidence throughout the Army and Navy series that the Union would prevail. He believed in the inherent superiority of northern society, and in its ability to transmit that culture across generations. Mrs. Somers taught her sons strong Protestant American values of courage, prudence, and self-possession, and the source of her commitment to the Union was "a vein of patriotism in her nature, which she had inherited from her father, who had fought at Bunker Hill, Brandywine, and Germantown, and which had been exemplified in the life of her brother," an 1812 veteran. This "genuine patriotism" contrasted with the mentality of the Pembertons, a northern family sympathetic to the Confederacy. Fred Pemberton initially opposes the war, and even when he ultimately enlists alongside Tom he does so because "he thought his friends were going off on a frolic, spiced with a little bit of peril and hardship to make it the more exciting, and he did not like being left behind. To the sentiment of patriotism he was a total stranger. He was going to war for the adventure, not for the insult toward the flag," and thus his "motive . . . could not be applauded."[11]

Throughout the latter half of the war and the transition into Reconstruction, children's magazines like Adams's *Student and Schoolmate, Our Young Folks,* and the *Youth's Companion* sold similar stories of northern virtue and competence contrasting with southern corruption and ineptitude. Union soldiers in these stories routinely outsmarted Confederates; even a Kentucky Unionist mother captured ten "secessionists," who then claimed "they had been wanting to get captured for some time past, and were heartily sick of the war." Other stories detailed horrifying examples of slaveholder cruelty, and claimed that the morally corrupt "slaveocracy" had imposed an ignorance on southern society that led to the downfall of the Confederacy.[12]

By the late 1860s, these war stories mostly disappeared. Adams presented a war-related story in nearly every issue of *Student and Schoolmate* until he left the magazine in 1867, but the *Youth's Companion* only published fourteen Civil War–related stories or articles between 1870 and 1900. *St. Nicholas* magazine, which subsumed *Our Young Folks* and *Student and Schoolmate* in 1873 and became the publication of choice for elite northern families, produced just fourteen stories connected to the war before 1900. After ending the Army and Navy series in 1866, Adams wrote stories about young men and women traveling abroad, migrating west, or working as farmers, fishermen, clerks, and even soldiers without returning to the subject of the Civil War. Best-selling English-language children's books of the era included boyhood stories like *Tom Sawyer* and *Huckleberry Finn*, domestic novels seeking to replicate the success of *Little Women*, adventure tales like *Treasure Island*, rags-to-riches myths such as *Little Lord Fauntleroy*, and fantasies like *Alice's Adventures in Wonderland*. Not one Civil War children's novel made a significant impact on the industry between the publication of Optic's Army and Navy finale, *Brave Old Salt*, in 1866 and *Taken by the Enemy*, the first of Adams's Blue and Gray books, which appeared in 1888.

This avoidance of wartime stories extended beyond children's literature. Dime-novel publishers Beadle and Adams produced stories about the American Revolution, the French and Indian War, and even the Mexican War, but not a single book about the Civil War during the 1870s or 1880s. The broader publishing industry followed the same pattern; very few of the popular or influential fiction and nonfiction writers of these decades focused on the central conflict of their generation. For the children's publishing industry, though, the end of the war provided additional reasons for retreating from its previous patriotic marketing strategy.

The war emergency had overwhelmed publishers' general reluctance to incorporate sensational material into children's books and magazines. Doing so in the midst and immediate aftermath of the conflict furthered the clear moral and social purpose of supporting the Union, while also providing a significant boost for sales within the industry. Once the afterglow of victory faded, the subject of the war lost its didactic purpose and risked alienating potential customers who wanted to return young readers to a more sheltered existence. In order to justify their still-contentious economic interest in providing thrilling stories for young consumers, and (perhaps more instinctively than consciously) continue to celebrate northern child-rearing practices, publishers shifted their focus to the more immediately relevant subject of how children should behave in rapidly expanding industrial cities. These stories did not explicitly focus on the superiority of northern child-rearing, but the examples of country boys who flourished in the city were nearly always from northeastern or midwestern states.[13] Writers for children mined the American past, the domestic present, and geographically and historically distant cultures for material, but once the immediate crisis faded the most dev-astating and consequential national event in recent memory seemed off limits.

This drought of war-related material began to change roughly a gen-eration after the end of the war. In 1884, the *Century* magazine launched a series of illustrated articles about the fighting told primarily by prom-inent military figures from both sides of the conflict. The series nearly doubled the magazine's circulation in six months and ran for three years, culminating in the publication of a popular four-volume book titled *Bat-tles and Leaders of the Civil War*.[14] In the immediate aftermath of this suc-cess, publishers of children's literature displayed renewed interest in the subject. Initially, their stories paralleled the fact-driven narratives that had launched the previous generation's wartime coverage. The most notable example of this genre were the stories of Adam Badeau, General Grant's aide and biographer who wrote several of the *Century* articles, and also contributed a series of battle descriptions to *St. Nicholas* (which shared a publisher with the *Century*) during 1887.[15]

Rather than addressing the morality or motivations of the combatants, the *Century* and *St. Nicholas* series focused on how the war was fought, and *Century* editors "structured the series and the subsequent *Battles and Leaders* as a means of reunion through the mutual recounting and under-standing of all soldiers' valor." This impulse toward reconciliation surged among late nineteenth-century white Americans, and the effort to feed it was integral to the commodification of the war. By offering large sums of money for stories from prominent veterans on both sides, the *Century* un-leashed a wave of Civil War memoirs by men and women seeking to cash in on their experiences.[16]

The year after the *St. Nicholas* stories, Adams capitalized on the trend—just as he had twenty-five years earlier—by launching a series of Civil War novels. *Taken by the Enemy* was the first time since 1866 that he placed the war at the center of an Oliver Optic book. It was also part of a wave of children's novels that appeared in 1888 and 1889, all of which explic-itly promoted the reconciliation impulse. Thomas Nelson Page published *Two Little Confederates*, a book for younger audiences that told a war story from a southern perspective and ended with a message of unification. Charles Fosdick, who wrote children's series books under the pseudonym Harry Castlemon, produced *True to His Colors*, his first Civil War novel since 1867, which focused on a southern Unionist who never abandoned his allegiance to the United States.[17]

Adams explicitly embraced reunion as part of his motivation for returning to the subject of the war. In the preface to *Taken by the Enemy*, he explains that

> at the conclusion of the war of the Rebellion, and before the writer had completed "The Army and Navy Series," over twenty years ago, some of his friends advised him to make all possible haste to bring his war stories to a conclusion, declaring that there could be no demand for such works when the war had come to an end. But the volumes of the series mentioned are as much in demand to-day as any of his other stories . . . and certainly the author has received more commendatory letters from young people in regard to the books of this series than concerning those of any other.[18]

Having established the popularity of his still-in-print earlier books, he pronounces that

> the writer had little inclination to undertake this task; for he has believed for twenty years that the war is over, and he has not been disposed to keep alive old issues which had better remain buried. . . . It is not, therefore, with the desire or intention to rekindle the fires of sectional animosity, now happily subdued, that the writer begins another series relating to the war. The call upon him to use the topics of the war has been so urgent, and its ample field of stirring events has been so inviting, that he could not resist; but, while his own opinions in regard to the great question of five-and-twenty years ago remain unchanged, he hopes to do more ample justice than perhaps was done before to those "who fought on the other side.[19]

Through this preface—and the use of Blue and Gray in the series name, an explicit contrast with the northern focus of the Army and Navy title—Adams sold these novels as part of the trend toward reconciliation that was pervading white American culture.

Yet unlike the Army and Navy books, which largely adhere to the ideals promoted in their preface, the Blue and Gray series offer far less appeasement than this introduction suggests. Instead, it celebrates the triumphs of Union military men, abandoning the emphasis on struggle central to Adams's previous Civil War series and incorporating only a few examples of admirable Confederate officers. Christy Passford develops a relationship of mutual admiration with Confederate captain Rombold, whom he takes prisoner and eventually brings home to his parents' New York mansion to convalesce. Rombold earns Christy's admiration by ordering his surgeon to attend to the wound of a Union officer before having his own examined, and when the young Union officer proclaims "this is Christianity in war, and I shall strive to emulate your noble example," the Confederate responds, "we are friends until the demands of duty require us to become technical enemies." Deck Lyon's relationships with Confederates are more transient in the Blue and Gray on Land books, but he does develop a friendship with a Texas cavalry officer with the unsubtle name Captain Makepeace, and develops respect for plantation owner Mr. Thornfield, who "proved that he could be a gentleman even while he was a secessionist."[20]

More often, southern characters in the Blue and Gray books are cowardly and ineffectual. Percy Pierson, a southern boy about the same age as Christy, offers a contrast to Optic's hero in patriotism, courage, and intelligence. Percy claims to want to join the Confederate army but says his father will not let him. If he does join the war effort, he expects to begin as a lieutenant because "he couldn't quite stand it to go in as a common soldier."[21] When they first meet, Christy tricks Percy into giving him vital information about the Confederate defenses in the Gulf of Mexico, and for the rest of *Taken by the Enemy* he uses the southern boy as an instrument for executing his plans to escape his captor.

That captor is Major Lindley Pierson, Percy's older brother and a failed suitor of Christy's sister, Florry. Major Pierson is "unkind, ungenerous," and behaves in a manner that is "rude, brutal, and tyrannical." Christy's father found it "exceedingly disagreeable" that a young Confederate officer should be attracted to his daughter, and once he met the young man, Horatio Passford determined that he "assuredly was not the person he would have chosen for Florry."[22] The young woman agrees with her father; she is not interested in Major Pierson, which in turn leads her suitor to attempt to abduct Florry from her New York home in a subsequent novel.

In addition to the often-troubling character of the books' native southerners, both Blue and Gray series feature northern-born men and their southern-born sons whose character has been corrupted (or at least more exposed) by migration to the South. Christy Passford and Deck Lyon each have an uncle who holds southern sympathies. Homer Passford owns a plantation in Alabama, where he has lived for two decades as a man of high standing and relative wealth, though "his fortune was insignificant compared with that of his brother." Throughout the series, Homer and his son Corny attempt and fail to thwart Christy's efforts to support the Union. Corny impersonates Christy, but his lack of intelligence and courage gives him away. Homer is deluded about the power of the South and the weakness of the North; he repeatedly claims that the removal of southern business will ensure that "grass grows in the streets of New York," and he believes Confederate reports that "business was paralyzed in the cities of the North." By the end of the series, Homer Passford is financially, physically, and emotionally ruined. While Christy charitably pronounces that he has never known anyone as "sincerely religious" as his uncle, and believes that Homer supported the Confederacy out of a sense of "pious duty," the uncle proclaims his nephew "the emissary of the Evil One, sent here to torment me."[23]

Deck Lyon's Uncle Titus is an even more flawed migrant to the South. While Homer Passford's major fault is blind dedication to the Confederacy, Titus Lyon is uneducated, "lazy, and greatly lacking in enterprise." He is a drunk and a spendthrift, an impoverished debtor who borrows money from Deck's father, Noah, and then publicly complains that he was cheated out of an inheritance. Adams describes him as a "more thorough-going pro-slavery" man than his deceased brother the planter, and a man who "associated with reckless and un-principled characters."[24] These associations lead him to become captain of the Home Guard, a group of local vigilantes who sought to benefit financially by expelling Union sympathizers from the region and taking over their properties. This group turned its wrath on Noah Lyon's plantation, and only the bravery of Deck, his father and brother, and the community that supports them kept these criminals from seizing the homestead.

After the Lyons and their newly formed Union regiment defeat and capture Titus and his cronies in *Brother against Brother*, the prisoner is sent to a Union camp in Illinois, where he gains sobriety, renewed religious faith, and a patriotic feeling toward the United States. With the departure of their father, Titus's wayward sons Sandy and Orly join their Uncle Noah's regiment (largely because they need to eat) and become similarly reformed. One of the boys dies fighting for the Union, and the other develops into a stalwart cavalryman under Deck and Noah Lyon's mentorship.

Thus, in the Blue and Gray series, Adams presents not only indomitable, successful northern boys, but also a collection of more susceptible males from the North who become corrupted by southern culture and (in the case of the Lyons) redeemed by reintegration into northern institutions. These books abandon the idea of superior northern "blood" that prevailed in the Army and Navy series, with environment seeming to replace genetics as the determinative factor in how American men develop. This presentation of northern cultural supremacy weakens the conciliatory message that Adams presents in the preface to several of the Blue and Gray books, and affirms Caroline Janney's argument that northerners "embraced reconciliation of a sort that left no doubt about who had been right."[25] While he proclaims a desire not to rekindle sectional animosity, Adams simultaneously asserts the North's preeminence as a producer of successful and upstanding young men.

The Blue and Gray books also implicitly subvert reconciliation by supporting the advancement of slaves and freed blacks. During the late nineteenth century, white Americans' embrace of a Civil War memory that celebrated the valor of soldiers on both sides undercut the emancipationist vision of the war, which emphasized the conflict as a reinvention of the republic through the freedom of black Americans. David Blight argues that during the 1880s and 1890s, the period when Adams was writing the Blue and Gray books, "forces of reconciliation overwhelmed the emancipationist vision in the national culture." In contrast, Adams's books feature black supporting characters who are vital to his protagonists' success, and who develop skills and confidence under the young white men's tutelage. Davis Talbot, a cabin steward rescued from slavery, serves as Christy's "very intelligent" and loyal aide, delivering crucial information and helping him to avoid capture by tricking his Confederate enemies. In return, Christy affirms Davis's worth, teaching him not to call white men "Massa" or himself a "nigger." Deck's assistant is a slave named Seef, who is a skilled engineer and navigator of steam launches on the Ohio River. He ferries Deck through a series of adventures, and the young man treats him as a peer, not allowing him to take food to the back of the boat but insisting he eat with the soldiers. The casual racism of Optic novels is cringeworthy for twenty-first century readers, but claims like "within reasonable limits, I am a friend of the colored man" made them anomalous for their era.[26]

This ideological disjunction, and the relative lack of commercial success of the Blue and Gray books, reflect that these children's Civil War stories of the 1880s and 1890s were in many ways not representative of children's books and magazines of the era or of broader industry trends.[27] St. Nicholas rarely returned to the topic of the Civil War after its 1887 articles, and Fosdick's series ended in 1893. The six-part Blue and Gray on Land series was popular enough that the publishers ordered Blue and Gray at Sea. Adams finished five of those books but died in 1897 before completing An Undivided Union. The young writer Edward Stratemeyer, who subsequently expanded the commercial possibilities of the series format that Adams had helped to launch, finished the series; among the thousands of Hardy Boys, Nancy Drew, and other books that emerged from his publishing syndicate, he never produced another Civil War collection. By 1898, when the Blue and Gray series ended, the children's literature industry's brief surge of interest in Civil War memory had been over for a decade, and Adams's publishers Lee and Shepard had fallen from the pinnacle he helped them achieve atop the juvenile book business (the firm closed in 1905). The most famous Civil War book of that decade (though not marketed to children) was Stephen Crane's *Red Badge of Courage*, a brutally realistic portrayal of the horrors of battle that was the antithesis of an Adams story.

Yet in a broader context these stories were consonant with the goals of the nineteenth-century children's publishing industry. Civil War narratives, whether written during or a generation after the conflict, illuminated and often served the industry's intertwined commercial and moral agendas. When those agendas aligned in Civil War novels, as happened during the 1860s, they offered young readers the thrills they demanded and adult purchasers the clear ideological vision they expected. When those interests collided in the reconciliation movement of the 1880s and 1890s, publishers revealed their complex assessment of market and moral influences, acknowledging public demands for unity while maintaining their traditional values (in Adams's novels and elsewhere) through promotion of the child-rearing practices of northern families and an absence of concomitant praise for the efforts of their southern counterparts.

Oliver Optic's Civil War novels, from both the 1860s and the 1880s–90s, exemplify a nineteenth-century U.S. children's publishing industry that remained steeped in and allegiant to the nation's middle-class, white, northern culture. With its cautious approach to legitimizing children's role as consumers, that culture was part of the reason why the Civil War was an uncommon subject in children's books and magazines. It also ensured that Civil War stories that did appear affirmed northern interpretations and memories of the national crisis, and followed the broader industry trend of validating the northern family as a vital institution for nation building. Indeed, even as the Lost Cause ideology that celebrated the antebellum South began to gain national support in other mediums as the twentieth century approached, publishers of children's literature, fueled by a combination of market and moral economic forces, continued to almost exclusively sell this northern ideal to American families.

NOTES

1. For this argument, see Paul Ringel, *Commercializing Childhood: Children's Magazines, Urban Gentility, and the Ideal of the Child Consumer in the United States, 1823–1918* (Boston: University of Massachusetts Press, 2015).

2. Lorinda B. Cohoon, *Serialized Citizenships: Periodicals, Books, and American Boys, 1840–1911* (Lanham, Md.: Scarecrow, 2006), 58.

3. The primary target audience for Adams's books, and for most Civil War stories for children, was boys, though on rare occasions girls were protagonists in the latter genre. Alice Fahs, *The Imagined Civil War: Popular Literature of the North and South, 1861–1865* (Chapel Hill: University of North Carolina Press, 2001), 263–279.

4. Oliver Optic, *The Boat Club or, The Bunkers of Rippleton*, new edition, revised and enlarged (New York: Mershon and Company, 1896), http://www.gutenberg.org/files/24557/24557-h/24557-h.htm.

5. Raymond L. Kilgour, *Lee and Shepard: Publishers for the People* (Hamden, Conn.: Shoe String Press, 1965), 26–34.

6. "The Patriot Boy," *Youth's Companion*, December 31, 1863, 209; "The Boy Soldier," *Youth's Companion*, July 9, 1863, 111.

7. Oliver Optic, "Teacher's Desk," *Students and Schoolmate*, June 1863, 189; James Marten, *The Children's Civil War* (Chapel Hill: University of North Carolina Press, 1998), 34.

8. Kilgour, *Lee and Shepard*, 44.

9. Oliver Optic, *The Soldier Boy; or, Tom Somers in the Army. A Story of the Great Rebellion* (Boston: Lee and Shepherd, 1863), 90, 132.

10. Ibid., 134, 314; Oliver Optic, *The Sailor Boy; or, Jack Somers in the Navy. A Story of the Great Rebellion* (Boston: Lee and Shepherd, 1863), 164.

11. Optic, *Soldier Boy*, 82, 103, 179; Optic, *Sailor Boy*, 14.

12. "A Brave Woman," *Youth's Companion*, March 12, 1863, 44; "A Southern Boy's Idea of the Yankees," *Youth's Companion*, October 15, 1863, 164.

13. See, for example, Amanda M. Douglas, "Larry," *Youth's Companion*, January 5, 1893, 1–2; William O. Stoddard, "Crowded Out O' Crofield," *St. Nicholas*, October 1890, 248–55.

14. David Blight, *Race and Reunion: The Civil War in American Memory* (Cambridge, Mass.: Belknap Press of Harvard University Press, 2001), 175.

15. Badeau wrote six articles for *St. Nicholas* in 1887, beginning with "Story of the Merrimac and the Monitor," *St. Nicholas* 14 (April 1887): 435–44, and ending with "General Grant at Vicksburg," *St. Nicholas* 14 (October 1887): 939–46.

16. Blight, *Race and Reunion*, 175–76.

17. Harry Castlemon, *True to His Colors* (Philadelphia: Porter and Coates, 1889).

18. Oliver Optic, *Taken by the Enemy* (Boston: Lee and Shepard, 1888), 6.

19. Ibid., 7–8.

20. Oliver Optic, *A Victorious Union* (Boston: Lee and Shepard, 1893), 198; Oliver Optic, *On the Staff* (Boston: Lee and Shepard, 1897), 73.

21. Optic, *Taken by the Enemy*, 105, 182.

22. Ibid., 129, 136.

23. Ibid., 25–26; Oliver Optic, *Fighting for the Right* (Boston: Lee and Shepard, 1892), 175, 184; Optic, *Victorious Union*, 215, 354.

24. Oliver Optic, *Brother against Brother: The War on the Border* (Boston: Lee and Shepard, 1894), 35–38.

25. Caroline E. Janney, *Remembering the Civil War: Reunion and the Limits of Reconciliation* (Chapel Hill: University of North Carolina Press, 2013).

26. Blight, *Race and Reunion*, 2; Oliver Optic, *On the Blockade* (Boston: Lee and Shepard, 1890), 43, 45, 76; Optic, *On the Staff*, 123–25; Optic, *Fighting for the Right*, 301.

27. Sales figures for Adams's series are not available, but the Army and Navy books were reissued six times between the 1860s and 1890s, whereas the Blue and Gray books never had a second reprinting.

Vigorous Men with Something to Say

Civil War Lecturers in Gilded Age America

JAMES MARTEN

By the late 1880s James "Corporal" Tanner was one of the "stars" among the lecturers and performers promoted by the Star Lyceum Bureau. As a teenaged soldier, Tanner had lost the lower third of both legs at Second Manassas. A longtime Republican operative and advocate for Union veterans, in 1889 he would earn infamy during his short-lived career as commissioner of pensions. Fired by President Benjamin Harrison, he remained extremely popular among veterans and remained a perennial favorite at Grand Army of the Republic (GAR) encampments and as a Republican stump speaker. He relished his nickname—"Corporal"—which happened to be his rank in the army; it made him unique among the generals and other officers with whom he often shared platforms.

Tanner's most popular talk was "Soldier Life—the Grave and the Gay," which he delivered countless times between the 1870s and 1890s. Apparently audiences loved it. "To say that [Tanner's] lecture was interesting," said one testimonial, "would convey but a faint idea of the manner in which the speaker entertained his listeners. His descriptive powers are excellent, his choice of language faultless, his relation of comical army incidents laughable in the extreme, and his more serious recitals are given with a pathos that brings tears to the eyes." Another review declared that "one minute his audience would be roaring with laughter, and as suddenly they would be moved to tears as he related some touching incident in his career."[1]

As his title suggests, Tanner's lecture featured a number of humorous and tragic stories of soldiers in camp and in battle. He paid homage to the women they left behind, and described his own excruciating wounds,

treatment, and recovery. Throughout, he emphasized sectional reconciliation: "No man who speaks of the war truly represents the feelings of the
veterans who served in it if he speaks anything in bitterness"—indeed, if
reconstruction "had been left to the front line of each army at Appomattox, they would have been settled lastingly [and] amicably" and would
have put the "politicians . . . out of business."[2]

Tanner was part of a small army of speakers and performers that provided an important element of popular entertainment in the nineteenth
century. This wildly varied community of entertainers helped to create what one historian has called a "public culture." Beginning in the
1820s and extending until well into the twentieth century, this "American Lecture-System" brought to the entire continent "the measured foot-
step of advancing civilization." Although its origins were in local organizations in which men and older boys gave lectures or participated in formal
debates, the system grew to include educational and religious gatherings
called Chautauquas, named after the lake in Upstate New York where they
began, which featured a mix of entertainment, serious speeches, and even
slide shows. But whatever their content, all of these presentations and performances were intended to elevate the character and values of Americans
of all classes, creeds, and backgrounds. As such, they became a classic part
of the self-improvement-minded Gilded Age.[3]

It was also a business. Speakers could earn a good living on the circuit, making an average of $75 (and as much as $250) per lecture, plus
expenses. An ambitious speaker could make as much as $30,000 a year.
Bureaus scheduled the talks, handled travel arrangements, and distributed catalogues of lecturers and their topics to fraternal organizations,
GAR camps, YMCAs, teacher institutes, and other potential audiences.
The vast network of railroads built during the Gilded Age made even the
smallest towns in the most remote places accessible to nationally known
entertainers and lecturers. Many towns and associations organized "sea-
sons" that often featured a couple of travel lectures, talks on historical
events, famous people, and recent inventions or scientific discoveries,
and presentations on practical hints for self-improvement. For instance,
the 1887 season in Brattleboro, Vermont, included Tanner, a humorist,
an elocutionist, a male quartet, a violinist, a "whistling soloist," and Albion Tourgee, the former soldier, Reconstruction politician, writer, and
lawyer (he would later serve as counsel for the plaintiff in the famous
Plessy v. Ferguson case that would lead to the legalization of racial discrimination by the U.S. Supreme Court).[4]

Just after the Civil War, J. G. Holland, himself a popular speaker, wrote that the lecture system would be replaced as a form of entertainment and education only if its successor offered something "more interesting, cheaper, simpler, or more portable . . . than a vigorous man, with a pleasant manner, good voice, and something to say." But Holland also argued that popular lectures represented important demonstrations of freedom, independence of thought, and democracy.[5]

The 1887 version of *Werner's Directory of Elocutionists, Readers, Lecturers and other Public Instructors and Entertainers* listed nearly 650 men and women hoping to provide interesting and cheap instruction and entertainment. The directory included short descriptive titles of the lectures and listed another thousand "elocutionists and readers"—people who would present poetry and prose in staged readings, complete with ethnic dialects and other dramatic flourishes. The others were professors and ministers, writers and poets, journalists and reformers. Their lectures covered literally thousands of different topics: "Three Lectures on Horace," "Turns on Life's Highway," "From the Useful to the Beautiful," "Bright Side of Things," "Is the World Better or Worse?," "Croaking and Crowing," "Beauty," "Cranes, Their Construction and Uses," "The Woes of Wooing." A few lecturers addressed hot topics of the day, such as "The Absurdities of Evolution," "The History of Communism," "Rum's Ruin and the Remedy," and "The Use of Electricity in the Arts." Perhaps thirty-five could be considered Civil War lecturers, although they offered nearly fifty different speeches. Among the speakers with connections to the sectional conflict included in the directory were Anna Dickinson, the abolitionist who had become famous as a teenaged lecturer in the early 1860s; Edward Everett Hale, who had written "The Man without a Country" a few years before; Mary Livermore, who had gained fame with the U.S. Sanitary Commission during the war; and Lew Wallace, the former general and author of the blockbuster novel, *Ben Hur*.[6]

Professional lecturers who drew on the Civil War for their inspiration communicated their versions of the Civil War directly to educated, and educatable, middle-class Americans. They likely confirmed their audience's preconceptions, but in so doing they ensured that certain interpretations and narratives of the Civil War era—from reconciliation to racial justice, and from women's roles to southern honor—would remain in the public consciousness for many years after the war. In many ways, audiences "bought" from Civil War lecturers a comfortable interpretation of the Civil War and a reiteration of noble, positive American characteristics. Attending a lecture was a way to learn things about the war and to find a place to store its memory safely away. The lecturers seemed to communicate a form of reconciliation that transcended politics and the fraught sectionalism of the previous decades.

But lecturers were also "selling" something more personal—values and memories shared with members of the audience. Some speakers, like Tanner, frequently appeared before fellow veterans, although most audience members would not have been old soldiers. Yet many audience members would have had family members who fought in the war. Some had been children of the sectional conflict, with dim childhood memories of the stirring debates that preceded the war (or at least the stark emotions that those debates had sparked), the tragic war years, and, by the time they had become teenagers or young adults, the bewildering Reconstruction era. For at least some audience members at any given Civil War lecture, the material no doubt sparked flashbacks to childhoods and youths fraught with danger and excitement.

Relatively few speakers on the Civil War were women. Dickinson's lecture career had declined by the early 1870s, when she began exploring opportunities in the theater. Mary Livermore, one of the leaders of the Sanitary Commission movement, spoke widely, but rarely about the war itself; after the war, her writing and speaking focused on women's rights. A number of southern women—particularly wives and widows of prominent generals—were active in perpetuating Lost Cause themes, but primarily through print media and talks at veterans reunions. Perhaps the best-known woman speaker on the war was LaSalle Corbell Pickett. Although not one of Werner's clients, she spent years writing and speaking about the Lost Cause and reconciliation, offering in print and in appearances at veterans' gatherings, Chautauquas, and even on vaudeville stages accounts of her husband's career and other Confederate topics. Desperately needing to make money, Pickett became one of the best known speakers of the late nineteenth and first two decades of the twentieth century, despite her precarious relationship with the truth. But she generally operated outside the traditional lecture circuit during her long career.[7]

As the following sampling of three representative talks by lecturers listed in Werner's 1887 directory indicates, Civil War lectures combined nostalgia, patriotism, knowledge, and entertainment. For Americans who followed the lyceum or Chautauqua circuits, the Civil War was never far from their consciousness. Indeed, at least part of the transaction completed when a speaker offered a lecture and an audience member paid their two or four bits for a seat, was to keep the meaning and drama of those bygone but legendary days fresh in their minds.

At the same time, performers like Corporal Tanner added several elements to this generations-old form of entertainment and civic education. Antebellum lecturers were engaged in a practice partly intended to knit the young nation together by highlighting Americans' common goals and interests. The war destroyed, at least for a time, that cozy if illusory notion. After the war, however, Civil War lecturers, deploying a familiar format and taking advantage of an ever-expanding transportation system, inserted the war into the lecture of halls of the Gilded Age. A few even broached the difficult subject of race in a postslavery world. Rather than avoid the bloody conflict that had nearly torn the nation apart, they drew from it important lessons about the national character, as well as important and entertaining stories of valor and human foibles.

Soldiers' Lives

Although he appeared in Werner's directory, unlike Corporal Tanner, the Reverend E. Livingston Allen was not one of the star speakers on the circuit in the late 1880s. A longtime Methodist minister in New Jersey and New York, he was also active in the GAR. At the age of eighteen he suspended his ministerial studies to enlist in the Thirteenth New Jersey. He served as a corporal in Company K until the last few months of war, when he was promoted to sergeant. Although the regiment did not suffer heavy casualties, it did serve with distinction, fighting at Antietam, Chancellorsville, and Gettysburg, and participating in the Atlanta Campaign and the March to the Sea. Allen may have been trying to cash in on Corporal Tanner's great success; his lecture, which he delivered at least a few times in the 1880s and 1890s in and around New York, was called "Both Sides of Army Life: The Grave and the Gay." Self-published as a sixteen-page booklet, it offers a sense of what many of the military-oriented lectures would have been like.

Clearly a transcription of a spoken performance, the printed lecture is filled with rhetorical flourishes and alliteration, cadences that work far better when heard rather than when read silently, and italicized and capitalized passages marking important thematic and emotional points. This formatting undoubtedly roughly captured the red marks, underlinings, and circles on the script from which Allen would have delivered his public lectures.

Allen's talk began with several paragraphs on past wars and on Fourth of July orators who inculcated ardent patriotism and emotional attachment to the American flag. "All this with reference to the flag and eagle was *sentiment*, but it educated Young America patriotically, so that when the glorious old stars and stripes—emblems of national unity—was fired upon at Sumter, the Northern heart was fired with indignation, and this *sentiment was to become crystallized into the solid steel of military activity*, and was to be proven the VERY EMBODIMENT OF INVINCIBLE FORCE!"[8]

Allen briefly described the assembling of "the boys" and their rush to the Maryland front, where, incredibly, they loaded their guns for the first time as they went into battle at Antietam. Allen peppered his talk with military terminology, and with phrases that are a little jarring to read but which must have drawn in audiences with dramatic repetition and clever word play: "As the gray dawn was pushing back the blackness of night, revealing the blue of day, we were ordered by the gray-haired Mansfield to push back the grey of treason and show the enemy the pure blue of loyalty." The battle scene that followed was particular to his experience yet also generic—similar scenes appeared in virtually every first person account of combat. As the Thirteenth New Jersey pressed forward, they passed a young soldier from the 107th New York, "with both limbs broken by a solid shot; and he, in his agony, knowing death must soon come, was calling, Mother! MOTHER! MOTHER! Brave hearts trembled—strong men wept—indescribable emotions swept over mind and heart—*Forward!* FORWARD! the command rose higher, and on we went."[9]

In addition to realistic accounts of the battles—his description of Chancellorsville captures perfectly the confusion on the Union right flank—Allen added a number of iconic facets of military reminiscences: rich, often funny characters, a no-hard-feelings approach to the enemy, and a few references to humorous incidents occurring at the height of battles, including a moment during a battle in Georgia when the regimental color guard (which included Allen) took cover behind a rock and spent part of the battle eating blueberries. One fellow member of Company K, Sam C. Davis, who the "boys" inevitably nicknamed "Jeff," was a "cross, crabbed, cranky, crusty, cantankerous" fellow—again, with the alliteration—who seemed most upset in the middle of a crucial battle when a bullet ruined the fry pan crammed into his knapsack. Another of Allen's stock characters, a German named John Icke, offered typical ethnic humor—popular throughout the United States during this time—when he remarked on the quantity of rations provided in winter quarters in early 1863: "see vat Hooker feeds us mit: he is fattenen us up fur de schlauter-house." Although played for laughs at first mention, Allen used the line with a greater sense of doom on other occasions when the regiment was preparing to go into battle. Later in the war, a new recruit arrived named Young—nicknamed, of course, "Brigham"—whose uniform is ill-fitting and whose cap is worn at an awkward angle, and whose feet were so large that they kept the fire from warming him. Always hungry, he became the camp thief, stealing provisions from company stores at every opportunity, until he was caught and court-martialed. One subtheme is the order of the army—even these hapless soldiers are kept more or less under control; moreover, when caught doing something wrong, they are simply fined ten dollars a month for six months. This indicates both the discipline and the mercy embodied by military justice.[10]

Like Tanner, most public speakers on the war—certainly the men who had fought in it—joined the reconciliationist movement of the late nineteenth century, and Allen was no exception. When reporting on the capture of his regiment's baggage by the Confederates at Chancellorsville, he admitted that although he still felt a twinge of regret at the loss of a package of letters ("tied up with a blue ribbon") from his girlfriend, Mary Ann, "the value of my own was not very great; and I have long since buried any ill-will harbored toward my late antagonists, having shaken hands 'across the bloody chasm' with many of them." Part of this reconciliationist imperative allowed Union soldiers to admire the bravery of their erstwhile enemies, which Allen does in dramatic present tense. At Chancellorsville, in the face of concentrated rifle and artillery fire, the Confederates advance "without flinching . . . close up the gaps made in their ranks, and, with their eyes, and hearts, and purposes fixed on the batteries, they reach the guns as the artillerymen fire the last shot, while the horses are being attached to take them away."[11]

The narrative is shot full of striking images. A soldier flees the firing line after convincing himself that the bullets were singing "where is he? where is he?" and the shells were answering "That's him! That's him!"[12] A sentry sets off a commotion when he fires into the dark—at what turns out to be an army mule rather than an enemy patrol. Individual soldiers bravely rescue comrades and resent their powerlessness to help wounded men caught between the lines. And there is the obligatory encounter with a young slave, who ends up the butt of a soldier's joke.

After describing a few more oddball soldiers, Allen spends the bulk of the last few pages of the lecture on more serious subjects that captured the pathos of sacrifice among Union troops, the tragedy of the contraband refugees who followed Sherman's army through Georgia, and the relief and pride the army felt when the war finally ended with the rebellion crushed. He finishes with a narrative of the regiment's mustering out and welcome home, a report on the charitable and educational activities of the GAR, and a tribute to the men and women who had supported the troops on the home front.

In addition to providing a sense of the drama captured by many speakers, Allen's lecture provides a feel-good narrative of a challenging time in American history. Devoid of politics, it invited audiences to embrace the pathos, heroism, and even humor of the conflict. Very much in keeping with reconciliationist narratives, *Both Sides of Army Life* also portrays easily identifiable, even stereotypical Americans and American values. The war is, of course, at the center of Allen's lecture, but the real message—and likely the product most appreciated by his audiences—was that the nation had endured the great conflict with its character and heritage intact.

The Race Problem

Even as other lecturers celebrated the end of the war, abolition, and the reunion of the states, Blanche K. Bruce took a very different tack. The former slave and schoolteacher rose to affluent comfort as a landowner in postwar Mississippi and spent nearly twenty years as an elected or appointed officeholder in Mississippi and as the first African American to serve a full term as a U.S. senator. Although he allied himself politically with the radical wing of the Republican Party, he remained a moderate on most issues and became friends with the unrepentant Mississippi secessionist senator Lucius Q. C. Lamar. After leaving the Senate, he was appointed to several federal sinecures and remained active in national Republican politics, earning a handful of votes for the vice presidential nomination in 1880 and 1888.

Bruce was also a popular speaker, often delivering his "Race Problem" lecture. That was his subject in July 1887, when he spoke at Mahtomedi, a town established by the Chautauqua association on the shore of White Bear Lake just northeast of St. Paul, Minnesota. The *Saint Paul Globe* reported that the largest crowd of the season, including at least twenty African Americans, had gathered under the big top to hear the man introduced as the "representative colored man from Mississippi" and as "Mississippi's colored orator." Preceded incongruently by the performance of a Spanish love song, Bruce—who the reporter took care to note was quite well dressed—framed his talk around the South's refusal to comply with the civil rights laws passed by Congress since the Civil War.

The *Globe*'s detailed report of the lecture suggests that at least toward the beginning this was an interactive lecture, as Bruce responded to audience questions or comments.[13]

Bruce showed that race issues had long preceded the sectional conflict. They had started with the settlement of America and Europeans' confrontation with the "red man." After seizing the land, they had forced Africans and "Asiates" to come to America, taking advantage of the "cheapness of their labor" for "selfish" reasons. As always happened when the races of the world collided, "the whites" were "dominant." Bruce devoted most of his lecture, however, to the aftermath of the peculiar institution, after slaves were emancipated by Abraham Lincoln, whose "memory would last as long as the English language." Exploding common myths about the freedmen and women, he asserted that they had worked not only as laborers in the immediate aftermath of slavery, but also as merchants, teachers, and preachers, and that they had worked "systematically" rather than "spasmodically." They proved themselves able to compete with whites and, after a few early political mistakes, they showed a "wonderful aptitude to learn" and "made a study of the requirements of a good citizen."

Despite these positive beginnings, African Americans in the South had been held back. The "crying evil in the South" in 1887 was the lack of educational opportunities for both whites and blacks. Education was the key to improving the lives of black southerners, but white northerners had been misled by white southerners about the qualities and potential of African Americans, causing them to withhold support for black schools. As an aside, Bruce briefly complained about northern elites sending their money abroad to help "foreign heathen" rather than black southerners. Emphasizing that the "black man" had neither "exceptional virtues" nor "exceptional vices," he contrasted the little that the country had done for African Americans versus "what the black man as done for himself."

By the end of the lecture, however, Bruce had retreated from such bold rhetoric. He suggested that others—citing the "expulsion of the Moors from Spain and the whites from San Domingo"—predicted "that a war of the races was inevitable." He denied such a claim, and "speaking for his people and for himself he wanted to say that he placed too implicit confidence in the American people to believe that they would allow the perpetuation of a wrong such as he had described." He believed that the "Christianizing influence would work out the ultimate salvation of the black race without any resort to the arbitrament of arms." Indeed, if the "churches of the land" would take it upon themselves to make Congress understand the purpose and value of education, it would be a matter of days before the "people's rulers" would come to their senses. "There [is] virtue enough in the world to take cognizance of and remedy the existing evil in the South, and thus remove the greatest obstacle to its future advancement."

This version of Bruce's lecture was not a transcription, but a summary, reconstructed by a white man, whose sympathy for the speaker was qualified by his personal prejudices and political opinions. But it is important to note that Bruce's lecture, while certainly not shying away from identifying the sources of the challenges facing African Americans in the South, also clearly made the case not just for the advancement of black southerners, but for all southerners. At the same time he maintained a generic confidence in "American" values to solve the racial issues that plagued the nation twenty years after the war.

A New South

The Georgian Bill Arp (the pen name of Charles H. Smith) would only partially have agreed. Arp was a regionally famous columnist and writer during the war whose wry commentaries on Confederate policies, the peculiar hardships on the Confederate home front, the plight of southern refugees, and his brief military service had earned him a reputation that carried into the postwar period. By the early 1880s he was a popular lecturer, with his best-known lecture, "Dixie Now and Dixie Then," published in *Wallace's Monthly* in late 1883.

A Georgia newspaper described Arp's style in great detail: "The grave and dry way he has of delivering himself of a remark is in itself sufficient to set the house to laughing, and then as a climax there comes, in answer to the applause, that innocent look of utter surprise, that is absolutely irresistible." Although "humor was the predominating element" of Arp's remarks, "when describing old plantation scenes and the deplorable misfortune of broken down families since the war, genuine pathos was not lacking." Another newspaper, apparently believing that the reputation that preceded Arp suggested that he was "a Georgia wire-grass cracker," instead emphasized that "he is a polished gentleman in appearance, manners and language." There was no talk of reconciliation, as such, nor relief, nor the end of slavery, at least as a political issue. Rather, Arp delivered a rather arch description of the old South, where planters ran things, the common folk got by, and slaves were content. This was no

"Old Kentucky Home"—inequality was built into the system, which was fixed to preserve the privileges of the wealthy.[14]

Arp made considerable fun of the old elite—and their sons—but he also revealed the stark reality that the old system was based on dominance. "The aristocracy of the South was, before the war, mainly an aristocracy of dominion." He captured the essence of slavery, of patriarchy, and of the class and race considerations that shaped the South in a passage that simply and casually exposes the racist bedrock of the system: "Dominion is the pride of a man—dominion over something. A negro is proud if he owns a yaller dog and can make him come and go at his pleasure. A poor man is proud if he owns a horse and a cow and some razor-back hogs. But the Anglo-Saxon aspires to a higher degree of master. They glory in owning men, and it makes but little difference whether the men are their dependents or their slaves."[15]

The lecture began with the premise that the prewar South was a social, economic, and political system controlled by the wealthy elite that the war had destroyed. Like other lecturers of the day, Arp filled his talk with biblical and literary references. "The dominion of the old aristocracy of the South was not over their own race," although "the poor white" could not compete with the slaves the elite owned. "This kind of slave aristocracy gave dignity and leisure to the rich, and Solomon says that in leisure is wisdom; and so these men became our statesmen and jurists and law-makers, and they were shining lights in the councils of the nation." But the "exclusive . . . aristocracy" had "shut out and overshadowed the masses of the common people, like a broad spreading oak overshadows and withers the undergrowth beneath it."[16]

Although Arp shared the casual racism of the time, freely using "darkey" and other racist terms for African Americans, he was honest about the status of slaves and former slaves, and the extent to which the lives of the white elite were built on the exploitation of the unfree. "When a white child was born it was five dollars out of pocket, but a picanninny was a hundred dollars in, and got fifty dollars a year better, for twenty years to come." He embraced the stereotype of the happy slave. He treasured the rural rhythms of the prewar years, the holidays, trips to town, slaves telling scary stories.[17]

All of that changed with the war. "No more the happy slave and the proud and happy master. The devil came along one day, and like Job they were put on trial. They lost their noble sons in the army, and their property soon after. The extent of their afflictions no one will eer know, for the heart knoweth its own bitterness, but they have long since learned how to suffer and be strong." The defeat created "two general classes of people at the South—those who have seen better days and those who haven't."[18]

But defeat had bred strength. "I believe the day of prosperity is coming back," Arp declared, "and the children of the present generation will yet reap an inestimable blessing from the great calamity." More to the point, the poor whites have risen up; "they now constitute the solid men of the State, and have contributed largely to the building up of our schools and churches, our factories and railroads, and the development of our mineral resources." Arp hesitated to heap too much praise on this coming generation—they were a little too proud of themselves, too enamored of gold, too selfish—but they were also "shrewd and practical and not afraid of work."[19]

Arp treated women somewhat condescendingly, but generally with respect. Elite women had borne the brunt of the Confederacy's loss. The daughters of the women who had suffered on the home front, the first postwar generation, would not have the leisure provided by "servants" to become cultured, to take advantage of the education that their privileged status allowed them. Even so, Arp seems to suggest that women continued to be the backbone of southern society, and that they were adapting to the new order more readily than men. At one point he only half jokes that there were not enough educated men available to marry the educated women in the South. In the old days, there were more educated men among the elite, and fewer educated women. Now, however, when women complete their education and "go home," they "can't find anybody good enough for them." He worried a little about these educated women having to settle for lives of drudgery and hard work on farms and in shops: "I never see ladies of culture and refinement doing the household drudgery, or the daughters of poor tenants plowing and hoeing in the field, but what it shocks my humanity." Yet the women of the South would adapt, he argued. During the war, the women left behind "lived cheaper and managed better than ever before." They demonstrated the difference between men and women; "if they can't do some big thing, or the crop ails, and they mope around and do nothing, but a woman never gives up. The more oppressed, the more she is aroused."[20]

Although Arp admitted "that the abolition of Southern slavery will eventually prove a blessing," he blasted the sudden emancipation of the slaves. He offered a long, if orthodox, defense of slavery, including the specious idea that "there is some kind of slavery everywhere; there is slavery at sea among the sailors, and slavery on land among the soldiers of the regular army. We are all of us under some kind of bondage." Slavery had prepared the slaves for a certain basic freedom, but they were not yet fully ready for independence.[21]

Focusing on the material conditions facing postwar southerners, Arp's gritty version of the New South, rising from the ashes of the values and assumptions that had buttressed the prewar South, showed southerners grimly adapting to defeat, the emancipation of slaves, and the destruction of their status and power. Arp himself fairly grudgingly accepts that the new order had improved southern society. "There need be no serious or gloomy apprehension concerning the future of the sons and daughters of the South," Arp declared as he began to wrap up his long lecture. The "common ancestry" of southerners, their loyalty to place and longing for home, their affection for the past, all combined to create a society designed to persevere and to rebuild. He got in a few licks at the North: their antebellum "jealousy of our power and influence in the councils of the nation," their anger at the South's "condemnation of their immoral practices in trade and the pursuit of money," their "fanatical crusade against slavery." There was no need to urge his audience to a cheerful reconciliation.[22]

Arp concluded by admitting that sometimes he felt "sad because our children know so little of what the South was in the good old times." Yet "the diffusion of knowledge is now bringing the masses up to the standard of education which these noble-men created. . . . The chances of men for fortune and for fame are more generally diffused and more nearly equal than they have ever been, and the rise of a man from the humblest walks of life is no longer considered a miracle." In the grand scheme of things, "the pendulum is always swinging. . . up to-day, down to-morrow—but still the pivot on which they play is rising higher and higher in Dixie."[23]

Arp's lecture combined a Lost Cause sentimentality for portions of Old South life and culture with a critical evaluation of other portions and a fairly full-throated admiration for the New South. Unlike many other southerners, however, he barely mentioned the Confederacy. Arp's subtlety no doubt disarmed listeners who were more nostalgic than he for the old ways. He was truly funny, and the humor dulled the barbs aimed at the ruling class that had led the South into war. Although this was hardly a reconciliation lecture, it nevertheless featured a South moving on and adjusting. Although it was also not a Lost Cause lecture, it heaped praise (in Arp's particular way) on the women who carried the torch for that cause in the 1880s and 1890s. And although it did not mourn the end of slavery, neither did it suggest a particularly prominent place for African Americans in the New South.

Donald Scott, writing of the prewar lecture system, argues that lyceum lectures imposed order on the chaos of information confronting modern audiences. "Audiences came away from a popular lecture with a sense that the lecturer had carried them to a state of 'enlarged understanding,' a mode of apprehension that went beyond mere empirical knowledge." Those Gilded Age lecturers on the Civil War introduced topics—personal recollections of bloody battles, race relations, and even class differences—that were virtually unheard of prior to the war. But they were adapted to familiar genres and marketing strategies, and even fit (if somewhat uncomfortably) into themes popular during the antebellum years. Despite the vast differences in subject matter and tone, in backgrounds and points of view, a single thread does run through these lectures: they were able to find a United States that their audiences would recognize, and a role in that version of America that they could fulfill. If the prewar lecture system was a means of bringing order to conflicting and confusing ideas, the same can be said for the Civil War lectures during the Gilded Age iteration, in which speakers sought to bring order to conflicting historical narratives. These stage-bound entrepreneurs, drawing on a shared history with multiple, conflicting facets, manufactured narrative products that consumers could recognize, digest, appreciate, and internalize. Frosted with nostalgia, leavened with a sense of loss, spiced with hope in the future, and often washed down with a draft of humor, the product purchased by listeners made the war understandable, matched their perceptions, and pointed them into the twentieth century.[24]

NOTES

1. Quoted in Capt. James E. Smith, "The Career of Corporal James Tanner in War and Peace," in *A Famous Battery and Its Campaigns* (Washington, D.C.: W. H. Lowdermilk, 1892), 178–216, quotes on 199, 197–98.

2. A long article on Tanner's standard lecture appeared in the *Brooklyn Eagle*, October 15, 1885. All subsequent quotes about Tanner are from that article if otherwise unattributed.

3. Angela G. Ray, *The Lyceum and Public Culture in the Nineteenth-Century United States* (East Lansing: Michigan State University Press, 2005), esp. 173–89.

4. Peter Cherches, *Nineteenth-Century Lecture Tours and the Consolidation of Modern Celebrity* (Rotterdam: Sense Publishers, 2017), 51; *Vermont Phoenix*, November 4, 1887.

5. J. G. Holland, *Plain Talks on Familiar Subjects: A Series of Popular Lectures* (New York: Charles Scribner and Co., 1868), 310.

6. Elsie M. Wilbor, ed., *Werner's Directory of Elocutionists, Readers, Lecturers and other Public Instructors and Entertainers* (New York: Edgar S. Werner, 1887), 381, 317, 319, 322, 315, 329, 328.

7. Caroline E. Janney, "'One of the Best Loved, North and South': The Appropriation of National Reconciliation by LaSalle Corbell Pickett," *Virginia Magazine of History and Biography* 116 (January 2008): 370–406.

8. Rev. E. Livingston Allen, *Descriptive Lecture: Both Sides of Army Life, the Grave and the Gay* (N.p.: The Author, 1885), 1.

9. Ibid., 2.

10. Ibid., 2, 3.

11. Ibid., 4.

12. Ibid., 5.

13. *Saint Paul (Minn.) Globe,* July 30, 1887. All quotes in the following paragraphs come from this detailed description of Bruce's lecture.

14. *Our Mountain Home* (Talladega, Ala.), March 16, 1881.

15. Bill Arp, "Dixie Now and Dixie Then," *Wallace's Monthly* 9 (November 1883): 747.

16. Ibid., 748.

17. Ibid., 749.

18. Ibid., 750, 748.

19. Ibid., 750.

20. Ibid., 752, 753.

21. Ibid., 755.

22. Ibid., 754.

23. Ibid., 755.

24. Donald M. Scott, "The Popular Lecture and the Creation of a Pubic in Mid-Nineteenth-Century America," *Journal of American History* 66, no. 4 (March 1980): 791–809, quote on 806.

A New and Unique Show

The Rise and Fall of Civil War Cycloramas

CAROLINE E. JANNEY

In October 1883, a "new and unique show" opened in Chicago. Painted by the famed Parisian artist Paul Philippoteaux, *The Battle of Gettysburg* proved an instant success. Two years earlier, Chicago investors had commissioned the cyclorama, a cylindrical painting depicting Pickett's Charge on July 3, 1863. The *Chicago Tribune* declared Philippoteaux's work to be "the most remarkable counterfeit presentment so far devised by the artistic talent of man." Others agreed. In the weeks and months that followed, tourists flocked to the brick octagonal building that held the painting to see if the hype was warranted.[1]

Panoramas and cycloramas were not born of the Civil War. They were not "new and unique." Nor had they proven particularly successful in the United States prior to the 1880s. But when investors began to leverage the war as their subject, the massive paintings became overnight sensations—and big moneymakers. Over the course of a decade, approximately forty to fifty cycloramas opened in cities from Boston to San Francisco, peddling an entertainment experience featuring the great battles of the war. The attractions not only made money for the individuals and companies that staged them, they also provided a new source of revenue for the studios who mass-produced them, the construction workers who built the enormous brick rotundas, and the streetcar operators who shuttled visitors to the doors. The cash flow did not end there. Souvenir booklets marketed items far removed from the battlefield, such as household goods, while portions of the grand artwork were sold as lithographs that appeared in advertisements for agricultural implements. On these massive pieces of canvas, the war could be both bought and sold.

Yet unlike the monuments erected by veterans and women's groups, the national battlefields established in the 1890s, or even the memoirs written by the war's veterans, the proprietors of the great Civil War panoramas did not create them as memorials to a particular memory of the war. The panorama companies staged the magnificent paintings chiefly as a moneymaking venture, altering the themes and messages to appeal to their audiences rather than to promote a particular interpretation of the war. The cycloramas, therefore, proved quintessentially Gilded Age: driven by a wealthy individuals, backed by joint-stock companies, outfitted with the latest technology, and intended to generate enormous profits, the exhibitions brought a new form of leisure to the nation's urban masses while opening new business ventures and marketing strategies to veterans and nonveterans alike.

Cycloramas appeared to burst onto the U.S. scene in the 1880s, but panoramas had been all the rage in Europe for nearly a century. In the late eighteenth century, Irishman Robert Barker imagined painting a "picture without boundaries"—a vast landscape with no beginning or end. Spectators flocked to see his *View of London* from the Albion Mills, which premiered in 1792. Panoramas then spread south to Paris, where artists painted scenes of Napoleon's armies. Throughout Europe, in Russia, and Japan, audiences who could not afford to own an oil painting or travel abroad flocked to see the panoramas.[2]

Panoramas arrived in the United States in 1795 when English landscape painter William Winstanley reproduced Barker's *View of London* from the Albion Mills. But they enjoyed much less initial enthusiasm than did those across the Atlantic. When American artist John Vanderlyn unveiled his *Panoramic View of the Palace and Gardens of Versailles* in New York in 1819, spectators refused to pay, leaving him bankrupt. In the decades that followed, artists took up American landscapes, including John Rowson Smith's panoramas of the Mississippi River (the first painted in 1838) and Frederic Church's *Niagara* in 1857. By the 1870s, panoramas had reached their golden age in Europe. As with so many other aspects of U.S. consumer culture in the Gilded Age, Americans looked again across the Atlantic for inspiration, importing paintings of Napoleonic battles, biblical scenes, and foreign vistas. In 1874, the Chautauqua Assembly of Upstate New York premiered a panoramic landscape featuring the Holy Land. That same year, Chicagoans welcomed their first panorama, *Paris by Moonlight*.[3] The rush to consume these massive paintings had commenced in the United States.

Cycloramas, a specific style of panorama, were truly pictures without boundaries, consisting of a single painting affixed inside a polygonal or round building with a viewing platform in the center. Most paintings measured slightly less than 50 feet high and 400 feet in circumference. The viewing platform was placed in the center of the space, approximately 15 to 20 feet above ground level and 40 feet from the painting on any side. The scene wrapped 360 degrees around the platform to encircle the viewer, and the canvas rose to an immense height while the bottom gave way to real three-dimensional objects, such as caissons, dirt, rocks, fence posts, and other battlefield detritus, thereby blurring the point where the painting ended and the objects began. All of this created an illusion, leaving the viewer with the sensation of being in the midst of the action. Yet experiencing the cyclorama involved much more than simply viewing a painting. At night, electric lights provided illumination, while lecturers offered "vivid and instructive explanation[s] of the battle as it actually took place."[4]

The first true cyclorama, the *Siege of Paris*, depicting the recent Franco-Prussian War, arrived in Philadelphia for the 1876 Centennial Celebration. "This wonderfully truthful cyclorama continues to gratify hundreds of well-satisfied and instructed gazers, who, for the first time in their lives, realize the striking and terrific violence of war" a newspaper reported in August (ignoring the fact that Civil War veterans were likely among the audience). After spending two years in Philadelphia, during the next decade the painting traveled to Boston, San Francisco, New York, Chicago, and Los Angeles. Without ever leaving their cities, spectators could travel across both space and time to distant lands. As one historian has noted, "panoramas provided the illusion of travel" becoming tourist attractions of places (and times) patrons might not be able to visit in person.[5]

The extravagantly wealthy department store magnate Charles L. Willoughby of Chicago was among those who paid to experience the *Siege of Paris* (and perhaps *Paris by Moonlight*). But Willoughby believed a U.S.-themed painting featuring the nation's own recent war might have even more appeal. The most prominent (and successful) of the painters had been trained in France and Germany, necessitating the need to once again look across the ocean. Willoughby selected French artist Paul Philippoteaux, who, along with his famous father, had created the *Siege of Paris*. He offered the painter a $50,000 commission to create a cyclorama featuring the climactic minutes of Pickett's Charge on the final day of Gettysburg. In 1883, under the banner of the National Panorama Company, Willoughby and his investors financed the exhibition, including the construction on the corner of Wabash Avenue and Hubbard Court in Chicago of a rotunda designed by architectural firm Bauer and Hill.[6]

The Gettysburg cyclorama was not the brainchild of a veteran or veterans' organization meant to memorialize their cause or fallen brethren. (Neither Willoughby nor his fellow investors appear to have been veterans.) The venture did not fall squarely into the category of documenting the war, as was the case with the goal of memoirs, battle accounts, or even the publication of the *Official Records of the War of the Rebellion* (beginning in 1881). Nor had the investors proposed the painting (or any others that followed) be located at the site of the battle. They intended the cyclorama to serve first and foremost as an entertainment that might generate massive profits as similar ventures had done throughout Europe. "Money has been made in every one of our enterprises except Madrid," reported a French company, adding that "the great expense is in the picture and the building; after that the expense is trifling." Gettysburg had become the most celebrated and well-known battle of the war, generating more publications and visitors annually than any other battlefield. This, alone, was reason to select it as a subject. Indeed, when *The Battle of Gettysburg* opened in October 1883 at the cost of fifty cents for adults (and twenty-five cents for children), a Chicago newspaper gushed that the city should "congratulate herself upon the permanent possession of a mise-en-scene of this kind which will add as much as a park or a great theatre to her attractions."[7]

The cyclorama proved a smashing success, with three hundred thousand people viewing the show during its first year. Willoughby thus commissioned Philippoteaux to produce a second painting of Gettysburg to be showcased in Boston.[8] As in Chicago, Willoughby hired crews to build a large, circular brick structure to house the painting, this one at 541 Tremont Street. Yet there would be some differences. With feedback from prominent veterans (the most discerning and perhaps important patrons), Philippoteaux altered some aspects of the scene. For example, he added troops to Brigadier General John C. Caldwell's division, converted a battery wagon in the area of the high water mark into a cannon, and moved Major General George H. Meade's headquarters closer to the viewer. (Philippoteaux's fourth *Battle of Gettysburg*, painted for New York in 1886, would be the first to include General Meade). And after hearing criticisms that the uniforms "looked too French," he improved the oversized backpacks (although he still included numerous Union soldiers with white pants, again a nod to the artist's French background).[9]

Days before the Boston exhibit opened on December 22, 1884, Willoughby took out large ads in the city's newspapers proclaiming the painting the "GREATEST and most EXPENSIVE work of art produced in ancient or modern times"—divulging that the entire enterprise cost $75,000. If the price tag was not enough to induce visitors, Willoughby thought peer pressure might do the trick. "You will come again and again, and will, by PERSUASION, THREATS, even FORCE, cause every person you know to visit this Magnificent Wonder of modern times." The ad mentioned only the name Gettysburg and the date of the battle. It said nothing of the war's legacy, its meaning, the virtues of saving the Union, or ending slavery. Spectators would come to see the enormous "50 feet high and 400 feet in circumference" painting—to experience this new entertainment venue.[10]

This cyclorama offered visitors a version of the Civil War unlike any other. It was one thing to read about battles in books, listen to a veteran lecture, look through a stereoscope, or play Milton Bradley's Myriopticon game (all popular formats during the 1880s–90s discussed in other essays in this volume). But cycloramas provided another level of *experience*. Standing on the viewing platform, urban patrons found themselves transported to the battlefield—to the very heat of battle. Even trips to actual battlefields could not evoke the same sensation of being in the midst of the action.

Civilians and veterans alike marveled at the authenticity of the experience. Major General John Gibbon, a division commander in the Army of the Potomac's Second Corps at Gettysburg, visited the Chicago cyclorama three times in mid-1884. "You may rest assured you have got a sight to see before you die. It is simply wonderful and I never before had an idea that the eye could be so deceived by paint and canvas," he wrote a fellow Union veteran. "The perspective and representation of the landscape is simply perfect," he continued, "and I say nothing more than the truth when I tell you it was difficult to disabuse my mind of the impression that I was actually on the ground." (Like others, however, he offered critiques of some military aspects including troop placements). Others concurred with Gibbon's praise. "You will find hard work to convince yourself that you are not standing on the top of the Cemetery Ridge in the very centre of the position occupied by the troops of the Northern army," observed the *Boston Globe* of the second painting. "On the ground at your feet lie broken cannon, guns, bayonets, and so finely is the work done that a person cannot tell where the artist ends and the painting begins." Some Union veterans claimed that "a better impression of the battle may be ob-

Spectators could purchase souvenir programs for the cycloramas that
included information about the battle as well as advertisements for household
items such as dinner sets, lamps, and water filters, suggesting that women
were a target audience. (Private collection of Caroline E. Janney)

tained in an hour spent in examining this cyclorama than in a month's
study of printed descriptions."[11]

It was not merely that veterans and their families admired the cycloramas' authenticity. They could also take home part of the experience
by purchasing souvenir programs for an additional five cents, which included biographical information on the painter, a map of the battlefield,
and other background information. Perhaps most important for the patrons, it included a fold-out key that denoted important individuals and
places on the field. Yet the souvenir program also engaged in the act of
selling: throughout the pages, readers found themselves inundated with
advertisements for dinner sets, lamps, and water filters that had nothing
to do with the experience or the Civil War. Moreover, only middle- and
upper-class women tended to purchase these items. While both men and
women visited the cyclorama, it remains telling that the overtly masculine
Civil War was being used to sell household items—items that could not
have been farther from the battlefield depicted in the painting.[12]

This cycle of buying and selling extended beyond the newspaper ads and souvenir programs. In the spring of 1885, Boston residents gathered for a carnival at Mechanic's Hall to raise money for the Soldiers' Home. Some attendees donated funds: the local Ladies' Aid Association gave twenty-five dollars while Mrs. Leopold Morse forwarded ten dollars. Charles Willoughby, too, contributed. He sent the hefty sum of fifty dollars—but in return, he asked the "privilege of distributing circulars of his war picture." Even in the act of donating to the Soldiers' Home, Willoughby intended to make a profit. Just a few weeks later, Willoughby decided to sell a portion of his company to stockholders, thus forming the Boston Cyclorama Company. In June, the local newspaper announced that the company was doing well—declaring a dividend of 4 percent from the earnings of April and May.[13]

Hoping to drum up more visitation, the company arranged for special excursion trains to run along the Boston and Providence Railroad. Tickets to and from Providence or Pawtucket, including admission to the cyclorama, cost a mere $1.50. Soon the exhibit spawned other ventures, such as horsecar companies that provided cars exclusively to and from the shows. Still the company looked for clever ways of profiting from the now not-so-new endeavor. In March 1888, it hired a quartet of male singers to perform old war songs on the platform. "Old soldiers will find much pleasure in joining with the quartet in several of the best selections," a newspaper column promised.[14]

The success of the Chicago and Boston Gettysburg cycloramas generated demand for more such paintings, and more paintings meant more studios. The most prominent and prolific of the companies were based in the Midwest. And as with Philippoteaux, most of the artists were foreign nationals or immigrants often trained in the academies of Munich, Duesseldorf, or Paris. In 1884, German-born and Chicago-based businessman William Wehner established the American Panorama Company in Milwaukee, the first large-scale company in the United States dedicated to producing panoramas. Wehner brought experienced German panorama painters, including August Lohr and Franz Biberstein, to the United States to work for American Panorama. Alongside a team of up to twelve artists, they painted several cycloramas, including *The Storming of Missionary Ridge* and *Battle of Atlanta* in a large, octagon-shaped studio at the corner of Wells and Fifth Streets. (In the years that followed, the firm changed names to Lohr and Heine Co., 1887–88, and finally the Milwaukee Panorama Company, 1888–ca. 1892).[15] In 1884, Paul Bechtner, Otto Osthoff, and Louis Kindt likewise incorporated the Northwestern Panorama Company in Milwaukee, while Chicago proved to be home to no less than four companies including Reed and Gross Panorama Co. and the Palentine Exhibition Company.[16]

For each of these companies, staging cycloramas required significant investments: construction of studios in which to paint the massive canvases and the rotundas in which they would be displayed, as well as the painters' labor. The American Panorama Company spent $60,000, for example, to produce *The Storming of Missionary Ridge* (to be paid for in shares of the company stock), not including the construction of a new studio in Milwaukee, which cost $8,000.[17] But companies—and the cities they called home—hoped such outlays would more than double their investments. Anticipating the opening of *The Battle of Gettysburg* at Philadelphia in 1886, an advertisement claimed that the Chicago cyclorama had been visited by more than five hundred thousand people—in two days alone $5,000 had been collected at the door. In less than a year, the Boston show had witnessed more than four hundred thousand visitors and taken in $1,850 in a single day. Philadelphia, the ad proclaimed, was "a greater city" than both Chicago and Boston. "One million dollars should be the receipts for the year 1886 in this great city," the ad boldly proclaimed.[18]

The profitability of the cycloramas continued throughout the late-1880s, as investors and artists expanded their subjects beyond the Civil War. In 1887, investors in Boston built "another great tubular building" to house *The Battle of Bunker Hill.*[19] Other subjects likewise found their way to the canvas, including *Christ's Triumphal Entry into Jerusalem* and *The Chicago Fire.*[20] Still, Civil War–themed paintings proved the most numerous. By October 1887, companies in Philadelphia, St. Paul, and Denver each had constructed round houses containing cycloramas of Gettysburg. St. Louis and Kansas City featured versions of the Battle of Missionary Ridge, Toledo showcased *The Monitor and Merrimac,* Milwaukee housed *General Grant's Assault on Vicksburg,* New York exhibited *Panorama of the Land and Naval Battles of Vicksburg,* and Detroit unveiled *The Battle of Atlanta.*[21]

But Chicago, the archetypal Gilded Age city, proved the most popular home for cycloramas. By 1884, the city had three cyclorama buildings. Two sat on opposite corners along Hubbard Court and Wabash Avenue, including the original Philippoteaux painting of Gettysburg and *Jerusalem at the Time of the Crucifixion.* In 1891, the city boasted five cyclorama rotundas, featuring such productions as Théophile Poilpot's *Battle of Shiloh* (1885). By the 1893 World Columbian Exposition, a sixth had been added, two of which featured Civil War battles.[22]

Notably, northern-based companies owned, commissioned, and dis-

The view south along Wabash Avenue and Michigan Avenue shows two of
Chicago's cyclorama buildings. The Battle of Gettysburg building is visible on
the west side of Wabash Avenue. (ICHi-05715, Chicago History Museum)

played the panoramas. Because the audiences tended to be Union veterans and their families, the paintings showcased Union victories. By 1886, companies had commissioned four different Battle of Gettysburg cycloramas. But other Union victories soon captured the nation's imagination. The *Panorama of the Land and Naval Battles of Vicksburg*, which opened in New York in May 1886, portrayed Union operations of May 22, 1863. The foreground featured hand-to-hand fighting by enlisted men in blue, but the artists had likewise included Generals Ulysses S. Grant, William T. Sherman, and John A. Logan. A Kansas newspaper reported that Grand Army of the Republic (GAR) veterans would find much to appreciate in the painting.[23] Similarly, the Atlanta cyclorama depicted that battle as a great Union victory centered on General Logan rallying the Union troops outside the city on July 22, 1864. When it debuted in Minneapolis in August 1886, more than eight hundred paying customers viewed the painting in a single day.[24]

In an effort to attract large crowds, companies invited famous generals to attend their openings. Generals Abner Doubleday, Dan Sickles, Henry W. Slocum, Joseph B. Carr, and Charles Graham all appeared at the pre-

mier of the New York *Battle of Gettysburg* in October 1886.[25] GAR members
and commanders were likewise usually in attendance. Before his death
in December 1886, General John A. Logan, commander-in-chief of the
GAR from 1868–71, proved a frequent attendee. Visiting alongside his
wife and other members of the Union League, Logan pronounced Minneapolis's *Battle of Atlanta* "very good . . . the best I ever saw."[26]

The panorama of the Second Battle of Manassas, exhibited in Washington, D.C., in 1886, however, gave some northern audiences pause.
Unlike the others, it featured a Confederate victory.[27] After its debut in
March, a local GAR post protested the painting. In the pages of the *National Tribune*, one Union veteran observed that "the selection of the subject and the manner of its treatment" deserved "most of the harsh criticism they have received." Central to his critique was the depiction of
havoc among the Union ranks and prominence in the foreground to pictures of Confederate generals Robert E. Lee and James Longstreet. There
had been no attempt to showcase "any Union success, or pictures of the
Union Generals who did gallant service upon that bloody field," he complained. "It is certainly straining severely all ideas of propriety to erect
in the Nation's Capital such a monument of a rebel victory," he continued, "especially when Washington contains no such testimonial to the triumph of the Union arms." But others objected to this critique, seeing no
indication that the painting glorified the Confederacy. Given the proximity to Virginia, and the potential to attract Confederate veterans and their
families, it made good business sense to paint the battle.[28] The GAR post's
response, however, revealed the distance between the veterans' feelings
about the paintings and the motivations of cyclorama companies. While
veterans might worry about honoring and perpetuating their memory
of the war, the market drove firms to produce paintings of Union rather
than Confederate victories.

Even as the cyclorama companies raked in profits, some individuals found other ways to capitalize on the paintings' popularity. In 1884,
Kurz and Allison of Chicago began printing a brightly colored lithograph
titled *The Battle of Gettysburg*, which could be displayed in one's home.
Louis Kurz, an Austrian immigrant and the firm's principal artist, had
served in the 165th Ohio. But Kurz had no battlefield experience—the
regiment formed the year after Gettysburg for one hundred days service,
and it primarily served guard duty. Yet he had clearly visited the Gettysburg cyclorama in Chicago and taken inspiration from it. As historians
Mark Neely Jr. and Harold Holzer observe, "the print openly copied vi-
gnettes from the painting and in at least one instance perpetuated a his-

torical error made by artist Philippoteaux" by depicting Confederate general Lewis Armistead leading the charge on horseback (rather than on foot). In the decade that followed, Kurz and Allison published the largest and most popular set of Civil War lithographs, thirty-six in all, several inspired by cycloramas.[29]

Other printers followed suit. In December 1885 (only months after Poilpot's *Battle of Shiloh* debuted in Chicago), Cosack and Company began printing a portion of the painting as a chromolithograph. In the lower right corner, a stamp noted that the image had been "copied by special permission from the Panorama Painting on Exhibition in Chicago." But this was more than just a print to display in one's home. It was issued as a premium by the McCormick Harvesting Machine Company. The printer had inserted a bright-red McCormick harvester and twine binder into Poilpot's painting. Tucked under a shed much dilapidated by the battle raging around it, the reaper remained intact. "The McCormick Machines Come Victoriously out of Every Contest, and Without a Scratch," declared the caption. Those old enough to remember the war would have recognized that the reaper had not been invented in 1862. Who was the intended audience? Those who had visited the cyclorama and wanted to continue to gaze on the image? Those in the market for a hay binder? Veterans? Was this intended as a merging of a romantic agrarian past and an industrial, mechanized present meant to appeal across generations? Whomever the audience, both Cosack and Company as well as McCormick Harvester believed the image worth copyrighting. In subsequent years, McCormick would add more lithographs derived from cycloramas to its advertising campaign, including *Terrific Engagement between the "Monitor" and "Merrimac"* (1885), *Battle of Mission Ridge* (1886), two versions of *The Battle of Gettysburg* (1886), and *Battle of Atlanta* (1888). In each advertising poster, the company inserted a McCormick machine into the scene, promising it would be indestructible—even in battle.[30]

Other veterans found employment with the cycloramas. When Philadelphia's *The Battle of Gettysburg* opened in October 1885, Captain Charles Hale of the Fifth New Hampshire who had fought in the battle began giving lectures on the platform. After the war, Hale had returned to New Hampshire and worked as a machinist to support his wife and two small children. By 1880, the family had moved into his father's home at Camden, New Jersey, where Hale labored as a paper material manufacturer. Perhaps it was this proximity to Philadelphia that drew him to the cyclorama in 1885. But the gig must have been a good one, because when the painting moved to Cincinnati in 1887, he followed and continued to serve as the main platform lecturer for the next three years. In the years that followed, he made a living as a battlefield guide with the Gettysburg Exhibition Company until 1899, when he was admitted to the Milwaukee branch of the National Soldiers Home and later died of a spinal infection.[31] By 1886, Captain John F. Chase was giving daily lectures for the Brooklyn-based *Battle of Gettysburg*. When Chase was positioned on Steven's Knoll on July 2 with the Fifth Maine Battery, shrapnel took his right arm and left eye and inflicted another forty-eight wounds, earning him the Medal of Honor. Like Hale, he levied these horrific experiences into a postwar career that included marketing his patented wringer and water still. But he also jumped on the cyclorama train. His business card indicates that he acted as a "lecturer and general manager" of the New York–based cyclorama, accompanying it on tour.[32]

Even as a handful of veterans cashed in on their ties to the paintings, cyclorama companies soon realized the limited scope of their market, because audiences tended to visit a painting only once. Investors therefore embarked on an effort to circulate the cycloramas among cities. A handful of companies even organized under the premise of rotating exhibits. In July 1888, for example, the Buffalo-based Queen City Cyclorama Company was incorporated. With capital of $200,000, the trustees planned to erect a large building that would become one of a circuit of cyclorama companies. The first painting, *Jerusalem at the Time of the Crucifixion*, would be a duplicate of one then on display in Chicago, itself a copy of the original, which hung in Munich. The company hired fifteen German painters, brought them to a studio in Milwaukee, and commissioned the painting to be exhibited by early September 1888. When audiences had their fill of the painting of Jerusalem, the company planned to bring battle images of Gettysburg (then on display in Chicago), Missionary Ridge (in San Francisco), Atlanta (in Detroit), and Sedan (in Toronto).[33] By 1890, between thirty to forty paintings featuring at least seven Civil War battles moved along the circuit that included cities from New York to Salt Lake City. Most of these paintings remained in a given city for a year or longer. For example, *Battle of Atlanta* debuted in Minneapolis (June 1886–March 1888) before traveling to Indianapolis (May 1888–May 1891).[34]

By the mid-1890s, however, visitation at cycloramas had declined precipitously. Boston's *Battle of Gettysburg* closed in 1888, and the following spring it was replaced by a new painting, *Custer's Last Fight* (the Gettysburg painting reopened briefly in late 1889 but permanently closed in December 1890).[35] After relocating from New York to San Francisco in 1887, *Panorama of the Land and Naval Battles of Vicksburg* remained open only three and half years.[36] In 1891, the proprietors of the Buffalo show attempted to increase visitation to the Missionary Ridge cyclorama by joining forces with the local newspaper. Those who purchased a Sunday paper (for five cents) would receive a free cyclorama ticket (a bargain at twenty-five cents—down from fifty cents a few years earlier—a common practice among many of the shows).[37] In 1892, a Baltimore newspaper announced the arrival of the circus, to be held in the former cyclorama building.[38] Chicago looked to its own past in 1892 with a cyclorama of the 1871 fire even as its *Battle of Gettysburg* greeted attendees at the Sioux City Interstate Fair in 1894 for ten days in a temporary building. The following year, the original Chicago rotunda was shuttered. By the turn of the century, only a handful of cycloramas remained. Many had been ravaged by poor storage and handling. Some fell victim to fires and storms, while others were cut into smaller sections to be used as theater backdrops. At least one, *Panorama of the Land and Naval Battles of Vicksburg*, traveled across the Pacific to open to Japanese audiences in 1890.[39]

The great heyday of the cycloramas had lasted a little more than a decade. But why the precipitous decline? Some art historians have suggested that motion pictures stole audiences when the first film debuted in New York in 1894. Yet the cycloramas had already experienced a sharp falling-off in attendance—and, more importantly—profits. The oversaturated markets in the North, Midwest, and even on the West Coast likely contributed to their demise. "The more or less popular cycloramas of the present day are so well known that a description of them is unnecessary," observed a Rochester, New York, newspaper in 1892. A Brooklyn paper provided an even bleaker commentary that same year, referring to a time when cycloramas "were all the rage."[40]

The rising popularity of new types of battle "recreation" may likewise have contributed to the cycloramas' short life. In 1886, a New York businessman began staging a panoramic pyrotechnical reenactment. An outdoor production, such shows used a large panorama as a background for reenactors portraying both Union and Confederate soldiers. Performed just before dark, pyrotechnics simulated exploding shells while the reenactors used blank ammunition to replicate musket fire. These dynamic exhibitions drew even larger audiences than the cycloramas. One Chicago show in 1895 reportedly attracted more than thirteen thousand spectators.[41]

While new forms of entertainment featuring Civil War battles appealed to audiences in the North, some of the cycloramas headed to the South. The *Storming of Missionary Ridge* enjoyed a stint in Atlanta in 1891–

92 before traveling to Nashville (where it was destroyed by a storm in July 1893).[42] In June 1891, *Battle of Atlanta* left Indianapolis bound for Chattanooga, where proprietors hoped southern audiences might flock to the show. In 1892, however, the painting's owner declared bankruptcy and put it on the market. Paul Atkinson of Atlanta purchased the cyclorama for $37,000 (and constructed the building for another $4,000).[43]

Like the northern entrepreneurs who had commissioned the Civil War–themed cycloramas, Atkinson recognized that he needed to appeal to his audience: white southerners. Other cycloramas had been altered during their lifetimes, but none inversed the narrative of a battle as did the changes commissioned by Atkinson.[44] He hired artists to recolor a scene depicting prisoners of war: the Union uniforms were changed to gray and the Confederate uniforms to blue while the captured Confederate battle flag was removed. No longer would *Battle of Atlanta* portray an effortless Union victory. Instead, artists manipulated the painting to show Confederates succeeding—a message Atkinson drove home in the advertising, which heralded the painting as a great Confederate triumph. "The painting is wonderful," lauded the *Atlanta Constitution*, "from the mere fact that is the only one in existence where the Confederates get the best of things."[45] This statement was incorrect on two counts: Atlanta was not a Confederate victory, and the Battle of Second Manassas, painted in 1886, had been a rebel victory.[46] Yet the praise continued. "Every [white] southerner will find in it the only cyclorama that does justice to the cause of the South. The glorious valor of her heroes is wonderfully portrayed," proclaimed the paper.[47]

No other cyclorama was subjected to such distortion. Perhaps that is because even the "revised" painting failed to generate sustained interest. Unable to generate the windfall he had hoped to land, Atkinson sold the painting in 1893 to another speculator. By August 1893, however, the new investor was forced to sell again to satisfy debts. Suggestions surfaced that the city of Atlanta should purchase the painting and permanently locate it in Grant Park "with the privilege of free access to the public." Two men soon purchased the cyclorama and immediately donated it to the city in 1898. Housed in a building too small for the massive painting, the city cut three sections to make it fit. Only ten years after the first *Battle of Gettysburg* opened in Chicago with the intent of generating great profits, the city of Atlanta had agreed to expend taxpayer money to sustain a *free* experience for its residents. But most attendees still visited only once. Not until 1939 during the premier of *Gone with the Wind* did the Atlanta cyclorama produce any real interest. Yet after the fanfare surrounding the movie faded, so too did interest in the cyclorama. Once more it fell into disrepair and obscurity.[48]

Today, only two original Civil War cycloramas survive. Philippoteaux's second *Battle of Gettysburg* painted for Boston (1884) has been housed at the battlefield that bears its name since 1913, property of the National Park Service since 1939. After more than fifty years of display in a building that caused more harm than good, in 2004 Gettysburg National Military Park reconstructed the painting before its reopening in 2008. Six years later, the city of Atlanta closed the Grant Park exhibit and turned *Battle of Atlanta* (1886) over to the Atlanta History Center (AHC). Raising $35 million for a new building to house the cyclorama on its campus, the AHC restored the painting to its original splendor and size (replacing the pieces removed in the 1890s). It debuted to the public in 2019.[49]

In a review of the Atlanta exhibit for the *New York Times*, art critic Holland Cotter observed that the AHC "doesn't treat the cyclorama as art, entertainment or monument. It presents it as a dynamic artifact of the past."[50] Such is the job of museums—a job done exceptionally well by the AHC. Yet the two remaining cycloramas still carry an admission fee. While that money sustains the nonprofits that house them rather than lines the pockets of wealthy entrepreneurs, the cycloramas have proved, yet again, the war could in fact be bought, sold, and perhaps sold once more.

NOTES

I thank Noel Harrison for his exceptional help on this project. As always, he was beyond gracious with his time and sources.

1. *Chicago Tribune*, October 21, 1883; Chris Brenneman and Sue Boardman, *The Gettysburg Cyclorama: The Turning Point of the Civil War on Canvas* (El Dorado Hills, Calif.: Savas Beatie, 2015), 21.

2. Robert Wernick, "Getting a Glimpse of History from a Grandstand Seat," *Smithsonian*, August 1985, 68–87.

3. Kevin J. Avery and Peter L. Fodera, *John Vanderlyn's Panoramic View of the Palace and Gardens of Versailles* (New York: Metropolitan Museum of Art, 1988), 9, 11; John F. Sears, *Sacred Places: American Tourist Attractions in the Nineteenth Century* (New York: Oxford University Press, 1989), 51; Kristin L. Hoganson, *Consumer's Imperium: The Global Production of American Domesticity, 1865–1920* (Chapel Hill: University of North Carolina Press, 2007); *New York Herald*, October 12, 1872; *Inter Ocean* (Chicago), June 2, 1874; Wernick, "Getting a Glimpse," 78.

4. Brenneman and Boardman, *Gettysburg Cyclorama*, 7–8; *Boston Globe*, December 18, 1884.

5. Brenneman and Boardman, *Gettysburg Cyclorama*, 12; *Philadelphia Inquirer*, August 4, 1876; Sears, *Sacred Places*, 51.

6. Brenneman and Boardman, *Gettysburg Cyclorama*, 12–16; *Chicago Tribune*, Nov. 28, 1883.

7. *Chicago Tribune*, July 29, 1882, and October 21, 1883; Wernick, "Getting a Glimpse," 80.

8. *Chicago Tribune*, December 1, 1884. By March 1884, another company organized in Chicago to bring a second cyclorama to the city, this one *The Battle of Montretout* (*Chicago Tribune*, March 1, 1884).

9. Brenneman and Boardman, *Gettysburg Cyclorama*, 64–65, 170, 200.

10. *Boston Globe*, December 20, 1884.

11. John Gibbon quoted in Brenneman and Boardman, *Gettysburg Cyclorama*, 21, 143; *Boston Globe*, December 21, 1884; *Fitchburg (Mass.) Sentinel*, June 16, 1885.

12. *Souvenir Cyclorama of Battle of Gettysburg* (Boston, 1885), author's collection.

13. *Boston Globe*, April 11 and June 26, 1885.

14. *Boston Globe*, November 19 and December 25, 1885, March 4, 1888; *Salt Lake City Herald*, August 14, 1888.

15. *Star Tribune* (Minneapolis), August 13 and September 3, 1886; *Chicago Tribune*, March 25, 1885; Harold Holzer, "What Happened to All the Other Cycloramas?," *American Heritage* 56, no. 4 (August/September 2005), https://www.americanheritage.com/vanished-heritage, accessed August 11, 2020; "Panorama Painters," cyclorama research files shared by Gordon Jones, Atlanta History Center (hereafter AHC).

16. *Saint Paul (Minn.) Globe*, November 17, 1884; Chicagology, https://chicagology.com/goldenage/goldenage049/, accessed July 10, 2019.

17. *Chicago Tribune*, May 16, 1885.

18. *Times-Philadelphia*, April 25, 1885.

19. *Boston Post*, June 9, 1887.

20. *Great Bend (Kans.) Register*, June 22, 1893; *Polk County News* (Bartow, Fla.), November 4, 1891.

21. *Hazelton (Pa.) Sentinel*, October 15, 1887; *Star Tribune*, Nov. 1, 1885; *New York Tribune*, June 20, 1886; Noel Harrison, "Vicksburg in the Round," *Civil War Times*, June 2010, 52–56.

22. Chicagology, https://chicagology.com/goldenage/goldenage049/, accessed July 10, 2019.

23. Harrison, "Vicksburg in the Round," 54; *Weekly News-Democrat* (Emporia, Kans.), June, 17, 1886.

24. *Star Tribune* (Minneapolis), August 13 and September 3, 1886.

25. Brenneman and Boardman, *Gettysburg Cyclorama*, 45.

26. *Star Tribune* (Minneapolis), August 13 and September 3, 1886

27. *Hazelton (Pa.) Sentinel*, October 15, 1887; *Star Tribune*, November 1, 1885.

28. *National Tribune*, March 11, 1886; *Critic* (Washington, D.C.), March 1, 1886.

29. CSR for Louis Kurz, NARA; Mark E. Neely Jr. and Harold Holzer, *The Union Image: Popular Prints of the Civil War North* (Chapel Hill: University of North Carolina Press, 2000), 209–18.

30. Neely and Holzer, *Union Image*, 116, 207–9; Jackson Lears, *Fables of Abundance: A Cultural History of Adverting in America* (New York: Basic Books, 1994), 107; "Battle of Shiloh," Prints and Photographs Online Catalog, Library of Congress, https://www.loc.gov/item/2013645344/; McCormick Harvesting Machine Company, "Monitor and Merrimac Advertising Poster," Wisconsin Historical Society, https://www.wisconsinhistory.org/Records/Image/IM41074.

31. *Philadelphia Inquirer*, October 14, 1885; 1880 Census; Brenneman and Boardman, *Gettysburg Cyclorama*, 40; U.S. National Homes for Disabled Volunteer Soldiers, 1866–1938 for Charles Hale, ancestry.com; *Our War* (blog), http://ourwarmikepride.blogspot.com/2013/09/a-gettysburg-veteran-who-knew.html.

32. Brenneman and Boardman, *Gettysburg Cyclorama*, 46–48; Jim Weeks, *Gettysburg: Memory, Market, and an American Shrine* (Princeton, N.J.: Princeton University Press, 2003), 78.

33. *Buffalo Weekly Express*, July 26, 1888.

34. *Salt Lake Herald*, August 11, 1888; *Buffalo Courier*, July 17, 1889; *Detroit Free Press*, February 26, 1887; Cyclorama Exhibit text, AHC.

35. *Boston Globe*, May 11 and December 31, 1889; Brenneman and Boardman, *Gettysburg Cyclorama*, 23, 30.

36. Harrison, "Vicksburg in the Round," 55.

37. *Buffalo Evening News*, June 23, 1891.

38. *Baltimore Sun*, June 15, 1892.

39. Brenneman and Boardman, *Gettysburg Cyclorama*, 22–23, 53; *Chicago Tribune*, April 1, 1892; Harrison, "Vicksburg in the Round," 57.

40. Harrison, "Vicksburg in the Round," 55–56; *Democrat and Chronicle* (Rochester, N.Y.), November 4, 1892.

41. Harrison, "Vicksburg in the Round," 55–57.

42. *Atlanta Constitution*, July 31, 1893.

43. Cyclorama research files shared by Gordon Jones, AHC; *Atlanta Constitution*, February 12, 1892, and August 1, 1893; Holland Cotter, "A Victory for the Civil War 'Cyclorama,'" *New York Times*, February 21, 2019.

44. Brenneman and Boardman, *Gettysburg Cyclorama*, 63–68.

45. *Atlanta Constitution*, February 18, 1892.

46. "Cyclorama: The Big Picture," AHC, https://www.atlantahistorycenter.com/explore/exhibitions/cyclorama-the-big-picture.

47. *Atlanta Constitution*, March 1, 1892.

48. *Atlanta Constitution,* August 1 and 15, 1893; Cotter, "Victory."

49. Brenneman and Boardman, *Gettysburg Cyclorama,* 32–38; Cotter, "Victory." Vanderlyn's *Versailles* is displayed at the Metropolitan Museum of Art in New York.

50. Cotter, "Victory."

COLT

Through All Wars the National Standard

Tried and trusted by "our boys" in their heroic defense of
our national honor, Colt's Firearms are to-day as they have
been for generations back, the great American weapon of
dependability. The best is none too good for Uncle Sam
in the field — nor for you in the home.

Revolvers

   Automatic Pistols

      Automatic Machine Guns

COLT'S PATENT FIREARMS MFG. CO.
HARTFORD, CONN., U. S. A.

*Illustrated Catalogue No. 26 mailed
free on request*

More than a half century after the Civil War, a pair of weathered old veterans—
one Yankee, one Rebel—are shown the latest weapon in the arsenal created
by Colt's Patent Firearms Mfg. Co. (*Literary Digest* 53 [March 23, 1918]: 86)

Epilogue

As the United States mobilized for the Great War in 1918, Colt Patent Firearms drew on the Civil War to advertise its newest line of pistols. The ad features a young officer proudly showing off his new pistol to a pair of aged survivors of the Union and Confederate armies, wearing their respective uniforms but seemingly joined arm in arm in unity. The image offered a couple of easy reference points to readers: the idea that Civil War veterans were the epitome of martial expertise, and the notion that the moral fiber that pulled the nation together after the war would inspire the strength of character and force for good necessary to win the current world war—and to protect citizens' homes from danger. "Tried and trusted by 'our boys' in their heroic defense of our national honor," Colt firearms are "the great American weapon of dependability"—and who would be better qualified to confirm their reliability than these brave old warriors?[1]

Civil War images and values were occasionally used to sell products right up to the Second World War: an ancient veteran drags a comrade out of a burning soldiers' home in a dramatic ad called "Once a Hero" for the Grinnell sprinkler company in 1920, while Stonewall Jackson's "foot cavalry"—famous for covering vast distances because of frequent short rest breaks—appeared in an ad for Coca-Cola promoting "the pause that refreshes" in 1931. In the first, the Civil War veteran symbolizes courage and perseverance in a crisis; in the latter, the famous Virginian and his men represent the well-known toughness of Jackson's men in particular and Civil War soldiers in general.[2] As it had during the Gilded Age, the Civil War provided language and meaning that informed the ways U.S. buyers and sellers thought about many common, everyday products and experiences, from handguns for self-protection to the latest in safe and reliable tires and the country's most popular soft drink.

Civil War memory also continued to shape politics in the 1930s and 1940s. As Nina Silber writes, the war remained an important reference point for "New Dealers, Popular Fronters, civil rights activists, white southerners with pro-Confederate leanings," who "came together and broke apart over various issues related to the Civil War, especially slavery and emancipation, Abraham Lincoln, and the Lost Cause."[3] But the use of Civil War memory to move product in the decade or two before the Second World War produced its own icons for commercial exploitation was no more political than it had been a generation earlier.

Rather, for advertisers, Civil War images served as a kind of common currency by both buyers and sellers, as businessmen and advertisers blended the Civil War into consumers' everyday lives for at least eighty years after the conflict ended. Throughout those four score years and more, Civil War memory followed two parallel but very different paths: as a touchstone for sectional identity and political "culture wars," and as a package of ideas, values, and comforting images that, in the commercial arena, at least, united rather than separated Americans.

NOTES

1. Colt's Patent Firearms Mfg. Co. advertisement, *Literary Digest* 53 (March 23, 1918): 86.

2. "Once a Hero," Grinnell Fire Protection Co. advertisement, *Everybody's Magazine* 2 (February 1920): 75; Coca-Cola advertisement, *Boys' Life*, September 1931, 2. The Coca-Cola ad ran well into the 1940s.

3. Nina Silber, *This War Ain't Over: Fighting the Civil War in New Deal America* (Chapel Hill: University of North Carolina Press, 2018), 6.

Contributors

AMANDA BRICKELL BELLOWS is a Lecturer at the Eugene Lang College of Liberal Arts at the New School in New York City. A 2016 PhD from the University of North Carolina at Chapel Hill, she is the author of *American Slavery and Russian Serfdom in the Post-Emancipation Imagination* (2020). She has also published articles on slavery and serfdom in the *Journal of Global Slavery* and *Novoe literaturnoe obozrenie* (New Literary Observer).

CROMPTON B. BURTON is an Internal Communications Manager in the Office of Human Resources for the University of Maine System, Augusta, Maine. He previously worked in other university administrations and spent time as a TV producer and broadcast news coordinator. He has a master of science in journalism from Ohio University. He has published numerous articles about Civil War topics in the *New England Quarterly, Maine History,* and other publications.

KEVIN R. CAPRICE is a PhD candidate in history at the University of Virginia. His dissertation explores the opportunities of the Republican majority allowed by the vacated congressional seats of secessionists, and the aftereffects of Republican aspirations for the expanding United States.

SHAE SMITH COX earned her PhD in history at the University of Nevada, Las Vegas. She is revising her dissertation, "The Fabric of Civil War Society: Uniforms, Badges, and Flags, 1861–1939," for publication.

BARBARA A. GANNON is Associate Professor of History at the University of Central Florida. She is the author of *Americans Remember their Civil War* (2017) and *The Won Cause: Black and White Comradeship in the Grand Army of the Republic* (2011); the latter won the Wiley-Silver Prize in Civil War History.

EDWARD JOHN HARCOURT is a Senior Vice President and Managing Director at Quacquarelli Symonds (QS), a higher education services company serving over 1,400 universities worldwide. Previously, he was pro-vice-chancellor at John Moores University in Liverpool, England. He earned a PhD in American history from Vanderbilt University and has previously published essays on the American Civil War in the *Journal of Social History, Southern Cultures,* and *Civil War History.*

ANNA GIBSON HOLLOWAY is the former museum services director at SEARCH. Now a Maritime Historian in Washington, D.C., she has nearly thirty years of experience with maritime art and material culture, museum collections management, curation, education, and interpretation. With a PhD in history from the College of William and Mary, she has served as a historian for the National Park Service as well as curator and vice president of Collections and Programs at the Mariners' Museum in Newport News, Virginia, where she led the effort to create the 20,000-square-foot, award-winning USS *Monitor* Center exhibition.

CAROLINE E. JANNEY is John L. Nau III Professor in the History of the American Civil War and Director of the Nau Center for Civil War History at the University of Virginia. She is a past president of the Society of Civil War Historians and the author or editor of several books, including *Burying the Dead but Not the Past: Ladies' Memorial Associations and the Lost Cause* (2008), *Remembering the Civil War: Reunion and the Limits of Reconciliation* (2013), and *Petersburg to Appomattox: The End of the War in Virginia* (2018).

JONATHAN S. JONES is a Post-Doctoral Scholar at the Pennsylvania State University's George and Ann Richards Civil War Era Center. He is currently revising a book manuscript on opiate addiction in the Civil War era, based on his dissertation, "Opium Slavery: Veterans and Addiction in the American Civil War Era" (Binghamton University, 2020).

JAMES MARTEN is Professor of History at Marquette University and a past president of the Society of Civil War Historians. He has written or edited a number of books on the sectional conflict, including *The Children's Civil War* (1998), *Civil War America: Voices from the Home Front* (2003), *Sing Not War: The Lives of Union and Confederate Veterans in Gilded Age America* (2011), *Children and Youth during the Civil War Era* (2012), and *America's Corporal: James Tanner in War and Peace* (2014).

MARGARET FAIRGRIEVE MILANICK earned a PhD in 2020 from the University of Missouri in art history with an emphasis in nineteenth-century American material culture. For nearly thirty years, she has given public tours of the Museum of Art and Archaeology at the University of Missouri and has given talks and published several articles on art and material culture.

JOHN NEFF was Associate Professor of History and Director for the Center of Civil War Research at the University of Mississippi. He authored *Honoring the Civil War Dead: Commemoration and the Problem of Reconciliation* (2005).

PAUL RINGEL is Associate Professor of History at High Point University. He is the author of *Commercializing Childhood: Children's Magazines, Urban Gentility, and the Ideal of the American Child* (2015), winner of the Children's Literature Association's 2015 Honor Book Award for outstanding scholarship in the field of children's literature.

NATALIE SWEET is the Program and Education Coordinator at the Abraham Lincoln Library and Museum. She is a former review editor for the *Lincoln Herald*, published by Lincoln Memorial University. She received an MA in history from the University of Kentucky before serving as a research fellow at the Abraham Lincoln Institute for the Study of Leadership and Public Policy. She has written numerous essays about Lincoln.

DAVID K. THOMSON is Assistant Professor of History at Sacred Heart University. He is the editor of *"We Are in His Hands Whether We Live or Die": The Letters of Brevet Brigadier General Charles Henry Howard* (2013) and has published articles on the financial component of the Civil War in journals including the *Journal of the Civil War Era*.

JONATHAN W. WHITE is Associate Professor of American Studies at Christopher Newport University. He is the author or editor of ten books, including *Midnight in America: Darkness, Sleep and Dreams during the Civil War* (2017), *Emancipation, the Union Army, and the Reelection of Abraham Lincoln* (2014), and *Abraham Lincoln and Treason in the Civil War: The Trials of John Merryman* (2011).

Index

UnCivil Wars

CPSIA information can be obtained
at www.ICGtesting.com
Printed in the USA
LVHW030428030822
725074LV00005B/413

9 780820 359656